Global Philosophy of Religion

A SHORT INTRODUCTION

"This book boldly goes to the heart of the matter . . . In so doing it opens up contemporary discourse to an exciting possibility, that the rational and nonrational dimensions of existence, far from being incompatible may be fully intelligible only when taken together."

ARVIND SHARMA, Mcgill University

"This ambitious textbook places philosophy of religion in worldwide context. It makes good use of resources from a variety of theistic and non theistic religious traditions while covering the full range of topics of a standard introductory course. It should be especially attractive to philosophy teachers who need course materials that will appeal to religiously diverse groups of students."

PHILIP QUINN, University of Notre Dame

"Runzo is abundantly successful in showing the importance (and the limits) of argument in matters of religion. I don't know another book that does this with as much success over such a range of materials."

PAUL J. GRIFFITHS, University of Chicago

Global Philosophy of Religion

A SHORT INTRODUCTION

Joseph Runzo

ONEWORLD

GLOBAL PHILOSOPHY OF RELIGION: A SHORT INTRODUCTION

Oneworld Publications
185 Banbury Road
Oxford OX2 7AR
England
http://www.oneworld-publications.com

ISBN 978-1-85168-235-5

Cover design by Design Deluxe
Typeset by Wyvern 21, Bristol, UK
Printed and bound by CPI Antony Rowe, UK

Reprinted in 2012

This book is dedicated to my wife

Nancy M. Martin

CONTENTS

FIGURES, TABLES, AND BOXES

ACKNOWLEDGMENTS

When I officially joined the church at the age of sixteen, I had one doubt. The church I joined was a large suburban church with a well-educated, middle-class congregation. The associate minister who ran the membership classes was a former Navy chaplain. When he asked at the very end of the classes if I had any questions, the one question I asked was, "What happens to people in other religions?" His answer was, "Unfortunately they are counted among the eternally damned." At the time, this did not seem like the correct answer to me, though it did not prevent me from joining the church. I suppose in a strange way I owe my journey toward a global perspective on religion, and so in some ways this book, to that first, not so gentle nudge.

Of course, in today's global world the issue which confronts believers is not just "what happens to those in other religions," but "what about those in my own tradition who come from a different cultural background than I do?" In the Japanese Christian novelist Shusaku Endo's magnificent last work *Deep River*, he portrays the experience of Otsu, a young Japanese Christian, when he travels to France to study for the ministry and encounters a very different Christianity. Otsu observes:

> I can't help but be struck by the clarity and logic of the way Europeans think, but it seems to me as an Asian that there is something they have lost sight of with their clarity and overabundance of logic, and I just can't go along with it...my Japanese sensibilities have made me feel out of harmony with European Christianity...As a Japanese, I can't bear those

who ignore the great life force that exists in Nature. However lucid and logical it may be, in European Christianity there is a rank ordering of all living things. They'll never be able to understand the import of a verse like Basho's haiku:

> when I look closely
> beneath the hedge, mothers-heart
> flowers have blossomed

Sometimes, of course, they talk as if they regarded the life-force that causes the mothers-heart flowers to bloom as the same force that grants life to human beings, but in no way do they consider them to be identical.[1]

When I did my doctoral work in philosophy at the University of Michigan, I had the privilege of working with William Alston, as well as some of the finest ethicists of the twentieth century: William Frankena, Richard Brandt, C.L. Stevenson, and John Rawls. I owe a great debt to William Alston for my development as a philosopher of religion. Alston later founded the journal Faith and Philosophy, which he asked me to join as a member of the editorial board. I might mention here two other friends who succeeded Alston as the editors of Faith and Philosophy, Philip L. Quinn and William J. Wainwright, both of whom have developed strong interests in the World Religions, which I have shared with them in more recent years. But when I was a graduate student in the philosophy department at Michigan, like most American analytic philosophy departments, there was little opportunity for working in the World Religions.

When I did further graduate work at Harvard Divinity School, the pattern was reversed. I had the opportunity to study with John Carman, and there were others who worked in the World Religions, but I did not have the opportunity to study under someone who combined philosophical acumen with a deep knowledge of the World Religions until I was a National Endowment for the Humanities Fellow at the East-West Center at the University of Hawaii where I got to know Eliot Deustch and Roger Ames. In the meantime, before going to the East-West Center, I first met John Hick in the early 1980s when he was Danforth Professor at Claremont Graduate University. Hick's work turned my interest increasingly toward comparative philosophy of religion, and I began to travel regularly to Britain to lecture at various universities. Through John Hick I met Keith Ward, Julius Lipner, Brian Hebblethwaite, Ninian

Smart, Don Cupitt, Stuart Sutherland, Janet Soskice, Richard Swinburne, Anthony Kenny, and Ronald Hepburne. These contacts, and particularly my lasting friendships with John Hick, Keith Ward, Julius Lipner, Brian Hebblethwaite, and Ninian Smart, showed me a new, more British, perspective integrating philosophy and religious studies, which took greater account of philosophical ideas in non-Western traditions. To these scholars and friends I owe much for my development both intellectually and as a person.

After studying at the East-West Center, I began to travel extensively in Asia, particularly Japan. My former philosophy student Yukihiro Aizawa, who is now the President of Alba Homes in Toyama, has generously accompanied me on each of my visits to Japan and translated for me in my conversations with temple priests and Rinzai Zen Masters. Four years ago I had the privilege of coming to know Arvind Sharma. I have since traveled at his invitation to the 1999 Parliament of the World Religions in Capetown, South Africa, to speak on human rights and religion, and he and I and Nancy M. Martin are currently producing a volume on human rights and the World Religions. In 1998, Julius Lipner had generously sponsored me as a Visiting Fellow at Clare Hall, Cambridge University, where I am now a Life Fellow. Clare Hall offered the extraordinary opportunity to meet a constantly changing set of international scholars along with the permanent Clare Hall faculty. Here I have come to know other Fellows combining interests in philosophy and religion, including John Hinnels and John Vathaki.

My colleague (and wife) Nancy M. Martin and I have had the privilege of developing an international society, The Global Ethics and Religion Forum (www.GERForum.org), of academic friends around the world who are committed to bringing an understanding of the global religions to the public, and helping educate the public about the contributions that the World Religions can make to ethical issues. Our work has been supported by the commitment of Novin Doostdar and Juliet Mabey, the publishers of Oneworld Publications, to make us General Editors of the book series "The Library of Global Ethics and Religion." I also want to thank my editors Victoria Warner, Rebecca Clare and especially Helen Coward of Oneworld Publications. I am grateful for the superb comments from Oneworld's reviewer which enabled me to avoid certain simplified characterizations which might have encouraged an overly simplified understanding of some of the philosophical and religious positions I address.

I owe much to many friends and colleagues, in addition to those already mentioned, who have been involved in these projects: James Kellenberger, Christopher Key Chapple, Nathan Tierney, Elliot Dorff, Charlotte Fonrobert, Philip Rossi, Masao Abe, John Berthrong, William LaFleur, Dale Wright, Zayn Kassam, and C. Ram Prasad. Jessie Rose Stevens has been the most remarkable and reliable student assistant in my career, not only helping with this text but participating with patience and joy in the process. Finally to Nancy M. Martin I owe more than can be expressed in the acknowledgments of a book. She has been friend and wife in the truest sense. I continuously learn more from her about the lived religious life of the World Religions than I have ever dreamed possible.

INTRODUCTION

As soon as definite knowledge concerning any subject becomes possible, this subject ceases to be called philosophy, and becomes a separate science...The value of philosophy is, in fact, to be sought largely in its very uncertainty...Philosophy, though unable to tell us with certainty what is the true answer to the doubts which it raises, is able to suggest many possibilities which enlarge our thoughts and free them from the tyranny of custom. Thus, while diminishing our feeling of certainty as to what things are, it greatly increases our knowledge as to what they may be.[1]

Bertrand Russell (1872–1970)

This is a book for those who wish to reason about religion, those who puzzle about the question "what rational sense can we make of religious beliefs and what do they mean?" I shall address topics as diverse, perennial, and timely as the nature of faith, arguments for and against the existence of God and arguments for and against the separateness of Brahman and *jivas*, the problem of suffering, the possibility of life after death, and religious approaches to moral issues and the meaning of life. I do not promise answers to these questions, and certainly do not promise definitive religious answers – for the latter are the purview of the science of theology. This is a philosophy book, and philosophy is the art of using reason to discover meaning and what is possible. My hope is to encourage the reader to enlarge his or her thoughts by comparing and contrasting the philosophical insights offered by the different World Religions and examining the global application of those insights for today. In the twenty-first century, there is no better way to free our ideas about religion "from the tyranny of custom" than to have an informed and *global* understanding of the great religious ideas of humankind.

The audience for this philosophical approach to religious issues includes both believers and non-believers. In our world, there are many who do not care to think about religion. But there are also those who are strongly religious, and those who, while they may not have religious conviction, wonder about the truth of religious belief. This book addresses the latter two groups – believers and non-believers alike who *wonder* about religion, who take religion seriously and see religion as at least potentially addressing the big questions of life.

THE PROBLEM OF RELIGIOUS COMMITMENT

Why be religious? In some ways this is an old question, yet it has a distinctly modern cogency. In our age, skeptics may ask this question, but more than ever committed religious people are inescapably confronted by it. For religious belief has come to appear irrational for the modern person. We are, it would seem, too scientifically sophisticated, too aware of other cultures and other ways of thought, too historically conscious, to believe in the old religious traditions of a pre-scientific, culturally parochial age. After all, science explains all – or at least can seem to hold out the promise of doing so. For example, belief in miracles can seem rather quaint today; the notion that God acts in history is often relegated to the disclaimer that the insurance company is not responsible for "acts of God," as when the branch of a tree falls on your automobile during a high wind.

Further, we live in the "global village," drawn together by instantaneous information and ubiquitous video cameras. While this often sensationalizes the trivial, it also means that we have not just heard of but actually *seen* the alternative thought worlds and the alternative lifestyles of others, in our own country as well as around the world. Within our pluralistic society and this international pluralistic outlook, belief in a specifically Hindu God, or Muslim God, or Jewish God, or Christian God, can appear parochial, a vestige of an earlier age. And even if some people believe in a particular God, that is all right *for them* – just as others in different social groups and cultures as a matter of fact believe in a different divine reality, or do not believe at all. From within the new perspective of cultural relativism, religious commitment may be accepted today, but only within its proper cultural place.

However, the global information age also challenges the non-believer. It is too facile for those without any particular religious beliefs to assume that there could not be good reasons for the religious life. If religious folk often err on the side of blind proselytizing, the a-religious often err on the side of uninformed disinterest. We wonder about the universe, are intrigued by the physiology of the brain, the mechanisms of the biosphere, and the possibility of black holes; we should equally wonder if there could be any good reasons for belief in a Transcendent. We question civil authority, argue about social issues like abortion and about international policies like environmental protection, work hard at our educations, our careers, our human relationships. It is at least odd, if not intellectually inexcusable, to ignore the completeness of this evolution of the modern mind by putting one's own mind in neutral when it comes to religious views.

To return to the believer, "Why believe in God?" was a virtually unthinkable question in the medieval period of the Judaic and Christian and Islamic and Hindu traditions. The appropriate question had become "What does God (the God of my tradition) require of humans?" Our world is different. In our world, even within the community of faith, Divine Providence is no longer an unshakable given. In *Crime and Punishment* Fyodor Dostoevsky expresses this culturally and historically transformed outlook of modern worldviews. Raskolnikov, the protagonist, discusses with Sonia, a devout Russian Orthodox Christian, her plight as a young prostitute. He suggests that Sonia's younger sister might also fall into prostitution for the sake of economic survival:

> "No, no! It can't be, no!" Sonia cried aloud in desperation, as though she had been stabbed. "God would not allow anything so awful!"
> "He lets others come to it."
> "No, no! God will protect her, God!" she repeated beside herself.
> "But, perhaps, there is no God at all," Raskolnikov answered with a sort of malignance, laughed and looked at her.[2]

Raskolnikov's words speak to our age.

While skepticism is not uniquely modern, skepticism about religion has become particularly widespread as a natural consequence of certain uniquely modern problems. But does the resistance of modern problems to easy religious solutions indicate a fatal deficiency in religious belief? Or instead, can religion adjust to the modern mind, and are these problems more like anomalies, that force one's worldview to evolve while leaving it intact? Whichever is the case, as we assess issues facing the believer and the non-believer, we will see a repeated pattern: in the modern age, what makes one person skeptical of religious belief is precisely what the religiously committed must confront if they seek a reasonable faith. Given modern grounds for doubt, what we shall be asking is what *could* justify the faith of the religious person in a global age.

RELIGIOUS EPISTEMOLOGY

Many of the issues addressed in this book concern religious knowledge, or epistemology of religion. These are not easy issues. Still, they are essential to an informed judgment, whether one of belief or disbelief. So in order to bring these issues to a wide audience, they are presented here in a manner intended to be accessible to the general reader, and not just to the specialist. However, since this book is introductory in nature, it is only possible to develop some potential solutions to certain trenchant philosophical issues in religion. For those who wish to pursue individual questions in finer detail, suggested readings are given at the end of each section. Likewise, a glossary, a chronology of the World Religions, and simplified schemes for classic arguments are offered for further clarification.

More specifically, this short introduction to global philosophy of religion addresses three interrelated epistemological problems: (1) what is the rational justification for holding one set of religious beliefs instead of some alternative religious (or even non-religious) worldview?; (2) how could one's own religious beliefs be rationally justified when there is insufficient proof?; and (3) are the non-rational elements of religion somehow rationally justified? In addressing these questions over the course of the book, I will set out what I take to be the inevitable failure of purely rationalistic, classic philosophical, psychological, and sociological arguments both for and against religion. This analysis will eventually lead us to ask: if reason cannot decide the issue for or against the religious life, what, if anything, is the value of the religious life? To answer this question, I will develop a rational defense of the non-rational – or, better, extra-rational – elements of religion: love, faith, compassion, and devotion.

The pluralism of the modern religious situation produces religious uncertainty, forcing people to choose between religious options. The sociologist Peter Berger calls this necessary choice the "heretical imperative."[3] There is often no immediate and uncontested right religious option for the modern person. So every religious choice has an element of heresy, because to choose any religious option is to reject other, well-received (orthodox) options. Further, as Paul Tillich notes, even within the faith stance one does choose:

> If faith is understood as being ultimately concerned, doubt is a neces-
> sary element in it. Faith is certain in so far as it is an experience of the
> holy. But faith is uncertain in so far as the infinite to which it is related
> is received by a finite being. This element of uncertainty in faith cannot
> be removed, it must be accepted.[4]

Given that genuine faith will be a "doubting faith," is religious commitment worth the risk?

> The risk to faith in one's ultimate concern is indeed the greatest risk [a
> person] can run. For if it proves to be a failure, the meaning of one's
> life breaks down; one surrenders oneself, including truth and justice, to
> something which is not worth it.[5]

Whether one should take this risk depends on whether there is a place for religion in the modern world (that is, the world as conceived by the modern mind). For while religious faith is not just a matter of rational belief, we do not want our faith to be irrational. And if there is no place, e.g., for God or Brahman or Nirvana in the modern world, directing oneself toward God or Brahman or Nirvana is not rational, and clearly not worth the risk. Against the prevalent modern sense that there is no place for the Transcendent, I hope to show that there is a place for rational faith in a Transcendent, even though a healthy skepticism should underlie that faith.

THE WORLD RELIGIONS

This book addresses philosophical issues in the World Religions. All of the World Religions are concerned with a Transcendent and the relation of humans to that Transcendent. Some traditions not addressed – such as nature religions like the Japanese Shinto tradition or ancient Greek polytheism – do not conceive of a Transcendent, while others – including Shinto but also native American traditions like Navajo or Hopi – while they have persisted over long periods of history, have remained ethnocentric and so are not World Religions. One cannot convert to being Navajo, and thus it is not a World Religion, whereas while the small but global tradition of Judaism is comprised today primarily of ethnic Jews, one can convert to this World Religion. Finally, there are religions which are not only ethnocentric but historical dead ends, such as the ancient Egyptian religion, and there are new religions which lack the historical longevity and global spread yet to be considered World Religions. In contrast to ancient Egyptian religion, Zoroastrianism is a World Religion with a now small but still living tradition in India as well as adherents in the Middle East.

Following the common demarcation of the World Religions, I will concentrate on the five traditions of Hinduism, Buddhism, Judaism, Christianity and Islam. But I will also include reference to the Chinese traditions as well as to some of the important if more modest sized World Religions like Zoroastrianism, Sikhism, and the Baha'i tradition.

THE RELATION OF SCIENTIFIC TO PHILOSOPHICAL APPROACHES TO RELIGION

Just as philosophical approaches to science must address the facts about science as well as the conclusions and processes of science, the philosophy of religion must address the facts about religion. Historical facts are particularly pertinent to global philosophy of religion. On the one hand, too often in Christian-oriented philosophy of religion, for example, there is either a naive dismissal of other religious worldviews or misleading generalizations are applied to other religious worldviews. More attention to the specific beliefs, individual philosophers, and historical developments of the World Religions can correct this. Still, on the other hand, mere facts will not settle philosophical issues in or about religion. Indeed, since philosophy is deductive, facts function primarily as counterinstances to any purported philosophical conclusion about religion. One example will serve to illustrate this.

A recent movement in America in biblical history is the Jesus Seminar, which is again pursuing the search of the late-nineteenth- and early-twentieth-century scholarship in Germany for the historical Jesus. As in the earlier search for the historical Jesus, the Jesus Seminar operates on the assumption that the philosophical importance of Jesus' ideas will be discovered when one knows the historical facts. The group's founder, Robert Funk, says in *Honest to Jesus*, "I am more interested in what Jesus thought about God's domain than what Peter the fisherman and Paul the tentmaker thought about Jesus of Nazareth."[6] And the reason he gives for this is:

> I am inclined to the view that Jesus caught a glimpse of what the world is really like when you look at it with God's eyes. He endeavored to pass that glimpse along in disturbing short stories we call parables and in subversive proverbs we call aphorisms...As divine Son of God, co-eternal with the Father, pending cosmic judge seated at God's right hand, He is insulated and isolated from His persona as the humble Galilean sage...there is not much left of the man who loved to laugh and talk at table.[7]

So rather than seeing Jesus as Christ, Funk prefers to think of Jesus as a "Galilean sage." There are a number of philosophical problems with this approach.

First, when compared to any significant historical philosopher, Jesus was not a philosopher. He did not, as far as we know, consistently develop rigorous arguments to defend his positions. So the interpretation of Jesus as a mere sage leaves us with an insignificant gnostic shadow, a sort of fortune cookie philosopher with a ready aphorism, rather than a seminal figure in the World Religions. This parallels often held views of Shakyamuni Buddha as a philosopher. While unlike Jesus, Siddhartha Gautama apparently *was* a philosopher, he too is philosophically insignificant compared to others if he is treated as a mere philosopher.

This brings us to a second problem. Funk speaks as if there were pure "facts" and uninterpreted experiences to which we could appeal to settle the nature of the historical Jesus and his philosophical-religious significance. So he proposes a quest to:

> Liberate Jesus from the scriptural and creedal and experiential prisons in which we have incarcerated him. What would happen if "the dangerous and subversive memories" of that solitary figure were really stripped of their interpretive overlay?[8]

This ignores the work of post-Kantian philosophy in the West, and *vis-à-vis* Asian philosophical thought is contrary to the long Indic tradition that humans always see with interpretation, indeed are always caught in *maya* (illusion), a view encapsulated in the Jain notion of *anekantavada*. On both ancient Indic views and post-Kantian Western views, there is no such thing as an uninterpreted experience, and there is no neutral standpoint from which to judge correct interpretation of historical fact.

And this leads to a third difficulty with the idea, exemplified by the work of the Jesus Seminar, that historical facts might settle philosophical issues. As Funk states the interpretive framework (hermeneutics) of the group:

> Since that symbolic world [that is ingredient to traditional Christianity] is crumbling or has crumbled the times call for a wholly secular account for the Christian faith, not just for the sake of its appeal to the third world, but primarily for the sake of those who inhabit the contemporary, scientifically minded Western world.[9]

The compatibility of science and religion will be addressed in chapter 10. But regarding Funk's suggestion, if a humanistic worldview is presupposed, it does not follow that the Christian (or any other religious) worldview is false. And of course if a humanistic worldview is presupposed as Funk does, the text would not be understood as expressing veridical experiences of the Transcendent. But this just begs the question. Again, philosophical issues are not settled by supposedly neutral historical facts. Nor is the significance of religious beliefs something which could be settled by historical facts. Whatever value the worldviews of the World Religions do have, as we will see throughout this book their value will depend on whether they can indeed direct humans toward a Transcendent. The rest is just history or sociology or psychology.

AGAINST GLOBAL THEOLOGY OR A GLOBAL PHILOSOPHY OF RELIGION

This book does not espouse a global theology – as for example Wilfred Cantwell Smith has proposed – not only because this book is not a theology, but also because a global theology is a philosophically impossible ideal. Global theology is an attempt to produce a single, universal religious perspective which all humans could hold. This necessitates obviating the specific doctrines of each tradition which, if true, would conflict with other traditions. For example, Jesus could not be the unique incarnation of God for Christians if Christians were to subscribe to a global theology which included Muslims, Buddhists, and Baha'is, just as Buddhists could not continue to hold the conception of *anatman* (no-self) if they were to subscribe to a global theology with those who hold that humans have souls. Moreover, precisely what does give a religious worldview its power as an action guide for a meaningful life is the specificity of the doctrines and moral directives which it sets out. Hence, the idea of a global theology does not really designate a religious worldview, for it is not a theology so much as a vision of general religious principles which humankind does, or could, hold in common. But such an abstraction, while having a certain philosophic interest, is of no practical interest for a lived religious life.

Likewise, this book does not set out a global philosophy of religion. There are global issues in the philosophy of religion, and a number of those are addressed here. But the idea of a single global philosophy of religion is specious. First, since there can be no global theology, there can be no correspondent global philosophic inquiry into that purported theology. Second, there are a multitude of philosophic approaches, and it seems highly unlikely that any one single philosophic approach could triumph over all others and so form the basis of a global philosophy. It simply does not follow from the commonality of humankind that there is a single, distillable essence of human philosophic inquiry. In short, both theology and philosophy certainly seem to be irreducibly plural, much as the world's religions, while sharing characteristics which make them all religions, are irreducibly plural.

THE WAY OF KNOWLEDGE VERSUS THE WAY OF LOVE

This brings us to the perennial question of whether, if there is a way to the Transcendent, it is a way of knowledge – i.e., a purely philosophical path – or a way of love. Typically those who conceive of the way (or the mystical path) to the Transcendent as a perfecting of the intellect, think of humans as sharing common intellectual capacities which enable all humans to follow this same ascent to the Transcendent. In a general sense this is, to use a Western term, "gnosticism." As a specific historical movement prevalent during the first centuries of the Christian Church, Gnosticism was the view that *gnosis* or knowledge is the way to salvation for humans, where humans are seen as sparks of the divine spirit, who are trapped in this world in the prison of the flesh. However, the later medieval domination of Aristotelian thought among Christian, Islamic, and even Jewish thinkers led to a form of gnosticism in the broader sense, where intellect was thought to take precedence over the heart.

A striking example of this gnostic emphasis on reason is found in *The Guide for the Perplexed* by the great Jewish theologian Moses Maimonides (1132–1204):

> A king is in his palace, and all his subjects are partly in the country, and partly abroad. Of the former, some have their backs turned towards the king's palace, and their faces in another direction; and some are desirous and zealous to go to the palace...some reach it, and go round about in search of the entrance gate; others have passed through the gate, and walk about in the ante-chamber; and others have succeeded in entering into the inner part of the palace, and being in the same room with the king in the royal palace.
>
> ...The people who are abroad are all those that have no religion...I consider these as irrational beings, and not as human beings...
>
> Those who are in the country, but have their backs turned towards the king's palace, are those who possess religion, belief, and thought, but happen to hold false doctrines...These are worse than the first class...
>
> Those who desire to arrive at the palace, and to enter it, but have never yet seen it, are the mass of religious people; the multitude that observe the divine commandments, but are ignorant. Those who arrive at the palace, but go round about it, are those who devote themselves exclusively to the study of practical law...but are not trained in philosophical treatment of the principles of the Law and do not endeavor to establish the truth of their faith by proof...But those who have succeeded in finding a proof for everything that can be proved, who have a true knowledge of God, so far as a true knowledge can be attained, and are near the truth, wherever an approach to the truth is possible, they have reached the goal, and are in the palace in which the king lives.
>
> ...The true worship of God is only possible when correct notions of Him have been previously conceived...man's love of God is identical with His knowledge of Him...the intellect which emanates from God unto us is the link that joins us to God.[10]

Though Maimonides sees knowing God as equivalent to loving God, it is clear that this is an intellectual love rather than an affective or emotive love. Thus he identifies nearness to God with "true metaphysical opinions" about God. As Maimonides' analogy so pointedly illustrates, this is an elitist view, reserving nearness to God for the intellectually endowed and culturally privileged, and relegating the common religious person to the outskirts of God's favor.

We will return to this in chapters 13 and 14, but for now we should note the alternative to this way of the intellect. That alternative is the way of love or what is known in Hinduism as *bhakti-yoga*: love of, and passionate devotion to, God. The way of love speaks of a love which involves knowledge but goes beyond knowledge, a love which is open even to those not intellectually or culturally privileged. The *Bhagavad-Gita* (Song of the Lord) enunciates three fundamental types of *yoga* (or discipline-methods): *jnana-yoga*, the way of contemplation; *karma-yoga*, the way of obligated action; and *bhakti-yoga*, the way of devotion. Arjuna asks his charioteer Lord Krishna:

> The ever-integrated come
> to worship You in love, while some
> the Imperishable, Unmanifest,
> but which know Discipline the best?[11]

Krishna responds:

> Their toil is weightiest
> whose thoughts pursue the Unmanifest,
> for hardly can the bodied soul
> achieve the unmanifested goal.[12]

Thus, having noted the difficulty of the way of the intellect, or *jnana-yoga*, Krishna does not reject it but says of *bhakti-yoga*:

> By undivided love alone
> can I be truly seen,
> in such a Form and as I am
> be known and entered in.[13]

In the West, we find this same idea of the way of love or passionate devotion to God in, for example, the Spanish mystics of the high Middle Ages. (Though they became marginalized figures in comparison to the reigning Aristotelian views of Thomas Aquinas.) However, not only are such famous mystics as St. Teresa of Avila or St. John of the Cross in effect Christian *bhaktas*, but so is St. Anselm (1033–1109), the Archbishop of Canterbury and author of the highly intellectualized "Ontological Argument" for God's existence (see chapter 4). Before presenting his ontological argument for the being "than which no greater can be conceived," Anselm says:

> Let me seek thee in longing, let me long for thee in seeking, and find thee in love and love thee in finding...for I do not seek to understand that I may believe, but I believe in order to understand.[14]

Similarly St. Bonaventure (1221–1274), the Franciscan opponent of the Dominican Thomas Aquinas at the University of Paris, who feels humans possess an innate idea of God and who accepts Anselm's Ontological Argument, himself turns to the mystical insight which St. Francis of Assisi has attained:

I breathlessly sought this peace, I, a sinner...I ascended to Mount Alverna as to a quiet place, with the desire of seeking spiritual peace and staying there, while I meditated on the ascent of the mind to God, amongst other things there occurred that miracle which happened in the same place to the blessed Francis [St. Francis of Assisi] himself, the vision namely of the winged Seraph in the likeness of the Crucified.[15]

Though Bonaventure develops a philosophical theology, and though he endorses an argument which is as intellectual as Anselm's, he concludes:

All truly spiritual men have been invited by God to passage of this kind...all intellectual operations should be abandoned, all the whole height of our affection should be transferred and transformed into God...

If you should ask how these things come about, question grace, not instruction; desire, not intellect; the cry of prayer, not pursuit of study; the spouse, not the teacher; God, not man; darkness, not clarity; not light, but the wholly flaming fire which will bear you aloft to God with fullest unction and burning affection. This fire is God.[16]

The first half of this book will focus more on the way of the intellect, or *jnana-yoga* (though the fulfillment of this path in Hinduism would also require meditative realization). In the later chapters we will turn more to a consideration of the way of love or *bhakti-yoga*. Thus, as we turn to the considerations of chapter 1 and the question of why religion needs philosophy, we should keep in mind that pure philosophy or gnosis or the intellect may not be the final way to the Transcendent.

1 RELIGION AND PHILOSOPHY

Empty the glass of your desire
    so that you won't be disgraced.
Stop looking for something out there
    and begin seeing within.

Jalalu'l-Din Rumi (1207–1273)

WHAT IS RELIGION?

As we begin the twenty-first century, religion is often regarded as something we invented in the distant past as a way to lessen our fear of nature and to help us control it. This conception of religion as part psychosomatic reaction, part magic, which is often shared in the mass culture of film and television, makes religion look infantile. But the wellspring of religion is not the desire to control nature. Indeed, genuine religion is inimical to the childish seeker of material pleasure: when Siddhartha Gautama saw sickness, old age, and death for the first time, he renounced the "pleasure palace" of his youth and began his search for liberation; Jesus went to his death mourning aloud "forgive them Father, for they do not know what they do," Christianity becoming established only after he suffered; and Muhammad had to flee for his life to remain true to his belief in Allah's revelation.

Genuine religion is fundamentally a search for meaning beyond materialism. This is also true of philosophy – as Socrates puts it in *Apology* 38a, "the unexamined life is not worth living." Thus, both philosophy and religion enjoin us in the Sufi poet Jalalu'l-Din Rumi's

A CHRONOLOGY OF THE WORLD RELIGIONS

Dates	Western World	Asian World
Ancient Period **3400–800 BCE**		
3400	Writing is invented in Mesopotamia; First recorded religious history	
3100	Statues of Min at Koptos, Kingdom of Upper Egypt	
c.3000		Evidence of Indus Valley Civilization
2630	First Pyramid at Saggara (Egypt)	
2600–2000		Indus images of possible proto-Shiva, bulls and goddesses are made
c.1500		Aryan migration into North India
1500–1200		*Probable composition of *Vedas*
c.1000	David; Solomon: Kingdom of Israel is founded	
First Axial Age **800–400 BCE**		
800–400		*Probable composition of *Upanishads*
640–546	Thales – first Western philosopher (Asia Minor)	
630–553		Zoroaster (Persia)
604		Traditional birth date of Lao-Tzu
596–587	Destruction of the Temple; Diaspora of Jews to Babylonia	
563–483		*Traditional dates of Buddha (Siddhartha Gautama)
551–479		Traditional dates of Confucius (K'ung Fu Tzu)

540–468		Traditional dates of Mahavira – 24th tirthankara of Jainism (India)
469–399	Socrates	

Middle Period
400–100 BCE

427–347	Plato	
399–295		Chuang Tzu – Taoist philosopher
384–322	Aristotle	
371–289		Mencius – Confucian philosopher
c.300		*Tao-Te-Ching* probably composed

Global Axial Age
100 BCE–800 CE

100 BCE–100 CE		*Bhagavad-Gita* is composed; Origins of Mahayana Buddhism; Buddhism spreads throughout South India, to Central Asia, and to China
30 BCE–50 CE	Philo Judaeus (Alexandria, Egypt)	
6 BCE	Birth of Jesus	
0 CE		
30 CE	Death of Jesus	
42–62	St. Paul's missionary journeys	
70	Romans destroy Second Temple of Jerusalem	
51–100	Christian Scriptures are composed	
c.100–200		Nagarjuna – founds Madhyamika school of Buddhism
125–202	Irenaeus – first Christian Church Father	
253–333		Ko Hung – founder of religious Taoism

300–500		Buddhism in Southeast Asia; Pure Land and Ch'an (Zen) arise in China
399		Buddhism arrives in Korea from China
354–430	St. Augustine – last Christian Church Father	
500–600		Development of Vajrayana Buddhism
538		Mahayana Buddhism arrives in Japan from Korea
570–632	Muhammad	
691–92	Dome of the Rock is built (Jerusalem)	
c. 700		Persian Zoroastrians settle in India
661–750	Umayyad Dynasty (Damascus): Islam extends from France to the Indus and Central Asia	
600–700		Buddhism is established in Tibet
700–800	Growth of Sufi tradition in Islam	
788–820		Shankara – founder of Advaita Vedanta

Development Period
800–1300 CE

750–1258	Abbasid Dynasty: High Islamic art, culture	
d.874	Abu-Yazid – Sufi (Persia)	
d.922	Al-Hallaj – Sufi	
870–950	Al-Farabi (Bhagdad)	
980–1037	Avicenna (Ibn Sina) (Persia)	
1017–1137		Ramanuja – founder of Vishishtadvaita Vedanta
1033–1109	St. Anselm of Canterbury	
1054	Eastern and Western Branches of Christianity permanently divide	
1058–1111	Al-Ghazzali – Sufi theologian (Bhagdad)	Buddhism disappears in India

1126–1198	Averroes (Ibn Rushd) (Spain)	
1141–1215		Eisai – founder of Rinzai Zen Buddhism in Japan
1132–1204	Moses Maimonides (Egypt)	
1133–1212		Honen – founder of Pure Land (Jodo) Buddhism in Japan
1165–1240	Ibn al'Arabi – Sufi (Spain)	
1173–1262		Shinran – founder of True Pure Land (Jodo Shin) Buddhism in Japan
1200–1253		Dogen – founder of Soto Zen Buddhism in Japan
1222–1282		Nichiren – founder of Nichiren Buddhism in Japan
1197–1276		Madhva – developer of Dualist Vedanta
1207–1273	Jalalu'l-Din Rumi – Sufi poet (Persia)	
1225–1274	St. Thomas Aquinas (France)	

Modern Period
1300–1965 CE

1325–1390	Hafiz – Sufi	
1440–1518		Kabir – nirguna bhakti (India)
1469–1539		Nanak – founder of Sikhism
1481–1533		Vallabha – developer of Shuddhadvaita (theistic Vedanta) and founder of the Pushtimarg (Krishna bhakti)
1486–1533		Chaitanya – founder of Gaudiya Vaishnavism (Krishna bhakti)
1450–	European exploration; Spanish, Portuguese, Dutch and British colonialism spreads Christianity to the Americas, Africa, Macronesia	
1500–1800	Major Islamic empires: Ottomans, Persians, Moguls in India, Indonesia and Africa	
1483–1546	Martin Luther (Germany)	

1517	Martin Luther "95 Theses"; Protestant Reformation	
1509–1564	John Calvin (Geneva)	
1596–1650	René Descartes (France)	
1632–1697	Baruch Spinoza (Holland)	
1724–1804	Immanuel Kant (Germany)	
1768–1834	Friedrich Schleiermacher (Germany)	
1806–1873	John Stuart Mill (England)	
1813–1855	Søren Kierkegaard (Denmark)	
1817–1892	Baha'u'llah – founder of Baha'i tradition (Iran)	
1834–1886		Ramakrishna "Paramahamsa"
c.1850	Beginning of West's interest in Buddhism	
1861–1947	Alfred North Whitehead	
1869–1948		†Mohandas K. Gandhi
1870–1945		†Nishida Kitaro – established the Kyoto school of philosophy
1872–1950		Aurobindo Ghose (India)
1886–1968	Karl Barth – initiates Neo-Reformed theology	
1893	World Parliament of Religion, Chicago; Vivekananda introduces Hinduism to West	
1878–1965	Martin Buber (Jerusalem)	
1886–1965	Paul Tillich (United States)	
1956		Ambedkar's conversion initiates the revival of Buddhism in India
1963–1965	Second Vatican Council	

*These dates are particularly uncertain.
†Gandhi and Nishida were educated in, and their thought heavily influenced by, the Western World.

words, to "begin seeing within." But unlike philosophy *per se*, the World Religions hold that the examined life points to a Transcendent – whether God or Brahman or Nirvana or the Tao – beyond the ultimately meaningless phantasmagoria of the physical world. A World Religious tradition is a set of symbols and rituals, myths and stories, concepts and truth-claims, which a historical community believes gives ultimate meaning to life, via its connection to a Transcendent beyond the natural order. Either this search for meaning beyond the material and human world is of no account, or human reasoning and endeavor is not a full account of reality.

The human drive to understand a value structure underlying the universe and to seek something beyond this world coalesced around 4500 years ago when the great World Religions began to form. As the Chronology (pp.14–18) shows, this occurs first in the form of Hinduism in South Asia, and continues with the rise of the Hebrew tradition some 3500 years ago, initially in Mesopotamia (one of several great seats of human religiosity) and then later in the ancient desert Mediterranean regions. These two great strands of Asian and Western world religiosity become marked by a hope for either liberation – a more Asian perspective – or salvation – the more Western understanding – from the merely material world.

After the Ancient Period of the World Religions (c.3400 to 800 BCE) the global history of humankind's search for salvation or liberation can be divided into four further eras. The first is what Karl Jaspers has called the Axial Age – around 800 to 400 BCE. Though the precise dates of texts and figures are contested, in this period the *Upanishads* are composed; the first Western philosopher, Thales, develops his ideas in Asia Minor; Zoroaster produces the seminal ideas of Zoroastrianism in Persia; Siddhartha Gautama and Mahavira develop Buddhism and Jainism, respectively, out of Hinduism in India; K'ung Fu Tzu develops Confucianism; and Socrates begins a new direction in Western philosophical thought. After this comes what we might call a Middle Period (400–100 BCE) which sees the further development of the ideas and movements of the Axial Age. Plato, the student of Socrates, and then his student, Aristotle, set the foundations of Western philosophical thought; the Chinese traditions see the further development and propagation of Confucianism under Mencius, and the *Tao-Te-Ching* is composed.

Next comes what I shall designate the "Global Axial Age," the period between 100 BCE and 800 CE, which is surely as profound in the development of the religious ideas of humankind as is the first Axial Age identified by Jaspers. For in this period, the traditions which are most expressly global arise: the great Hindu *bhakti* text the *Bhagavad Gita* is composed; Mahayana Buddhism develops in India and spreads north and east into China; after Jesus' death in 30 CE, the Christian scriptures are composed and the Church Fathers develop key doctrines for Christendom as this new religion spreads. Meanwhile in the East, Nagarjuna (second century CE) founds the Madhyamika school of Buddhism; Pure Land and Ch'an (Zen) Buddhism arise in China; and Vajrayana Buddhism develops in Northern India. The Global Axial Age is capped with the arrival of Mahayana Buddhism in Japan (538 CE) and the life of the great Prophet Muhammad from 570–632 CE.

Next is a long period of development, from 800 to 1300 CE. This period sees the rise of the Sufi tradition as well as the development of philosophical Islam in the works of such theologians as Al-Farabi, Avicenna, Al-Ghazzali, and Averroes; the great Hindu Vedanta philosophers Shankara and Ramanuja develop opposing Advaita (non-dualist) and Vishishtadvaita (qualified non-dualist) views of Hinduism; Moses Maimonides writes *The Guide for the Perplexed*; and after Eisai the various schools of Zen Buddhism flourish in Japan. This period of development is capped with Madhva's development of a fully dualist Vedanta in India, the Sufi poetry of Jalalu'l-Din Rumi in Persia, and the work of the greatest Christian theologian since Augustine, Thomas Aquinas, who is the Aristotelian theologian *par excellence*.

Finally, from 1300 CE to the twentieth century we enter the Modern Period of religious thought. *Bhakti* develops rapidly in India, and Nanak founds Sikhism; Martin Luther initiates the Protestant Reformation, and Immanuel Kant produces a great philosophical system rivaled only by Aristotle's in the West. Finally, Friedrich Schleiermacher and Søren Kierkegaard begin to change Western theology in ways which only become fully evident in the work of Karl Barth and the Neo-Reformed movement of the twentieth century, while in India Mohandas Gandhi brings the Jain and Hindu traditions of *ahimsa* to the world stage, and Nishida Kitaro establishes the Kyoto school of philosophy in Japan.

Strictly on empirical grounds, the pervasiveness of the World Religions today is an astonishing fact about humanity. As we begin the twenty-first century, there are over four and a half billion adherents of the World Religions: Christianity has nearly two billion global adherents,[1] while Islam, the other aggressively proselytizing World Religion, itself has a billion adherents around the globe; Hinduism has nearly one billion adherents, and Buddhism some 350 million. Important, smaller traditions in the world today include about twenty million Sikhs, fourteen million Jews, six million Baha'is, and perhaps four million Jains, as well as millions whose thought has been influenced by Confucianism. But whereas being religious was a cultural assumption in earlier ages, our age of scientific skepticism may well leave us wondering how this ever happened in the modern world, for surely blind genes, or a struggle for survival, do not foretell this pervasive religiosity in the family of humankind.

WHAT IS PHILOSOPHY?

Despite their diversity, what the World Religions share is a search for meaning via a Transcendent. Now, philosophy also fundamentally involves a search for meaning beyond the mere material world. As Socrates, the Athenian, says:

> I have never lived an ordinary quiet life. I did not care for the things that most people care about – making money, having a comfortable home, high military or civil rank, and all the other activities, political appointments, secret societies, party organizations, which go on in our city. I thought that I was really too strict in my principles to survive if I went in for this sort of thing. Examining both myself and others is really the very best thing that a man can do, and that life without this sort of examination is not worth living.[2]

But philosophy, unlike the World Religions, is not necessarily concerned with a Transcendent. Indeed, one open philosophic question is whether there is a Transcendent. As William James says, "Philosophy in the full sense is only man thinking; thinking about generalities rather than about particulars."[3] Philosophy is committed to the use of reason to question and understand our assumptions, but it is not inherently committed to any particular conclusion. In the words of Bertrand Russell:

> As soon as definite knowledge concerning any subject becomes possible, this subject ceases to be called philosophy, and becomes a separate science...The value of philosophy is, in fact, to be sought largely in its very uncertainty.[4]

Moreover, it is not the place of philosophy *per se* to endorse what has been concluded in the past (history) or is concluded in the present (sociology). For as the American pragmatist C. I. Lewis notes:

> Philosophy is, so to speak, the mind's own study of itself in action; and the method of it is simply reflective...Though it rises from what is implicit in experience, its procedure must be critical, not descriptive.[5]

Another way to see the difference between philosophy and religion is through the example of a philosophic conclusion which is not religious. Materialism is the view that everything is explainable purely in material terms, or reducible to material terms. One might use philosophical reasoning to arrive at a materialist (or, as it is sometimes called, a naturalist) view that once the universe has been described in terms of the laws of physics, chemistry, biology, and so on, there is nothing left to describe. This common form of contemporary materialism is usually expressed as scientific humanism. For a scientific humanist, all values come from the human or humanity, especially the values that science imparts. But scientific humanism, while a philosophic view, is an a-religious view. Scientific humanists may be rather interested in the meaning of life, but not in reference to a Transcendent.

In the loose and popular sense of philosophy as the seeking of wisdom, philosophy and philosophical religion or philosophical theology are not different in kind. However, in the strict, disciplined sense of philosophy, as a critical inquiry into the nature of reality and the meaning of life via "the mind's own study of itself in action," while philosophy complements, it is different in kind from philosophical theology. Philosophy begins with the supposition that the universe, despite its apparent chaos, is amenable to or understandable by human reason. It is the supposition that the universe can be understood as having an order, or alternatively, as susceptible to being ordered (by reason). It is the supposition that there is not just a world, but a world order, even if an underlying principle is, *à la* the Greek philosopher Heraclitus, one of universal flux – for that principle too can be brought under reason.

Philosophical theology shares this supposition with philosophy that the universe is ordered and understandable. The difference between these disciplines is not just that the philosopher, working within this broad compass, will often pause to inquire in depth about a subject which may be of only peripheral interest to the philosophical theologian – say the complexities of formal logic, or the meaning of art. The crucial difference is that the philosophical theologian works from within the "theological circle" (to use Paul Tillich's phrase). Thus, the explicit faith commitment of the theologian distinguishes philosophical theology and philosophical religion from philosophy (which is not to suggest that the distinction between philosophy and philosophical theology or philosophical religion is either hard and fast or always easy to determine). In the West, philosophy first developed virtually independently of religion, or theology. After the rise of the Christian and then Islamic traditions, philosophical advances came largely at the behest of theological needs, more closely paralleling the Asian world, until the Enlightenment.

DOING PHILOSOPHY AND USING PHILOSOPHY

It is important to differentiate here between engaging in the methodology of philosophy and a philosophic system reached as a conclusion of philosophical reflection. With respect to the former, philosophy is a critical, reflective enterprise employing methods of reasoning for clarifying, elucidating, and justifying any particular analysis within one or more of the branches of philosophy – for example, metaphysics or ethics or epistemology or philosophy of science. A philosophy or a philosophic system, on the other hand, consists in an interrelated set of particular conclusions, together with their reasoned justification, about one or more of the subject matters of these branches of philosophy.

However, being committed to engaging in the enterprise of philosophy does not entail a commitment to producing a philosophic system, or even to using any particular philosophic system. One can clarify, elucidate, and justify some specific philosophical subject without in any sense producing or exclusively adhering to a philosophical system. Were this not the case, professional philosophers would be the only rightful sellers, as it were, in the philosophic market place. And in fact philosophical theologians frequently only need to work with a portion of some branch of philosophy and do not require a complete philosophic system. Only in the case of more extensive and systematic religious philosophical reflection is it necessary for the theologian or religious thinker to engage to any considerable extent in philosophy and, thus, to produce or use a complete philosophic system. Much of what we will analyze philosophically in the following pages is philosophic theology coming from within the traditions. Thomas Aquinas's *Summa*

Theologiae or Maimonides' *Guide forthe Perplexed* , with their especially heavy reliance on Aristotle, are examples of philosophical theologians borrowing philosophic systems. Yet for the most part, the primary use of philosophy for religion, especially insofar as the amount of required philosophic reasoning is modest, is for purposes of clarification and justification.

ARE RELIGION AND PHILOSOPHY ENEMIES?

The Asian traditions have traditionally had a close relationship between philosophy and religious thinking. In Hinduism, philosophical reasoning becomes scriptural in the *Upanishads* (800–400 BCE), so that by the medieval period it is perfectly consistent that the three major schools of Vedanta are founded by philosophers: Shankara, Ramanuja, and Madhva. Siddhartha Gautama himself had a philosophical mind, and the early tradition of philosophical Buddhism continues through the initial developments of Mahayana and then the Madhyamika school, developed by Nagarjuna in about 100–200 CE, down through the highly philosophical approaches of Zen which develop in the work of Dogen and others in Kamakura Japan. Even more so, Confucianism is a philosophical system first under Confucius and then Mencius, only later developing its more religious orientation, partially through interaction with Taoism and later Buddhism.

This tight connection between philosophy and religion in Asian traditions is undoubtedly due in part to the fact that these are both orthopraxic and not primarily revealed traditions. The ancient Hindu *Vedas* are *shruti* ("heard") and the *Bhagavad Gita* is given as revealed by the Lord Krishna, but scriptural texts like the *Upanishads* and the Buddhist *Sutras* record the insight and wisdom of advanced practitioners, resulting in an emphasis on the acquisition of wisdom.

The religious traditions of the West emphasize revelation, from the *Avesta* of Zoroastrianism and the *Torah* of the Hebrews to the "Word of God" of Christianity and the *Qur'an* of Islam. This leaves a potential divide between Western scripture – which is largely non-philosophical – on the one hand, and the philosophical reasoning of the Western traditions, on the other hand. In the West, it is more common to think religion can proceed without philosophy, and for philosophy to be opposed to religion. So ancient Greek philosophy is not particularly religious, though Pythagoras headed a religious cult, Socrates felt his calling came from the gods, and Aristotle thought there was a supreme "unmoved mover."

Christian thought, beginning as it did with a remarkably slender set of uniquely Christian scriptural texts (the Hebrew Bible was also accepted as scripture), soon developed extensive philosophical explanations of various doctrines. Over the first four centuries the philosophical perspective of each Church Father was incorporated into the tradition, ending with Augustine, whose theology is heavily Platonistic but also influenced by his youthful commitment to Manicheanism (an offshoot of Zoroastrianism). As Christianity developed into the modern period, while Thomas Aquinas's theology was Aristotelian, modern theologians like Friedrich Schleiermacher and Karl Barth are strongly influenced by Kant, Rudolph Bultmann closely follows the work of Martin Heidegger, and more recently the process philosophy of Alfred North Whitehead has spawned a whole movement of process theologians. (Islamic thought after Muhammad developed along two lines, the Sufis being especially influenced by Plato, and other theologians influenced equally by Aristotle, to the extent that among the latter group Averroes is "the Commentator" who so strongly influences Thomas Aquinas's understanding of Aristotle.) Generally, Western theology tends to be heavily philosophical because it particularly focuses on the justification and assessment of both ethics and metaphysics.

Until the end of the medieval period in the West, theologians modified the work of previous philosophers, thereby creating their own philosophical theologies. But this positive, symbiotic relationship between philosophy and theology changed dramatically in the West after Descartes, the father of modern philosophy. René Descartes addresses his *Meditations* to the "Dean and Doctors of the Sacred Faculty of Theology of Paris," asking them to give his arguments "your approbation and publicly testify to their truth and certitude." But Descartes's philosophic reasoning, which became the model for modern Western philosophy, is in fact carried out apart from any appeal to or grounding in the authority of the church. With philosophy thus removed from church tradition and authority, the opposition, real or imagined, between theology and philosophy could arise without restraint. Thus, the twentieth century saw the celebrated atheism of a towering philosophic figure like Bertrand Russell, the attack of the logical positivists on any metaphysics or theology, and the rise (ironically enough from the religiously centered work of Kierkegaard) of atheistic existentialism, encapsulated in Jean-Paul Sartre's "I am going to tell you a colossal joke: God does not exist."[6] A recent problem for theology in the West, then, has been the question of how it should perceive its relationship to philosophy.

WHY RELIGION NEEDS PHILOSOPHY

Insofar as theology or philosophical religion strives to present a rational case, rather than to be merely polemical or poetic, it will need to conform to the clarificatory demands of coherence, cognitive significance, intelligibility, and parsimony, and to the justificatory demands of plausibility, consistency, logic of proof, and provision of firm evidential support – and this is to engage in *doing* philosophy. As Etienne Gilson, echoing Kant (see chapter 9) has said about even Christian theologians like Augustine and Anselm who hold that unless one first believes, one shall not understand the Christian faith:

> We cannot believe something, be it the word of God Himself, unless we find some sense in the formulas which we believe. And it can hardly be expected that we will believe in God's Revelation, unless we be given good reasons to think that such a Revelation has indeed taken place.[7]

Good reasons are produced by philosophical methods.

Now, philosophy always deals with the frontiers of human thought, the leading edge of our concepts, and not just the replication of an already articulated and fully accepted worldview. In *Philosophy and the Mirror of Nature* Richard Rorty draws a distinction between what he calls "systematic" and "edifying" philosophy that may be helpful here. Rorty suggests that typical systematic philosophers say, in effect:

> Now that such-and-such a line of inquiry has had such a stunning success, let us reshape all inquiry, and all of culture, on its model, thereby permitting objectivity and rationality to prevail in areas previously obscured by convention, superstition, and the lack of a proper epistemological understanding of man's ability accurately to represent nature.[8]

Examples of Western philosophers who have taken this position, Rorty suggests, are Aquinas (using Aristotle to conciliate the Fathers), Descartes (criticizing Scholasticism), and Carnap (using logic to attempt to overcome metaphysics). In contrast, Rorty points to such figures as Kierkegaard, William James, the later Wittgenstein, and the later

Heidegger as philosophers engaged in edifying philosophy. In defending the revolutionary work of these philosophers, Rorty argues that knowing the facts, knowing "what is out there," is not the only way to be edified. For besides the quest for truth (or The Truth), there is the equally valuable quest for "new, better, more interesting, fruitful ways of speaking."[9]

Theology, and more generally philosophical religion, needs both systematic and edifying uses of philosophy. With respect to systematic philosophy, traditional ways of argumentation and concept usage, and traditional questions, will guide much of the philosophical theologian's use of philosophy. But for any religious thinker, the problem is always how to say old things in new ways, how to "satisfy two basic needs: the statement of the truth of the...message and the interpretation of this truth for every new generation."[10] The quest within edifying philosophy for new lines of argumentation, new concepts, and new questions will ultimately provide help for the religious thinker. As Rorty points out, edifying philosophy, being essentially reactive, is necessarily built upon systematic philosophy. So these two ways of doing philosophy proceed together, but edifying philosophy remains crucial in our global age.

In order to think in ways that can cross between the differing worldviews of the World Religions in our global age, the task of both philosophy of religion and philosophical theology is as much one of innovation as it is one of discovery, and religion needs edifying philosophy for its ability to break through the "tyranny of custom." When religion ceases to engage continually in philosophy, in rigorous clarification, analysis, and especially in the redefinition which is the purview of edifying philosophy, religion ceases to be a fair claimant to providing a rational approach to the meaning of life, and it leaves the field to the secular philosophers.

Further reading

Descartes. *Meditations*. Indianapolis, Hackett Publishing, 1960

Grube, G. M. A., trans. *Plato's Republic*. Indianapolis, Hackett Publishing, 1974

Grube, G. M. A., trans. *The Trial and Death of Socrates*. Indianapolis, Hackett Publishing, 1975

James, William. *Some Problems of Philosophy*. New York, Greenwood Press, 1968

Kant, Immanuel. *Prolegemena to Any Future Metaphysics*. Indianapolis, Hackett Publishing, 1977

Lewis, Clarence Irving. *Mind and the World Order: Outline of a Theory of Knowledge*. New York, Dover Publications, 1929

Nozick, Robert. *The Examined Life*. New York, Simon and Schuster, 1989

Radhakrishnan, Sarvepalli and Moore, Charles A., eds. *A Sourcebook in Indian Philosophy*. Princeton, Princeton University Press, 1957

Russell, Bertrand. *The Problems of Philosophy*. New York, Oxford University Press, 1959

Smith, Wilfred Cantwell. *The Meaning and End of Religion: A Revolutionary Approach to the Great Traditions*. Oxford, Oneworld, 1963

2 WORLDVIEWS AND RELIGION

Why in the name of common sense need we assume that only one...system of ideas can be true? The obvious outcome of our total experience is that the world can be handled according to many systems of ideas.[1]

William James (1842–1910)

Religious affiliation, like every cultural construction of self, is largely an accident of birth. If you are born in India, you are likely to be a Hindu, Jain or Sikh; if born in the United States, you are likely to be a Christian, especially a Protestant; and if born in Indonesia, you are likely to be a Muslim. Moreover, it is not only geography but history which largely determines religious affiliation. Until rather recently, the vast majority of the world's population was either Hindu or Buddhist or Confucian or belonged to an African tribal tradition.

The present global pattern of religion (see the Chronology pp.14–18) was produced first by the rapid spread of Islam under the great Umayyad Dynasty centered in Damascus (until 750 BCE), which extended Islam up the Iberian Peninsula into France, displacing Christian influences, and into central Asia and western India, where even today (in Pakistan) it has displaced Hinduism. This expansion was followed by the flowering of the Abbasid Dynasty, which until 1258 remained the greatest Western culture, as the Western and Eastern branches of Christendom fatally fractured, and Western Christianity was largely relegated to a culturally and materially impoverished Medieval Europe. Under the Abbasids the growth of the Sufi tradition and the crowning achievements of Islamic philosophical theology came to fruition: Al-Farabi in Bhagdad, Avicenna in Persia, Al-Ghazzali also in Bhagdad and Averroes in Spain, among others.

More recently, the Christian population has surged past the huge Islamic, Hindu and Buddhist populations, primarily through colonialism during the last few hundred years. With its trinity of "gold, God, and glory," colonialism spread Christianity to the Americas in the west, central and southern Africa to the south, and to the Philippines, Australia, and New Zealand, though it was largely unable to penetrate the established geographic home of Islam, Hinduism, Buddhism, or Confucianism/Taoism.

Of course, despite this history of dispersion and the limited geographic locus of their traditions, the adherents of each of the great religious traditions believe that their own religious worldview is rationally justified. However, with our global awareness of other traditions and a clear sense of the historical and geographic inception of each tradition, the philosophical problem of religious plurality confronts us: is only one system of religious truth-claims correct, is more than one system correct, or are all religious systems mistaken? In this chapter we will set out and assess the possible alternative responses to this problem, before turning in subsequent chapters to the specific arguments given for the rationality of particular types of truth-claims within each tradition.

THE PROBLEM OF RELIGIOUS PLURALITY

A religious way of life rests most fundamentally on specific claims about the nature of reality, about how meaning and value are to be achieved, and about what is the desired *telos* for humankind. A religion is not in itself true or false. Religion, like any other human institution, is only more or less effective in meeting certain goals. It is the underlying, specific truth-claims of such systems which are potentially true or false. And it is these truth-claims which are the basis of conflict between the systems. A great number of the secondary truth-claims of each of the World Religions are expendable and need not cause conflict. But for each tradition there is a fundamental or vital core of beliefs, which are definitive of the tradition.[2] The problem of religious plurality arises from the fact that the vital core beliefs of the World Religions are incompatible.

As noted in chapter 1, a religion or a religious tradition is a set of symbols and rituals, myths and stories, concepts and truth-claims, which a community believes gives ultimate meaning to life, via its connection to a Transcendent beyond the natural order. Thus religion is a human construct (or institution) which fundamentally involves beliefs at two levels: (1) at one level religion involves the meta-belief that the religious life can effectively orient one towards the Transcendent; and (2) at a level below that it involves specific beliefs – including vital core beliefs – about the nature of the Transcendent and/or the way in which the Transcendent gives meaning to life. The first level of meta-belief, (1), is shared by the World Religions. The second level beliefs, (2), are the point of conflict among the World Religions.

CAN DIFFERENT WORLDVIEWS BE COMPARED?

If you are attempting to compare the views of different cultures or traditions, there are two approaches that you can take. One approach is to look for transcultural universals. The other approach is to look for

FIVE WORLD RELIGIONS: COMPARISONS AND CONTRASTS

	Hinduism	Buddhism	Judaism	Christianity	Islam
Transcendent	Brahman	Nirvana	YHWH	God: Trinity	Allah
World	manifested	appearance	created	created	created
Self	atman	anatman	body/soul	soul	soul
Telos	moksha: liberation or union	nirvana: liberation	presence of God	union in heaven	union in paradise
Means to telos	Orthopraxy: yoga and good karma	Orthopraxy: meditation and good karma	Orthodoxy: divine justice and law	Orthodoxy: divine grace and law	Orthodoxy: divine mercy and law
Ethics	Dharma	Dharma	Divine Commands and Mishnah	Divine Commands and theology	Divine Commands and Hadith
Adherents in 2000	900 million	330 million	17 million	1.9 billion	1 billion

differences among the cultures. The first approach was emphasized in the nineteenth and early twentieth century in the search for a comprehensive understanding of newly (re)discovered world cultures. This often led to the homogenization of cultural difference and the reduction of the achievements and ideals of other cultures to the status of mere reflections of one's own values. This process has been resisted more recently in a desire to emphasize the value of each culture for its own sake and thus the differences among cultures. However, this latter movement has led sometimes to the supposition that one can only accept another culture, one cannot ever really understand another culture. But how could we accept another culture unless we know that it is another culture, and how would we know that it is another culture if we cannot understand it? Of course we cannot understand another culture fully (or then it would be our culture), but there must be elements which it shares with our culture for us even to consider it a culture.

Imagine the following situation. There are two computers in two different rooms. One is your personal computer, and you are having difficulty interfacing with the other computer. There are three possible sources of the incompatibility. Level one: the hardware, that is the computers themselves, are so different that they are incommensurate – e.g., the computer motherboards are entirely different. Level two: the two computers are using different meta-programs – e.g., one is running on DOS and one on Windows. This will leave the computers incommensurate unless one of those meta-programs can supervene on the other. For example, if you are using Windows with an embedded DOS program, then you can communicate with the DOS based system. Level three: the two computers are running different software programs. This last is not an instance of incommensurability but rather one of incompatibility as long as the meta-programs of the two computers are compatible. One just needs to load the appropriate software into each computer.

Our bodies are like the computers, our processes of thinking are like the meta-programs, and our religious worldviews are like the software. At the first level, given our shared biologies, ultimately our worldviews and ideologies are embedded in the same biological "wetwear" (though the restricted brain of the Down's Syndrome person or the undeveloped brains of young children are much like early computers, incommensurate with developed brains in mature adults as early computers would be incompatible with today's advanced computers). Moving to the second level, do humans have the same meta-programs? It is to be hoped so. It has been claimed that Buddhist adepts or certain mystics have a different logic, but as considerations in chapter 9 will show, this does not make sense. So let us assume that humans do employ the same meta-programs of rationality.

This brings us to the third level, the difference of software. It would be absurd to suggest, for example, that because of the richness of their iconography Hindus and Tibetan Buddhists have better brains than either strict adherents of the Islamic Shari'a or Calvinist Protestants (the sometimes self-described "frozen chosen"), for surely Hindus and Tibetan Buddhists just use more complex graphics. So it would be best to say that Hindus and Buddhists and Muslims and Christians and so on run different software programs. Still, their respective worldviews can only count as different religious software because they share enough similarities to be different examples of a type.

Here is another example. In a symphony orchestra of fifty or sixty members, if the players literally had different brain types, different auditory systems, and so on, harmony would be impossible. Again, if the players had radically different training, then once again there would be little chance of harmony. But as long as the members of the orchestra have roughly similar brains and roughly similar musical training, then even though their instruments are irreducibly different – cellos cannot produce the same sounds as French horns and violins not the same sound as timpani – there can be a universal harmony as long as they play from overlapping scores. Similarly, the World Religions can share universals but remain irreducibly different. Indeed on the one hand, if there were no religious universals, there would not be any religious differences, and on the other hand if we did not perceive differences, we would not be able to see the universals behind the differences.

Assuming then that the "software" of the World Religions can be, to some extent, compared and contrasted, how might one respond to the conflicting truth-claims of at least the vital core beliefs among the World Religions? For each response to this question, there is a response to that response. Six main responses, then, to the problem of religious plurality, placed in an order in which, as we shall see, each can be a response to views preceding it, are the following: (1) Exclusivism: only one World Religion is correct, and all others are mistaken; (2) Antipathy: all World Religions are mistaken; (3) Subjectivism: each World Religion is correct, and each is correct insofar as it is best for the individual who adheres to it; (4) Pluralism: ultimately all World Religions are correct, each offering a different path and partial perspective *vis-à-vis* the one Ultimate Reality; (5) Inclusivism: only one World Religion is fully correct, but other World Religions participate in or partially reveal some of the truth of the one correct religion; (6) Henofideism: one has a faith commitment that one's own World Religion is correct, while acknowledging that other World Religions may be correct.

EXCLUSIVISM AND ANTIPATHY

His Holiness Tenzin Gyatso, the Fourteenth Dalai Lama, characterizes the relation between Buddhism and other World Religions this way:

> Other religious traditions possess many good instructions for cultivating love and compassion, but no other religious tradition explains that things lack intrinsic existence and that everything is dependent on something else. Only the Buddhist tradition explains a state of liberation that is achieved by realizing emptiness, the real nature of all phenomena. Therefore, only the Buddha, Dharma, and Spiritual Community, or the Three Jewels, are the infallible objects of refuge for those desiring liberation or *nirvana*. This is what the compassionate Buddha Shakyamuni has taught.[3]

This is a quintessential statement of religious Exclusivism, though it should be noted that the doctrine of reincarnation mitigates this exclusivism in the long run. (For as long as all humans are eventually reincarnated as Buddhists, all persons ultimately have access to the Three Jewels.) While this is a Tibetan Buddhist statement, other strands of Buddhism such as Theravada, with its emphasis on the Path of the Tradition, lend themselves to Exclusivism. Exclusivism is the view that salvation or liberation can only be found either inside a particular institutional structure – as exemplified by the traditional Roman Catholic dogma, *extra ecclesiam nulla salus* – or on the basis of a specified tradition of religious beliefs, symbols, and rituals.

Every World Religion has been exclusivist in its own way. But unqualified Exclusivism seems more and more untenable in the face of global interaction and the problem of religious plurality. The Fourteenth Dalai Lama's own way to resolve this problem is to seek an accord between Buddhist ethics and secular ethics (though he also edges at times more toward religious Inclusivism).[4] Since it is largely a matter of history and geography whether one grows up as a Hindu or Buddhist, Christian or Muslim, etc., and since even the extent to which one understands the parameters of one's own tradition is largely determined by family circumstances, religious Exclusivism casts those who have privileged knowledge, or who are intellectually astute, or who are socially fortunate as a religious elite, while penalizing those who either have no access to the putatively correct religious views or who are incapable of advanced understanding. In this vein we find the Fourteenth Dalai Lama suggesting that, "People who have been born in a place where the Dharma is practiced and have at least some sense of compassion and concern for the welfare of other sentient beings are regarded as free and fortunate human beings."[5] However, it is hard to see how one could know with certainty that there is only one correct set of religious truth-claims or only one institutional structure providing a path to salvation or liberation. This is exacerbated for those in the World Religions who have a global awareness by the fact that every other World Religion than one's own also makes exclusivist claims. Exclusivism would seem to underestimate the degree to which all religious truth-claims are human constructs, subject to the limitations and fallibility of the human mind.

One obvious response to Exclusivism is response (2), Antipathy. Given the enormity of the conflicting truth-claims of the World Religions, and given the typical exclusivist claims of all World Religions, is it not rational to conclude that all religious traditions are simply false in different ways? In the absence of a generally acceptable proof of some sort for the existence of God or the Transcendent (see chapters 4 and 5), there is no incontrovertible reply to religious Antipathy. Indeed, there are important atheological arguments, like the problem of evil (chapter 6), sociological and psychological arguments, like those of Feuerbach and Freud, and arguments derived from physics and biology (chapter 10), which lend support to religious Antipathy. Atheism is the common form of Antipathy in the West.

SUBJECTIVISM AND PLURALISM

It is, of course, possible that the Exclusivism of some particular religious tradition is correct. But given some of the weighty considerations against Exclusivism, let us turn to responses (3)–(6), responses that hold that in some form each of the great World Religions is or at least might be correctly directed toward the Transcendent. This brings us to various pluralistic views. They share an idealist epistemology that the world we experience and understand is not a world independent of our perceiving but a world at least in part structured by our minds. They also share the sort of view expressed by William James in the passage from *The Varieties of Religious Experience* cited at the beginning of this chapter that more than one set of human concepts – more than one worldview – is valid for understanding the world.

Pluralistic religious responses are based on the view that one's perception of religious truth is in some sense relative to one's worldview. The most radical of the pluralistic responses to the conflicting truth-claims of the World Religions is Subjectivism, which holds that religious truth is relative to each individual's idiosyncratic worldview. This would make religion a radically private affair, purely a matter of one's individual relation to the Transcendent. However, religious Subjectivism is conceptually incoherent. Only statements or propositions are true or false, statements or propositions are comprised of concepts, and concepts, in turn, are social constructions. Concepts cannot be purely private, individual understandings,[6] and therefore truth cannot be idiosyncratically individualistic. Religious Subjectivism must be rejected.

A very different pluralistic view is religious Pluralism. John Hick, who puts forth a systematic powerful religious Pluralism which is one of the most important developments in philosophical theology in the latter half of the twentieth century, offers this concise description of Pluralism as the view that, "There is not merely one way but a plurality of ways of salvation or liberation...taking place in different ways within the contexts of all the great religious traditions."[7] John Hick's own religious Pluralism holds that there is only one Ultimate Reality, but the World Religions offer different enculturated images of that one Ultimate Reality.[8] Thus, each of these religious perspectives is both partially accurate and does not ultimately conflict with the other perspectives. For Hick proposes that religion definitively concerns "the transformation of human existence from self-centeredness to Reality-centeredness,"[9] and that the apparently conflicting truth-claims of the world's religions are, in the final analysis, irrelevant given this more fundamental shared goal of moving from self- to Reality-centeredness. On Hick's account, specific forms of religious awareness "are formed by the presence of the divine Reality...coming to consciousness in terms of the different sets of religious concepts and structures of religious meaning that operate within the different religious traditions."[10] Thus, the divine Reality comes to consciousness as divine *personae* (e.g. YHWH,

Allah, etc.) for theists and as divine *impersonae* (e.g. *nirguna* Brahman, the Dharma, the Tao, etc.) for non-theists.[11]

However, in response to Hick it seems that differences of belief among the World Religions *are* soteriologically important. The cognitive content of religious faith provides the necessary cognitive map for purposive religious action and a guide to salvation/liberation. The cognitive content of a religion is what determines one's specific path to salvation/liberation, a path which is not just a means to an end, but is itself an integral part of the goal. This is the idea in Christianity that the "Kingdom is now" (Luke 17: 20–21); in Hinduism that *bhakti-yoga* puts one in the presence of Brahman/Ishvara, and in Mahayana Buddhism that *samsara* is *nirvana*. Indeed this is concisely captured in Buddhism with the idea that your individual *dharma* (path) is part of the universal *Dharma*.

Another difficulty faced by Hick's position is this. The idea of a personal God is a vital core belief of Jewish, Christian, Muslim, Zoroastrian, Hindu *bhakti*, Sikh, Baha'i, and, in a certain way, even Pure Land Buddhist worldviews. Atheistic Hindu Advaita Vedantists, Confucians, Taoists, and Theravada and Zen Buddhists hold an opposing vital core belief that the Transcendent is not personal. Hick attempts to account for this by suggesting that among the world's religions the "Ultimately Real" is only experienced as *either* personal or non-personal. Yet this contradicts the understanding of the first group of religious traditions that a personal God *correctly* reveals, indeed is the proper form of, the immanence of the Transcendent. While a personal reality might have non-personal aspects, it could not be identical to something which is non-personal. Hence, Hick's pluralist account would entail that the monotheist's and henotheist's experiences of a personal divine reality ultimately fail correctly to represent the Transcendent. And this runs counter to the monotheistic and henotheistic majority of both Western and Asian views, obviating the views of Maimonides and Aquinas, Ramanuja and Madhva, Zoroaster and Al-Ghazzali, and Nanak and Baha'u'llah alike.

INCLUSIVISM AND HENOFIDEISM

A natural alternative to turn to in order to meet these concerns is Inclusivism. Religious inclusivists fully retain the core doctrinal content of their traditions but hold two additional theses: (1) other religions convey part of the truth about the Transcendent and the relation of humanity to the Transcendent, and (2) only one's own tradition most fully provides an understanding of the Transcendent, and the most adequate path to salvation or liberation. For example, for those who believe in a God who is not a mere tribal deity, but the "being than which a greater cannot be conceived," the very ground of Being, a Creator-God who has providence over creation, it would seem to follow that the Spirit of God must be present somehow in all the World Religions. So it would seem that the monotheist, at least, must somehow include other religious worldviews.

Inclusivism has become the official view within Roman Catholicism since Vatican II. Thus, the dogmatic constitution *Nostra Aetate* from Vatican II states that "The Catholic Church rejects nothing which is true and holy in [other] religions," and that "...all peoples comprise a single community, and have a single origin...God...One also is their final goal: God," and the cross of Christ "is the sign of God's all-embracing love" and "the fountain from which every grace flows."[12] Karl Rahner, the eminent twentieth-century Catholic theologian, develops Inclusivism in some detail with the suggestion that those in the non-Christian traditions can be "anonymous Christians," emphasizing "the universal salvific will of God's love and omnipotence."[13] And R. C. Zaehner offers this historical argument for Roman Catholic Inclusivism:

> The drive towards the integration of...the personal and the collective, has been characteristic of the most original thinkers in [all religions] during the first two-thirds of the twentieth century...This unity in diversity is the birthright of the Catholic Church... all the other religions, in their historical development, grow into "other Catholic Churches"... [For while one God] is the inspiration of all religions and peculiar to none...The only religion that has from the beginning been both communal and individual is Christianity.[14]

It might be argued, however, that of all the World Religions, Hinduism is the most inherently inclusivist. The inclusivist orientation of Hinduism is exemplified by the absorption of Buddhism back into Hinduism by conceiving of Shakyamuni, the historical Buddha, as an *avatar* of Vishnu (see the chart "Metaphysics of Hinduism" in chapter 4, p.66).

Fundamentally, Inclusivism supposes that a specific sort of religious experience and understanding of the Transcendent is elemental to all religion (indeed, is elemental for all humans). This is reminiscent of John

Calvin's idea that all people have a *sensus divinitatis* and René Descartes's idea that one of the clear and distinct ideas all humans have is the idea of a God who is not a deceiver.[15] Though these claims may have been thought of as empirical claims, they express faith commitments. And as we shall see in chapter 13, the sort of powerful faith stance we find in Inclusivism and Exclusivism is, in itself, an important and appropriate religious disposition. But how could we *know* – except as an article of faith – that all humans have the same sort of elemental apprehension of the Transcendent? The empirical evidence of religious experience supports precisely the opposite conclusion. Even in the broadest terms, the notion of an elemental apprehension of the Transcendent is understood in personal terms in monotheistic and henotheistic traditions, while it is non-personal in Confucian, Advaita Vedanta Hindu, and Theravada and Zen Buddhist traditions. Moreover, each World Religion has a different idea of this elemental apprehension, and tends to see itself as the culmination of the elemental apprehension of the Transcendent.[16] So for example when Rahner says that the Christian has, "other things being equal, a still greater chance of salvation than someone who is merely an anonymous Christian,"[17] this is clearly a statement of faith.

Now, for those who reject the inclusivist and exclusivist views that one's own tradition must be the fullest if not the sole arbiter of the path to the Transcendent, there are two choices about how to deal with the irreducible plurality of religious conception and experience. As we have already seen, one can subscribe to the approach of religious Pluralism and treat the incompatible beliefs among differing religious worldviews as ultimately inessential. Or one could instead respect the doctrines which adherents of different World Religions so devotedly profess and passionately follow and treat them as essential to their faith. In our increasingly global world, many people are moving toward the latter stance of religious tolerance and acceptance while retaining the specific claims of their own personal faith. I shall call this view "Henofideism," from the Greek *heno* (one) and the Latin *fide* (faith) – a multicultural term for a multicultural perspective.

A henofideist is one who has fidelity to a single religious worldview, while acknowledging that other religious worldviews might be correct. So a henofideist is aware of other cultures and their religious perspectives. A henofideist might be a henotheist, but a henofideist might just as well be a monotheist. "Monotheism" and "henotheism" refer to one's metaphysics, "Henofideism" to one's faith commitment. The parallel in Hinduism would be between *ishtadevata* ("the god of one's choice") and *ishtavishvas* ("one's chosen faith"). The henofideist is an *ishtavishvasi* (or one inspired by a chosen faith), and may or may not hold to the *ishtadevata* of henotheism.

There are general meta-criteria that can be applied across world-views to assess the acceptability of a worldview. These criteria include the internal coherence of a worldview, its comprehensiveness, thoroughness of explanation (e.g. that it does not depend on *ad hoc* hypotheses), the efficaciousness of the worldview in producing its intended end, considerations of parsimony, and so on. The henofideist can employ these meta-criteria to assess other faiths. The henofideist can recognize that salvation or liberation could come to others in other traditions, without either attempting to assume the external stance of an impossible neutral global theology (as pluralists tend to do) or diminishing the strength of commitment to his or her own tradition. Yet in acknowledging that we humans cannot transcend our socio-historical worldviews, Henofideism recognizes the fundamental potential fallibility of every human conception.

Exclusivists and inclusivists might object to Henofideism on the grounds that it subverts one's faith. But what might be the problem? There are three ways in which one's beliefs might subvert faith. First, one might hold a belief (or cluster of beliefs) which is actually opposed to a core belief of one's tradition. Thus atheism, or a denial of life after death, subverts Islamic, Hindu *bhakti* and Christian faith. This is to use faith in a cognitive sense, so let us call this "belief subversion." Second, one might hold a meta-theory of one sort or another – meta-ethical, or epistemological, or metaphysical – which could subvert one's faith because it prevents one from consistently holding vital core beliefs of one's tradition. Thus, antinomianism which is against all laws, or belief in the complete preeminence of scientific explanation, prevents one from believing, respectively, in God's commands or the acts of God. That is, one's theoretical beliefs can preclude commitment to vital core religious beliefs, even though the converse of the theoretical beliefs in question are not themselves vital core beliefs. Let us call this "theory subversion." Finally there is a third sort of subversion of faith which concerns attitudes or character traits: e.g. being egotistical, unable to accept responsibility for one's actions, hatred of others, or hatred of God. Let us call this "commitment subversion."

Commitment subversion is the most insidious for any religious life, for it is a moral danger. Belief subversion is a danger to one's adherence to any specific tradition. But the least significant of the three types of subversion is theory subversion, precisely the type of subversion with which the exclusivist or inclusivist might charge Henofideism. Theory subversion is an epistemological issue. But surely the correctness of one's epistemology is not salvific or liberating – unless one is promoting a sort of gnosticism where bad epistemologists shall crowd out all others in hell or in the number of turns they take on the wheel of *samsara*! All the World Religions hold that it is actions, attitudes, and affective states which are salvific and liberating. So under what conditions does one have an obligation to change one's epistemology, to be an inclusivist, say, rather than an exclusivist, a henofideist rather than an inclusivist? The greatest dangers to the religious life are commitment subversion and belief subversion, so the most important obligation to consider is our moral obligation to give up beliefs which we come to realize we hold for immoral reasons – such as greed, self-centeredness, and pride. Assessed on this count, Henofideism fares well, for it promotes a religiously appropriate humbleness: a faith commitment is either correct or incorrect, but it does not improve the correctness of a faith commitment also to believe and so judge that others are necessarily wrong.

A ROAD MAP OF WORLD RELIGIOSITY

To see the relation among all these responses to the problem of religious plurality, consider an analogy drawn from the pattern of roadways which come into London like the spokes on a wheel from the surrounding countryside. Those who travel in from the outlying shires hope to reach London. Some come down from Cambridge to the northeast on the M11, some from Oxford to the northwest on the M40, some from Bristol to the west on the M4, and others on various routes in between as well as from the east and even from the south from across the Channel.

From the perspective of the apathetic traveler, there is no London and all the travelers are deluded and destined to be disappointed. For the more provincial, exclusivist traveler, the M11 from Cambridge is the only way to get to London, or the M40 from Oxford is the only way to get to London, etc. The free-spirited subjectivist traveler listens to the tales of the various exclusivist travelers and declares that all routes lead to London, and it is just a matter of personal preference. The more highly organized pluralist travel agency insists that not only is there a London, but, if you just imagine greater London from a "God's eye view," you will see, even if dimly and through a fog, that all the great routes do indeed lead to London. The pluralist travel agency cautions against disorganized tours and urges travelers not to waste their time in minor byways on their travels to London.

Inclusivist travelers are found among the exclusivists on the major thoroughfares. Inclusivists are committed to their favored route – the M11, M40, M4, etc. – but they feel that all the other supposed routes to London (at least the other major routes) are in actuality just branch routes which inevitably feed into their favored route. The henofideists also travel among the exclusivists and the inclusivists. Henofideists admire the fidelity of the inclusivist and the exclusivist, while rejecting the faithlessness of the apathetic traveler and the mercurial approach of the subjectivist traveler. The henofideists do not understand how the pluralist travel agency can be certain what a God's eye view of greater London really looks like. But while the henofideists are firmly committed to their favored route into London, they do not discount the reports of other travelers and allow for the possibility of alternative routes. However, while the henofideists do not disparage alternative routes, if asked about a recommended route, they will always recommend the route they themselves are on, on the grounds that they have only heard about but have not themselves traveled the other routes.

Finally, there are rumors that there actually is a divine travel agency in London itself. One version is that from the perspective of the divine travel agency, the travelers themselves should be henofideists, but the agency is inclusivist:

> Driven by their very Nature,
> deprived of knowledge by their lust,
> adopting various religious rules,
> some men in other gods may trust.
>
> Whatever form a devotee
> may worship in his faith,
> 'tis I ordain the same to be
> for his unswerving faith.

Some with faith may offer worship
to other gods as devotees,
yet it is only Me they worship
tho' not as law decrees.

I am Recipient and Lord
of every sacrifice,
but those will fall if Me in truth
they do not recognize.

I am the same to every being,
none is despised or dear,
but they're in Me and I in them
    who love Me and revere.[18]

Krishna speaking to Arjuna in The *Bhagavad Gita*

Further reading

Endo, Shusaku. *Deep River*. Van C. Gessel, trans. New York, New Directions Book, 1994

Hick, John. *God and the Universe of Faith*. Oxford, Oneworld, 1993

Hick, John. *An Interpretation of Religion*. London, Macmillan, 1989

Mahfouz, Naguib. *The Journey of Ibn Fattouma*. Denys Johnson-Davies, trans. New York,   Doubleday, 1992

Mullan, David George, ed. *Religious Pluralismin the West* . Oxford, Blackwell Publishers, 1998

Nostra Aetate (Declaration on the Relationship of the Church to Non-Christian Religions) in *The Documents of Vatican II*. Walter M. Abbott, S.J., ed. The America Press, 1966

Smart, Ninian. *Worldviews: Crosscultural Explorations of Human Beliefs*. New Jersey, Prentice Hall, 1995

Ward, Keith. *Concepts of God*. Oxford, Oneworld, 1998

3 RELIGIOUS METAPHYSICS WITHOUT GOD

> It is prohibited to understand that [Atman] is different [from Brahman].
> [The pupil may say:] "How is it prohibited to understand that [Atman] is different [from Brahman]."
> Then the teacher replies:
> "So whoever worships another divinity [than his Atman], thinking that He is one and I another, he does not know"[1]
> (Brh. Upanishad I, 4, 10)
>
> Shankara (d. 874 CE)

A religious metaphysics is any expressly religious view of the structure of reality. Let us begin our assessment of particular religious truth-claims by assessing the general religious metaphysics of those traditions among the World Religions which have a metaphysics without God. It will be important to keep in mind that these non-theistic traditions have a religiously realist metaphysics. Within the World Religions, a realist metaphysics holds that the structure of reality includes (or on some views just is) a Transcendent reality. Monotheisms, which we will address in the next chapter, are obviously realist because they postulate the existence of God. But for instance the Hindu Shankara's Advaita Vedanta (nondualism), from which the opening quote comes, is also a realist metaphysics: while there is no God or individual soul (no individual *atman*), all that is is Brahman, and Brahman is the Plenitude of Being. And while it is less obvious, Buddhism similarly holds a realist metaphysics: *nirvana* is designated as "Nothingness," but *nirvana* is not nothing, for it is pure bliss, the bliss of selflessness, the as it were "Fullness of Emptiness." This is why the Mahayana Buddhist formula which was eventually developed, that *"nirvana* is *samsara* and *samsara* is *nirvana,"* still expresses a realist metaphysics: the true nature of this world of *samsara* is emptiness; hence *samsara,* if understood correctly, is recognized as identical to the Fullness of Emptiness, or *nirvana.* In sum, whatever differences there are among the World Religions, they agree insofar as they all have a religiously realist metaphysics. We will return later in the chapter to this important issue about the nature of religious realism.

THE MATERIAL WORLD VERSUS THE TRANSCENDENT

Any philosophic system which includes the idea of a Transcendent, and this includes every World Religion, demarcates between the mere world of appearance and things as they really are, where the latter either includes or is identical to the Transcendent. One of the most famous Western examples of this demarcation is found in the writings of Plato when he relates the Allegory of the Cave in the *Republic*:

> Imagine men to be living in an underground cave-like dwelling place, which has a way up to the light along its whole width, but the entrance is a long way up. The men have been there from childhood, with their neck and legs in fetters, so that they remain in the same place and can only see ahead of them, as their bonds prevent them turning their heads. Light is provided by a fire burning some way behind and above them. Between the fire and the prisoners, some way behind them and on a higher ground, there is a path across the cave and along this a low wall has been built, like the screen at a puppet show in front of the performers who show their puppets above it...
>
> See then also men carrying along that wall, so that they overtop it, all kinds of artifacts, statues of men, reproductions of other animals in stone or wood fashioned in all sorts of ways, [thus projecting shadows of the artifacts on the wall in front of the prisoners].

Plato then goes on to explain the Allegory in this way:

> The realm of the visible should be compared to the prison dwelling, [and the shadows of the figures which the prisoners see on the wall] and the fire inside it to the power of the sun...interpret the upward journey and the contemplation of things above as the upward journey of the soul to the intelligible realm, ... in the intelligible world the Form of the Good is the last to be seen, and with difficulty; when seen it must be reckoned

to be for all the cause of all that is right and beautiful, to have produced
in the visible world both light and the fount of light, while in the intelligible world it is itself that which produces and controls truth and intelligence, and he who is to act intelligently in public or in private must
see it...the capacity to learn and the organ with which to do so are present in every person's soul.

It is as if it were not possible to turn the eye from darkness to light
without turning the whole body; so one must turn one's whole soul from
the world of becoming until it can endure to contemplate reality, and
the brightest of realities, which we say is the Good.[2]

Plato's Allegory illustrates the basic metaphysics, or theory of the structure of reality, of the World Religions *vis-à-vis* the idea of a
Transcendent: the things of this world partake of, or are mere shadows
of, or are illusory, compared to the Transcendent. In Plato's particular
metaphysics, that Transcendent is the world of the Forms – especially
the Form of the Good – and the things of this world, the world of shadows, are shadows of imitations of the Forms of Beauty, Justice, the
Good, and so on.

Christian and Islamic theology easily assimilated this Platonic conception into the dichotomy between the material world (creation) and
God (the Creator in whose mind reside the perfect ideas which inform
our imperfect world). But religion can also develop in another direction
vis-à-vis the Transcendent, not, as in the West, seeing this world as a distinct created reality separate from the Creator, but seeing this world as a
mere illusion which hides the only reality. As the quote commencing this
chapter indicates, the great medieval Hindu philosopher Shankara developed this latter view in his Advaita Vedanta, where the final realization
(*moksha*) is that *Atman* is *Brahman* and there are no distinct real souls
(*jivas*). Shankara's own position will be made clearer in the next chapter
when his opponents, Ramanuja and Madhva, who disputed Shankara's
non-dualistic interpretation of the classic Hindu scriptures, the *Vedas* and
the *Upanishads,* will be addressed. In this chapter, to understand better
a religious metaphysics without God, let us focus on another tradition
which also first arose within Hinduism, namely Buddhism.

BUDDHISM AND METAPHYSICS

Compared to the Hindu tradition from which it separated, Buddhism
is metaphysically more like the extreme non-dualism of Advaita Vedanta
than it is like other Hindu philosophical systems. Ramanuja and

Madhva even accused Shankara of being like a Buddhist. But Buddhism opposes the Advaitist's postulation of a transcendent *Brahman/Atman*, so much so that it is often said that Buddhism has no metaphysics, or that Buddhism is anti-metaphysical. On this characterization, the Buddhist metaphysics looks like this:

There is no statement about metaphysics in this box.

Of course, just as the statement in the box contradicts itself, anti-metaphysical claims are themselves metaphysical claims.

The misunderstanding that Buddhism is a view without a metaphysics is rooted in early texts about the historical Shakyamuni himself. In the parable of Malunkyaputta in the Pali Scriptures we find this account of the Buddha's words:

> It is as if, Malunkyaputta, a man had been wounded by an arrow thickly smeared with poison, and his friends and companions, his relatives and kinfolks, were to procure for him a physician or surgeon; and the sick man were to say, "I will not have this arrow taken out until I have learnt whether the man who wounded me belonged to the warrior caste, or to the Brahmin caste, or to the agricultural caste, or to the menial caste."
>
> ...Or again he were to say, "I will not have this arrow taken out until I have learnt whether the arrow which wounded me was an ordinary arrow, or a claw-headed arrow, or a calf-tooth arrow, or a karavirapatta." That man would die, Malunkyaputta, without ever having learnt this.
>
> The religious life, for this Malunkyaputta, does not depend on the dogma that the saint both exists and does not exist after death; nor does the religious life, Malunkyaputta, depend on the dogma that the saint neither exists nor does not exist after death. Whether the dogma obtain, Malunkyaputta, that the saint both exists and does not exist after death, or that the saint neither exists nor does not exist after death, there still remain birth, old age, death, sorrow, lamentation, misery, grief and despair, for the extinction of which in the present life I am prescribing.
>
> ...And why, Malunkyaputta, have I not elucidated this [life after death]? Because, Malunkyaputta, this profits not, nor has to do with the fundamentals of religion, nor tends to aversion, absence of passion, cessation, quiescence, the supernatural facilities, supreme wisdom, and *Nirvana*; therefore have I not elucidated it.[3]

Here the Buddha is not saying that all metaphysics is mistaken. What he says instead is that getting caught up in metaphysical speculation – such as whether or not the same person survives death in rebirth – is like examining a poison arrow rather than extracting it. To live is to suffer, and to die is to be reborn into suffering, and what the Buddha wished to convey to his hearers was a way out of this cycle of *samsara*, not to encourage further speculation which would prevent them from focusing on rectifying their human plight.

Likewise, Plato sees that the person caught up in this world and in ordinary religious ritual and speculation will not advance to a higher level of understanding:

> Hence, as long as true knowledge does not present itself, there is no reason why the ordinary course of secular and religious activity should not hold on undisturbed. The case is analogous to that of a dreaming man who in his dream sees manifold things, and, up to the moment of waking, is convinced that his ideas are produced by real perception without suspecting the perception to be a merely apparent one.[4]

However, Plato thinks that the individual self can save itself, for he holds that the individual soul is both real and immortal. Shakyamuni's metaphysics denies that there is any self (*atman or jiva*) to save (or liberate), for even more fundamentally he denies that there are any substantial things, any substances at all.

The usual starting point for explaining Buddhism is the path which the historical Buddha encapsulated in the Four Noble Truths. The Four Noble Truths enunciate a progression of ideas: in the endless cycle of life and death, to live is to suffer; we cause our own suffering on this

---

THE FOUR NOBLE TRUTHS

1. The Truth of Suffering

2. The Truth of Arising

3. The Truth of Cessation

4. The Truth of the Noble Eightfold Path:
   Wisdom: (1) Right Views and (2) Right Resolve
   Morality: (3) Right Speech, (4) Right Action, and (5) Right Livelihood
   Meditation: (6) Right Effort, (7) Right Mindfulness, and (8) Right Meditation.

---

wheel of life and death through craving (i.e. inappropriate attachment to, or aversion from, "things"); there is a way out of our suffering; and finally, that way is to follow the Eightfold Path. The Eightfold Path, in turn, can be divided into three things one must do to achieve enlightenment or liberation from *samsara*: achieve wisdom, act fully morally, and meditate (both literally and as mindfulness in all our actions). The key to the Four Noble Truths is the Second Truth, that we cause our own suffering. We can see what the Buddha had in mind if we consider Leo Tolstoy's magnificent novella *The Death of Ivan Ilyich* in which the life of the protagonist illustrates this realization that material attachments cause suffering and keep us from a meaningful life.

Ivan Ilyich lives a contented life in nineteenth-century Russia as a municipal judge, marrying properly, having the proper friends, living in a proper house, and having a proper family. As he reaches the pinnacle of success as a judge:

> Ivan Ilyich's life had been most simple and most ordinary and therefore most terrible...But now, as an examining magistrate, Ivan Ilyich felt that everyone without exception, even the most important and self-satisfied, was in his power...Ivan Ilyich never abused his power; he tried on the contrary to soften its expression, but the consciousness of it and of the possibility of softening its effect, supplied the chief interest and attraction of his office.

Then Ivan injures himself, ironically while absorbed in pridefully working on his perfectly proper and perfectly ordinary house, and becomes gravely ill. He is disturbed when those around him begin to treat him as he had treated others who were ill:

> The awful, terrible act of his dying, he could see, was reduced by those about him to the level of casual, unpleasant, and almost indecorous incident (as if someone entered a drawing-room diffusing an unpleasant odour), and this was done by that very decorum which he had served all his life long.

He finds that even his own children exhibit these disturbing attitudes:

> Their daughter came in in full evening dress, her fresh young flesh exposed (making a show of that very flesh which in his own case caused so much suffering), strong, healthy, evidently in love, and impatient with illness, suffering, and death, because they interfered with her happiness.

He comes to reassess his attitude toward life and its meaning:

> It is as if I had been going downhill while I imagined I was going up. And that is really what it was. I was going up in public opinion, but to the same extent life was ebbing away from me. And now it is all done and there is only death...Then what does it mean? Why? It can't be that life is so senseless and horrible. But if it really has been so horrible and senseless, why must I die and die in agony? There is something wrong!

Finally, realizing the value of genuine relationship, near the end of his life he reaches, like Socrates, a reconciliation with death:

> He sought his former accustomed fear of death and did not find it. "Where is it? What death?" There was no fear because there was no death.[5]

Similarly, in the words of the Fourteenth Dalai Lama, Buddhism offers a release from the fear of death:

> As a great practitioner you will welcome death, as a moderate practitioner you will not fear death, and even as an inferior practitioner, you will have nothing to regret at the time of death.[6]

Buddhism teaches a realization much like that which we find in *The Death of Ivan Ilyich* that the mundane life of materialism ending in death "is so senseless and horrible." Again in the words of the Fourteenth Dalai Lama:

> No lasting satisfaction can be derived from sensual pleasures or desirable objects. These things are like honey smeared on the sharp blade of a sword. When you lick it, you may be able to taste the honey's sweetness, but at the same time you lose your tongue.[7]

But Buddhism ultimately posits a different root cause of our suffering than that proposed in the Western monotheism of Tolstoy.

On the Buddhist view, our own craving causes suffering because the things (including the self) to which we attach ourselves as if they were permanent (i.e. as if they were persistent substances) are impermanent. In attaching ourselves to what we think is permanent, we are doomed to suffer loss: those we love die and disappoint, material objects are transient, and we ourselves are mortal. Thus, the elemental principle of metaphysics in Buddhism is impermanence (*annica*) and the related notion of the dependent origination (*pratitya-samutpada*) of everything from every-

THE ARGUMENT FROM IMPERMANENCE

1. Experience is the test of truth.
2. To live is to be an experiencing ego (*anatman*).
3. Only impermanence and interdependence is experienced in life (*annica* and *pratitya-samutpada*).
4. Therefore everything which can be experienced (including our egos) is impermanent and interdependent.
5. In life we egoistically have attachment to, or aversion from, the "things" we experience as if they were permanent.
6. Through this ignorance (*avidya*), our own cravings (attractions and aversions) cause suffering (*duhkha*): this is the Second Noble Truth.
7. To be an ego is to be reborn and to be reborn (*samsara*) is to suffer: this is the First Noble Truth.
8. Therefore, if humans hope to avoid suffering, they must avoid rebirth.
9. Rebirth is caused by ignorance and bad *karma*, which is the result of craving and a false sense of self (karmic law).
10. We have no experience of a higher power which could save us from our bad karma.
11. However, there is a way out if we cultivate egoless non-attachment and non-aversion: this is the Third Noble Truth.
12. The Eightfold Path leads to non-attachment and non-aversion: this is the Fourth Noble Truth.
13. Therefore, we must follow the Eightfold Path to cultivate non-attachment and non-version and eradicate the false sense of self.

thing else so that nothing is a subsisting thing (substance) in itself. This means that there is no *atman*, a fundamentally mistaken view in Hinduism according to Buddhists. Rather Buddhism holds *anatman* (noself). But impermanence and dependent co-origination also means there is no God (or no Brahman, another Hindu "mistake"), for the concept of God is the concept of infinite substance (we will see this clearly when we look at Anselm's Ontological Argument in the next chapter).

The Buddhist metaphysics entails a line of reasoning which is actually more foundational than, indeed it even undergirds, the Four Noble Truths. That reasoning is formalized as "The Argument from Impermanence", see above. The karmic law (premise 9) which the Argument from Impermanence assumes is the idea that reincarnation is caused by ignorance and resulting bad character traits (bad *karma*) acquired during the past life (or lives) – where bad character traits are formed through repetitive inappropriate (craving) attachment to a false sense of a permanent self and permanent things outside the self. Thus, habitual lying produces a deceitful character, repeated acts of possessiveness produces a greedy and stingy character, and so on. Likewise, good character (good *karma*) is produced by habitual acts of truth-

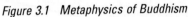

Figure 3.1 Metaphysics of Buddhism

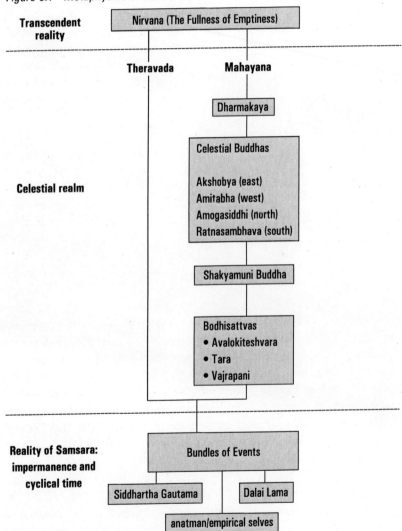

telling, benevolence, compassion, etc. This is put concisely in the Buddhist proverb "sow an act, reap a habit; sow a habit, reap a character; sow a character, reap a destiny."[8]

We are all aware to some extent that we habitually act in ways that cause us grief. So why do we not change ourselves? Unfortunately, the human condition is summed up in the Tibetan saying "engaging in virtuous practice is as hard as pulling a tired donkey up a hill, but engaging in negative, destructive activities is as easy as rolling a boulder down from a steep slope."[9] On the Buddhist view, to overcome this human condition, we most fundamentally must eradicate our ignorant attachment to the idea of self as a substance that can acquire things. Likewise on this Buddhist perspective, we must not think that there is an infinite substance – Brahman or God – which could offer permanent succor from suffering.

But if there is no God and no soul, what is the metaphysics of Shakyamuni's historical existence, or our existence, or that of the Dharmakaya (the later Mahayana idea of a Buddha Nature)? We might sketch the alternative Theravada and Mahayana metaphysics using figure 3.1, opposite. Where Theravada is highly teleological and more oriented toward individual liberation, Mahayana is oriented toward communal liberation and adds an emphasis on liberation now (*"nirvana* is *samsara"*) as well as final *nirvana*. But we see from the schematic that even in Mahayana, with its celestial Buddhas like Amitabha, etc., only *nirvana* is Transcendent. Within both traditions, the historical Shakyamuni is a bundle of events, a collection of transient thoughts, bodily actions, etc., which we categorize as a person but which is not additionally some underlying substance. (More will be said about this notion of *anatman* when we discuss life after death in chapter 8). And for Mahayana, even the *bodhisattvas*, like Avalokiteshvara, and the Dharmakaya are ultimately transient. For ultimately all is the Fullness of Emptiness, *parinirvana*, or final *nirvana*. Put another way, only *parinirvana* is transcendent and only this final *nirvana* parallels the transcendent God in the Western monotheisms and Brahman in Hinduism (see chapter 4).

THEOLOGICAL REALISM VERSUS RELIGIOUS NON-REALISM

As we have seen then, while Buddhism appears non-realist, it is not. In contrast, it might appear that all those who subscribe to monotheism and henotheism are obviously religious realists, but this is not so. There are philosophic positions, albeit a small minority, within historic monotheism which are non-realist. True, talk of God is essential to Jewish, Christian, Islamic, and Hindu *bhakti* understanding. But even though one may talk of God, theological realists conceive of God as Transcendent; the theological non-realist does not. So there is a minority who describe themselves as belonging to the nominally monotheistic traditions but who do not include a realist God as part of their metaphysics. What exactly do theological non-realists deny that theological realists hold and in what sense is God transcendent for religious realists who are monotheists?

God might be regarded as transcendent in either a metaphysical or a conceptual sense. Metaphysical transcendence is the idea that God is not identical with either the whole or part of the natural world. In this sense, Benedict Spinoza does not refer to a transcendent God when he identifies God with Nature, and when process thought, based on the ideas of Alfred North Whitehead, identifies God with the originating conditions and the consequent of the process of nature, this is not a transcendent God. Another use of transcendence is conceptual transcendence. This concerns *otherness*, and in its strongest form this is the view that the transcendent is so "wholly other" that it is impossible that any of our concepts can strictly apply to God. On a strong view of conceptual transcendence, no positive attributions can be made of the Transcendent. As we saw in the Introduction, for instance, the great Jewish theologian Moses Maimonides holds that God is metaphysically transcendent, but he also holds strong conceptual transcendence and so employs the *via negativa* as the only means to talk about God.

Religious realists hold metaphysical transcendence and sometimes conceptual transcendence regarding the Transcendent. Religious realism, in brief, is the view that there is a Transcendent which is independent of nature, and so independent of human thought (metaphysical transcendence). God is not a mere projection of the human mind. However, many realists – systematically throughout the history of Hinduism and Buddhism and in the West largely among post-Kantians – hold that the mind structures all of perception. So it is accurate to say that religious realists hold that there is a Transcendent which is metaphysically transcendent and therefore is, at least in part, conceptually independent of human thought, action, or attitudes. Religious non-realists deny this.

Most forms of Hinduism and Buddhism share a deep suspicion about the material world – the deluding world of *maya*. Western monotheism, on the other hand, sees the material world as God's creation and hence as both real and good. So Western monotheism is more susceptible to an interior challenge by religious non-realists who agree that the material world is real enough, and religion valuable enough, but hold that the Transcendent is either non-existent or so transcendent as to be irrelevant. In his mid-nineteenth-century novel *The Brothers Karamazov*, Fyodor Dostoevsky addressed the rise of atheistic nihilism in Western culture and the resultant moral threat which was felt among theists. If "God is dead," would not everything be permitted? Contemporary theological non-realists reject this idea that the death of (the old) God must lead to moral anarchy. As Don Cupitt, one of the most significant proponents of this theological non-realism, puts it:

> A God out there and values out there, if they existed, would be *utterly* useless and unintelligible to us. There is nothing to be gained by nostalgia for the old objectivism, which was in any case used only to justify arrogance, tyranny and cruelty. People [forget]...how utterly hateful the old pre-humanitarian world was.[10]

As the theological non-realist knows, the question raised in the West in the last two centuries has often been less "Why believe in God?" than "Why talk about God at all?" or "Why think of God as existing?"

Theological non-realism poses a particular challenge to the religious realism which claims a Transcendent God is needed to clarify, support, and extend our understanding of the ethical. For example, Don Cupitt says in *The New Christian Ethics* that:

> While the old God was about, he prevented Christian ethics from becoming truly creative...Only through the death of that God does Christian ethics at last acquire the duty and the authority to create value *ex nihilo*, which marks it as truly Christian and enables it to redeem our life...the more "objective" your theology is, the more you will suppose yourself to be in possession of a kind of literal account of God's nature and dealings with men, and the more open your belief will be to severe moral criticism...it is the most highly developed dogmatic theologies which represent God in the most repellent light. And it will not do to say, "It's only symbolism", if the symbolism is in fact morally repellent.[11]

On Cupitt's view, the most fundamental feature of truly ethical action is autonomy.[12] The moral deficiency of the old theological realism is that it proposes a relation with God in which morality is treated as a set of divinely promulgated "guide rails" which constrain autonomy and direct humans from the outside.[13] Cupitt argues that this view of morality undermines autonomy and produces a sense of one's own worthlessness. He then concludes that "The *first* task is to create enough value, to inject enough meaning and weight into our human world to make life worth living at all;" this is "the life that is ethically creative...creat[ing] value where previously there was no value..."; we now "have to do what God used to do for us...Our immediate task is to *secularize* and humanize the Christian self."[14] To see whether contemporary religious non-realism could succeed in this ethical task, let us look at several possible problems with Cupitt's well-articulated version, which he refers to as "Christian humanism."[15]

First, Cupitt argues that Christian humanism is superior to secular humanism because it

> Explicitly presents itself as a temporalization and humanization of God. Thus the human being acquires a dignity and a status that is directly derived from the ancient holiness and worshipfulness of God. God indeed just was a symbol of the goal towards which our moral development is heading and of the dignity to which we should ultimately attain.[16]

But this encourages self-deception. What is being proposed is that one acknowledge that God does not exist but continue to use traditional language about God because this will transfer a special holiness and nobility to the struggle to be moral. This seems no better than suggesting that if, as we grow older, we recognize that our parents have no particular moral authority, we should continue to use the language of deferential respect to parental moral authority because this will enhance the sense of the importance of morality.

A second deficiency of religious non-realism is that the religious element becomes extraneous. Representing the sort of scientific humanist view which we will address again in chapter 10, Julian Huxley starts from a view like Cupitt's, saying that "it is among human personalities that there exist the highest and most valuable achievements of the universe," and suggests that "many men and women have led active, or self-sacrificing, or noble, or devoted lives without any belief in God."[17] This raises the question of "Why be a *religious* humanist, and not simply a secular humanist?"[18] Why would a call to raise our ethical sights be any stronger or more motivating if it is cast in religious terms, when belief in a Transcendent is rejected? If all that is at stake is the moral life, secular humanitarian institutions and symbols like UNICEF, Amnesty International, and The International Red Cross can be as morally effective and affective as religious institutions and symbols.

A third problem with severing religious morality from religious realism can be seen if we consider why the World Religions have had a realist notion of a Transcendent to ground morality. Cupitt suggests that "The best Christian life is the life that is dedicated to those who are of the least account, those who are the most victimized – and your own vocabulary will give you a pretty good idea of who they are."[19] Unfortunately, the vocabulary of a community cannot *per se* serve as the criterion of what is moral, of who is the oppressed and who the oppressor. All too often oppressors actually see themselves as the original victims. Rather, for the religious realist, the moral standards by which we judge the Nazis and Pol Pot and Idi Amin to have acted wrongly, and the generous, the compassionate, and the benevolent to be morally laudatory, are indicative of real structures independent of humans, such as the *Dharma* or the *Tao* or the *Torah* or the *Shari'a*, which in turn are indicative of the Transcendent. On this view, morality is not simply a matter of doing the right thing but a matter of aligning oneself with the deep moral structure of a Transcendent source of all value.

In sum, religious non-realists hold that the true significance of the religious life can be found apart from metaphysical conceptions of the Transcendent. This effectively reduces the religious life to the moral life. In contrast, religious realists hold that unless there is a Transcendent, there is little if any point to religion. It does seem that, everything considered, the adherents of any of the great World Religions need to be religious realists. For not to be a realist about the Transcendent, yet to devote one's life to a humanly invented path to salvation/liberation amounts to being simply a humanist.

THE ADVANTAGES OF NON-THEISM

Adherents of worldviews without God within the World Religions claim that the advantage of such a metaphysics is that the notion of God is irrelevant to morality. Here is Bhikku Chao Chu speaking for Buddhism:

> The many contradictory conceptions of god held by various revealed traditions have no place in the Buddhist teaching...Faith in a particular god or scripture – to the exclusion of others – is a weak and insupportable

basis for a system of ethics...[For people] all perceive, however dimly, the same universal laws inherent in the world itself.[20]

If this is right, a clear consideration in favor of religious worldviews without God is parsimony, or simplicity and elegance of explanation. A system which includes both the notions of nature and of a distinct, self-existent God is more complex than one, such as Buddhism, in which there is only a Transcendent. Generally in choosing among alternative systems, we do choose that which is more elegant in its explanations. But as Einstein said about overemphasizing parsimony, "elegance is for tailors." Even more fundamental than parsimony to the acceptability of a system over its competitors is comprehensiveness of explanation. Monotheism and henotheism, to which we now turn, are religious worldviews which claim that the nature of reality and the presence of value, including moral values, are only sufficiently explainable if there is a God.

Further reading

INTRODUCTORY

Berthrong, John. *Confucianism: A Short Introduction*. Oxford, Oneworld, 2000

Cupitt, Don. *The New Christian Ethics*. London, SCM Press, 1988

Cupitt, Don. *Taking Leave of God*. New York, Crossroad, 1980

Deutsch, Eliot. *Advaita Vedanta: A Philosophic Reconstruction*. Honolulu, University Press of Hawaii, 1973

Keown, Damien. *Buddhism: A Very Short Introduction*. Oxford, Oxford University Press, 1996

Lopez, Donald S. Jr. *The Heart Sutra Explained*. New York, State University of New York Press, 1988

IN-DEPTH

Abe, Masao. *Zen and Western Thought*. William LaFleur, ed. Honolulu, University of Hawaii Press, 1985

de Bary, William Theodore, ed. *The Buddhist Tradition in India, China, and Japan*. New York, Vintage Books, 1969

Chan, Wing-Tsit. *A Source Book in Chinese Philosophy*. Princeton, Princeton University Press, 1963

Deutsch, Eliot and van Buitenen, J.A.B. *A Source Book of Advaita*

Vedanta. Honolulu, The University Press of Hawaii, 1971

Dumoulin, Heinrich. *Zen Buddhism in the 20th Century*. Joseph O'Leary, trans. New York, Weatherhill, 1992

Fingarette, Herbert. *Confucius: The Secular as Sacred*. New York: Harper and Row, 1972

Hartshorne, Charles. *Man's Vision of God and the Logic of Theism*. London, Yale University Press, 1948

Koller, John M. and Patricia. *A Sourcebook in Asian Philosophy*. New Jersey, Prentice Hall, 1991

Runzo, Joseph, ed. *Is God Real?* New York, St. Martin's Press, 1993

Taylor, Rodney L. *The Religious Dimensions of Confucianism*. New York, State University of New York Press, 1990

Whitehead, Alfred North. *Process and Reality*. New York, The Free Press, 1929

4 RELIGIOUS METAPHYSICS WITH GOD

Those, however, who understand the Vedanta, teach as follows: There is a highest Brahman which is the sole cause of the entire universe, which is antagonistic to all evil, whose essential nature is infinite knowledge and blessedness, which comprises within itself numberless auspicious qualities of supreme excellence, which is different in nature from all other beings, and which constitutes the inner Self of all.[1]

Ramanuja (1100–1200 CE)

GOD AND MONOTHEISM

Ramanuja is an ideal philosophical theologian with whom to begin a chapter on monotheism. Monotheism is obviously definitive of the Abrahamic faiths of the West – Judaism, Christianity, and Islam – which we will be addressing especially in the next two chapters. Too often however the seminal Indian tradition, Hinduism, is philosophically identified with non-theistic Advaita Vedanta, ignoring the ancient and dominant strands of Hindu theism. Alfred North Whitehead once suggested, in an often quoted misunderstanding, that Christianity is a religion seeking a metaphysics while Buddhism is a metaphysics seeking a religion.[2] It is important to keep in mind that Buddhism and Hinduism are orthopraxic traditions, while the Western monotheisms like Christianity are orthodoxic. The Indic traditions emphasize right practice; the Western traditions emphasize right belief or doctrine. So to parody Whitehead, as we saw in the last chapter Buddhism is a religious practice founded on a metaphysics; Christianity is a metaphysics which is sometimes taken to be the whole of religion; and Hinduism – not Christianity – is a religion seeking a metaphysics. A prominent focus of this quest for a metaphysics within Hinduism has been various forms of Hindu dualism, especially Hindu monotheism.

A word must be said about the use of the term "monotheism" and also "God." Consider Benedict Spinoza's (1632–1677) view that God – the one infinite substance – is identical with the universe (Nature). Though Spinoza uses the term "God," his classic pantheism has sometimes been referred to as "God-intoxicated atheism." In a literal and not just pejorative sense Spinoza's view is atheistic. For normally when we ask "Why believe in God?", we do not mean anything like "Why believe in the universe?" Contrary to Spinoza, we mean to refer to the traditional God of theological realism, a God who is distinct from the natural order.[3] Now, sometimes a theological realist's use of the term "God" is more narrowly employed to refer to Western ideas of the Divine. But here "God" will be used in its broad philosophic sense of theological realism as referring to the infinite source of the universe, who is not dependent on anything else (who possesses *aseity*, or self-existence), who is maximally loving, caring and wise, and who is, most fundamentally, a personal God. On this theological realist view, God is distinct from nature, and God is not just a figment of the human imagination but a transcendent reality.

HINDU THEISTIC VEDANTA

While the Western monotheisms were founded in the Pentateuch's insistence on a single god (the "Lord your God...you shall have no other gods before me" of Exod. 20:2–3 and Deut. 5:6–7), the multifaceted complexity of the huge corpus of Hindu scripture (the *Vedas* and the *Upanishads*, the *Bhagavad Gita* and much more) lends itself to multiple metaphysical interpretations of the Transcendent. While Christian theologians fairly narrowly constructed the idea of the Trinity from suggestive passages in the comparatively short New Testament text, Shankara developed a non-dualistic understanding, and Ramanuja, Madhva, and others developed monotheistic alternatives based on the extensive Hindu *shruti* (the sacred literature). Both the Hindu non-dualists and the Hindu monotheists, working from the same text, accused the other of misinterpreting scripture, just as medieval Islamic philosophers and Christian philosophers each accused the other of heresy,

Muslims accusing Christians of being polytheists and not holding to the *Tawhid* (divine unity), and Christians accusing Muslims of denying the divinity of Jesus and the Triune God. (Illustrating the latter, the *Qubbat al-Sakhrah* – the Dome of the Rock in Jerusalem – the oldest intact surviving Islamic building, includes a long *qur'anic* inscription proclaiming the Oneness of God against the Triune conception of God.)

Regarding differences of interpretation within Hinduism, a major point of dispute within philosophic Hinduism focuses on the *"tat tvan asi"* saying ("Thou art That") in the ancient *Chandogya Upanishad*. The non-dualist Shankara takes this phrase as indicating the identity of Atman and Brahman:

> [A]s the passages, "I am Brahman," "That art thou," and others, prove, there is in reality no such thing as an individual soul absolutely different from Brahman, but Brahman, in so far as it differentiates itself through the mind (*buddhi*) and other limiting conditions, is called individual soul, agent, enjoyer.[4]

In contrast, the monotheistic Ramanuja analyses the same text rather differently:

> In texts, again, such as "Thou art that," the co-ordination of the constituent parts is not meant to convey the idea of the absolute unity of a non-differenced substance; on the contrary, the words "that" and "thou" denote a *Brahman* distinguished by difference. The word "that" refers to *Brahman* omniscient, etc., which had been introduced as the general topic of consideration in previous passages of the same section, such as "It thought, may I be many"; the word "thou," which stands in co-ordination to "that," conveys the idea of *Brahman* in so far as having for its body the individual selves connected with non-intelligent matter. This is in accordance with the general principle that co-ordination is meant to express one thing subsisting in twofold form. If such doubleness of form (or character) were abandoned, there could be no difference of aspects giving rise to the application of different terms.[5]

Further, while Shankara employs the *via negativa*, arguing that central Upanishadic statements like *"Brahman* is reality, knowledge, infinite" should be understood as the denial that Brahman is illusory or bound by space, Ramanuja and Madhva apply the *via positiva* to these terms of divine attribution. Thus, Madhva develops the line of reasoning against Shankara and Advaita Vedanta presented on the facing page as the "Argument Differentiating Brahman and Individuals."

◆

ARGUMENT DIFFERENTIATING BRAHMAN AND INDIVIDUALS

1. There is nothing that is not either real or unreal (Law of the Excluded Middle).
2. Therefore *jivas* are either real or unreal.
3. We should believe experience unless it is shown to be unreliable (doxastic practice: innocent until proven guilty).
4. We experience the defects of *jivas* (sorrow and suffering).
5. Dialectical reasoning cannot prove the invalidity of direct and immediate experience and scripture cannot overturn direct experience, for scripture is misconstrued if it is taken to show something that is directly contradicted by experience.
6. Therefore *jivas* are real.
7. *Brahman* is real.
8. Either *jivas* and *Brahman* are identical, or *jivas* and *Brahman* are not identical (Law of the Excluded Middle).
9. To take the second case, if they are not identical, then *jivas* and *Brahman* are distinct realities.
10. To take the first case, if *Brahman* and *jivas* were identical, we would not be able to perceive a difference between them.
11. Since *jivas* suffer defects, if *Brahman* and *jivas* were identical, *Brahman* would suffer defects.
12. *Brahman* has no defects (by scripture and definition).
13. Therefore, *Brahman* and *jivas* cannot be identical and are distinct realities.

◆

Now Shankara can accept the empiricist epistemology expressed in premise 5 of this reconstruction of Madhva's line of reasoning[6] – that we should believe our experiences unless they are shown to be unreliable. But Shankara's own empiricist claim which would go against Madhva's conclusion is that there is an ultimate mystical experience of the Oneness of Brahman and Atman. Ramanuja's response to Shankara on this score is this:

> To assert that the theory of a substance free from all difference (does not require any further means of proof but) is immediately established by one's own consciousness, we reply that he also is refuted by the fact, warranted by the witness of the Self, that all consciousness implies difference: all states of consciousness have for their object something that is marked by some difference, as appears in the case of judgements like "I saw this."[7]

So far then we have conflicting claims about the data of experience which lead to a stand-off: Shankara takes the data to be about the experience of a non-dual monism, and Ramanuja takes the data to indicate experiences of a distinct God, experiences which qualify the non-dualist view. (Hence Ramanuja's view is called Vishishtadvaita or qualified non-dualism.) It is worth noting, though, that Ramanuja gives another argument about the nature of consciousness itself which is much like Madhva's longer argument above:

> Moreover, you yourself admit that to consciousness there actually belong different attributes such as permanency (oneness, self-luminousness, etc.), and of these it cannot be shown that they are only Being in general.[8]

However, even though Ramanuja and Madhva are in agreement in offering a monotheism in opposition to Shankara's monism, their understanding of God, or rather God's relation to nature, is not the same. Madhva espouses a view remarkably close to Western monotheism. In particular, he rejects univocal predication and employs analogical predication (see chapter 7) – which the great Christian theologian Thomas Aquinas also was noted for employing – to explain the relation between those properties held by humans and their counterpart held by God:

> If it be said that on account of the statement that (on release) the self, the subject of the experiences of mundane life, becomes one with the Supreme Being, there is absolute identity, we deny it...Accordingly the *shruti* says, "Just as pure water poured on to (another quantity of) pure water, becomes only such (water)" [*Katha Upanishad* IV.15]..."Even so the self too, those said to be in a state of non-distinction from *Brahman*, does not, however, become absolutely the Lord Himself; for there exists the attributes of absolute independence, wisdom, etc., which differentiate *Brahman* from the self." And, "O Hari, thou art of that pure essence and character to which it is not possible for Brahma, and Rudra and other gods to attain." "Lord, they do not make approaches to Thy glory." [*Rig Veda* VII.99.1].[9]

Madhva even holds a direct causal view about how God, being distinct from us, brings about the rewards and punishments of our behavior:

> Though the Supreme Being and *karma* (action) are both the cause of fruit, *karma* does not guide the Supreme Being; on the other hand it is the Supreme Being that guides and rules (our) action.[10]

In contrast, Ramanuja holds a view of the relation of nature to God not so much like Aquinas's, say, as like that espoused by Sallie McFague[11] and others in contemporary feminist Christian theology, who conceive of the world as "God's body" (see chapter 7):

> The individual self also has *Brahman* for its Self, owing to the fact of *Brahman* having entered into it – From all this it follows that the entire aggregate of things, intelligent and non-intelligent, has its Self in *Brahman* in so far as it constitutes *Brahman*'s body.[12]

Now, Ramanuja's notion of the world as God's body is highly integrative: individuals are actually modes of God:

> Of this *Brahman*, the individual selves – whose true nature is unlimited knowledge, and whose only essential attribute is the intuition of the supreme Self – are modes, in so far, namely, as they constitute its body. The true nature of these selves is, however, obscured by ignorance, i.e., the influence of the beginningless chain of works; and by release then we have to understand that intuition of the highest Self, which is the natural state of the individual selves, and which follows on the destruction of ignorance.[13]

Still, it is important to keep in mind that Ramanuja retains the distinction between God and nature more fully than, for example, the integrative views of contemporary Christian process theology have tended to, where God's "consequent nature" just is the sum total of that into which the universal processes. Ramanuja preserves a devotional (*bhakti*) stance toward a loving (and separate) God which would be harder to achieve with the abstract God of Christian process thought (though in the latter God is referred to as "luring" humans with the aesthetic).

HINDU HENOTHEISM

At first glance, the practice of Hinduism seems highly complex and even chaotic. The person who comes to Hinduism from the outside is confronted with a plethora of deities: the "trinity" of Brahma, Vishnu, and Shiva – conjointly referred to as creator, sustainer, and destroyer; Ganesha, the elephant-headed deity who is son of Shiva; Goddesses like the fierce dark-skinned Kali, Durga, and Chamunda; as well as a multiplicity of local deities. But in fact, as figure 4.1 on the following page indicates, this amazing array of divinity actually fits a clear and logical

Figure 4.1 Metaphysics of Hinduism

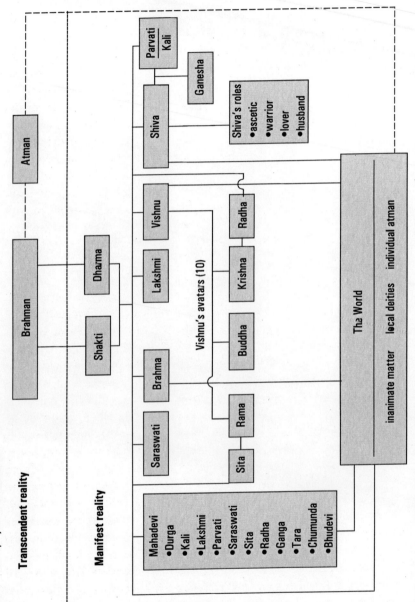

pattern. The only Transcendent is Brahman. Brahman is understood by Advaita Vedanta as both the only true existent and as identical with Atman. But in the other philosophical variations of Hinduism, both qualified non-dualism (Vishishtadvaita Vedanta) and dualism (Dvaita Vedanta), Brahman, as the fullness of being, becomes manifest, (rather than undertaking intentionally creative action as in Western monotheism). Brahman becomes manifest first as *Shakti* (i.e. power, which is female) and *Shakti* is re-manifest in combination with *Dharma*, or the law of the universe, as the level of being we might think of as universal deities. This includes male gods like Shiva and their female counterparts or consorts like Parvati-Kali as well as independent goddesses (for all power is female, and while males need a female counterpart, females do not necessarily need a male counterpart). These are all manifestations of Brahman, and the chart indicates the various lines of connection between this universal level of deity. The final level is the level of local deity, which again is a manifestation of Brahman. Or, going from the bottom up, village deities are incarnations of the universal deities, which in turn are manifestations of Brahman.

Hinduism is henotheistic (it is not polytheistic), which is to say that each practitioner is devoted to a particular deity, or *ishtadevata* ("the god of one's choice"). So a person who is a devotee of Shiva is not a devotee of Krishna (who is an avatar of Vishnu), but would not reject Vaishnavites and would affirm that the One Reality might manifest in multiple forms. To understand how this works, consider the following analogy: imagine that all television broadcasts are beamed down to earth by a single satellite. And imagine that the satellite itself is the origin for all the programming carried on the radiation waves emanating from the satellite. Now imagine a large community of people, each with his or her individual television. The people in the community are divided into groups: some watch CBS while other groups are devoted to alternative major networks like NBC, ABC, CNN, BBC1, and BBC2. Throughout the day the programming on each of the major networks changes: there are major programs which everyone can receive on their television sets, and there are more local programs that are tailored for smaller neighborhoods in the community. However, even if a particular individual only tends to watch local programming or only consistently watches one of the national programs on one of the major networks, everyone in the community knows that all the levels of programming and all of the networks are connected to the one satellite far above. Moreover, while members of the community are fiercely loyal to their own programs, they do not despise or reject those who have a program of a different choice.

Brahman is like the satellite; *Shakti* is like the composite television signal emitted from the satellite; *Dharma* is like the structuring of that signal into invariant wavelengths; Vishnu, Shiva, Kali and Durga are like CBS, CNN, BBC1, BBC2; Krishna, Rama, and Buddha are like major programs within the CBS/Vishnu network; and village deities are like the local news on the major networks. The system is orthopraxic, so everyone knows that what matters is watching and learning from television. That is what makes one a member of the community (a Hindu). It neither matters which particular program one is devoted to watching – for everyone understands that all comes from Brahman – nor does it matter how others practice – for what matters for yourself is that you are in the system, not whether others are right about their view of the system.

YHWH, THE TRINITY, AND ALLAH

The monotheisms of the Western traditions have a metaphysics which is at the same time very much like *bhakti* Hinduism at the macro level and radically different from *bhakti* Hinduism at the micro level. As figure 4.2, metaphysics of Western monotheism, on page 69 indicates, there is only one Transcendent, designated as YHWH or God or Allah. Christianity insists on the notion of one God, but traditionally adds the metaphysical notion of the Trinity, three divine persons in one. As the connective lines on the schematic indicate, the Trinity is connected to the notion of the Incarnation (of Christ as human) and the third person of the Trinity is associated with the ongoing body of believers, the *ecclesia* or church. The historical connection between the three Abrahamic faiths is also indicated on the figure, Christianity arising out of Judaism and Islam arising out of both Judaism and Christianity.

Thus, the Western monotheisms do share with Hinduism the overarching idea of a single Transcendent which is the Plentitude of Being, as opposed to the Buddhist notion of the Fullness of Emptiness (*nirvana*). At the same time, Hinduism shares more with Buddhism than the Western monotheisms when it comes to the nature of the non-Transcendent world. For the Abrahamic faiths, the division between the Transcendent and the natural order is sharp: the creator God inten-

Figure 4.2 Metaphysics of Western Monotheism

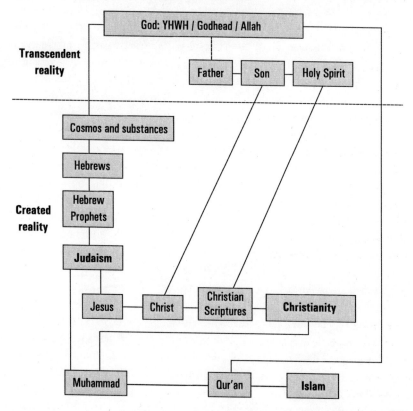

tionally brings about the created (natural) order, which in turn is real. For *bhakti* Hinduism, the natural order is metaphysically real, but it is a manifestation, not intentionally created but produced by *lila* or serendipitous divine play. The natural order is illusory in the epistemological sense that it can produce in us the illusion of being the only thing that is real, whereas Brahman is in actuality the Transcendent and ultimate source of value. From this it follows, for example, that the "trinity" of Hinduism – Brahma, Vishnu, and Shiva – is not comparable to the Trinity of Christianity. Deity such as is focused in Brahma, Vishnu, and Shiva is a manifestation of Brahman, not Brahman in Itself. In contrast, on the traditional doctrine of the Incarnation within Christianity, Christ is Godself, not just a manifestation of Godself.

AN ONTOLOGICAL ARGUMENT FOR GOD'S EXISTENCE

Monotheists believe that God exists, but how might one go about proving that God does exist? In our everyday life we attempt to prove many things. We wish to prove things to ourselves, and we wish to communicate with others, showing them that our views are well-founded. Some of the most obvious sorts of proofs are in mathematics and its application. Suppose I am learning how to make Thai lemon-grass soup. The recipe calls for a quart of liquid. I wonder how many cups that is. I prove to myself that a quart is equal to four cups by pouring four consecutive cups of water into a quart container until it is full. Attempting to prove that God exists is not quite that simple. But it involves the same sort of processes of inference from data or assumptions to arrive at a rational proof.

Potentially the most powerful of all types of arguments for God's existence are ontological arguments, the most famous of which was constructed by St. Anselm (1033–1109), the Archbishop of Canterbury. These are called ontological arguments because they argue from the nature of God (the being, or *ontos* in Greek, of God) to God's existence. The potential power of ontological arguments comes from the fact that they are deductive arguments which argue *a priori* that God must necessarily exist. There is no stronger reasoning than a deductive argument because it proves (or is intended to prove) a truth rather than a mere probability. And there is nothing stronger than *a priori* considerations – the use of pure reason – as a means for supporting an argument, because if we are careful about constructing the argument, there is no chance that the errors of sense perception, which we so often commit, will undermine our reasoning. However, as we shall see, ontological arguments are famous in part because they have been among the most puzzling of all arguments. Generally, the stronger the conclusion of an argument, the more difficult it is to prove; the weaker the conclusion, the easier to prove. And ontological arguments with the unequivocal conclusion that God must exist set a goal which is extremely difficult to prove.

Anselm begins by suggesting that the fundamental notion of God is of a being "than which nothing greater can be conceived." Putting this another way, Anselm suggests that the core definition of "God" is "the greatest conceivable being."[14] He then argues that a person can understand this concept. And if someone understands this concept, then the thing they understand at least exists in their understanding. He then reasons:

For, suppose it [the greatest conceivable being] exists in the understanding alone: then it can be conceived to exist in reality; which is
greater.

Therefore, if that, than which nothing greater can be conceived, exists
in the understanding alone, the very being, than which nothing greater
can be conceived, is one, than which a greater can be conceived. But
obviously this is impossible. Hence, there is no doubt that there exists
a being, than which nothing greater can be conceived, and it exists both
in the understanding and in reality.[15]

To clarify what Anselm is proposing here, the main lines of this kind
of attempted proof are formalized on page 72. Though Anselm later
provides a second ontological argument, for simplicity I shall refer to
this as "Anselm's Argument." It is easier to understand Anselm's
argument if we notice that it has two stages: steps 1–3, and then steps
4–9.

In premises 1–3 it is first asserted that we can understand the notion
of "a being than which nothing greater can be conceived." Think of
something. If it is not the greatest being you can conceive of, you are
not yet thinking of God. Keep thinking. When you reach the limits of
conceivable greatness for a being, then and only then are you conceiving of God. By way of explication, after he presents his ontological argument, Anselm argues further that the greatest conceivable being would
have such attributes as being infinite, omnipotent, perfectly just and
compassionate, self-existent, etc. Another way to sum up what "greatest conceivable" means is "a being more worthy of worship than which
cannot be conceived" and another way, closer to *bhakti* Hinduism, is
"a being more worthy of loving devotion than which cannot be conceived." It is not that we can understand everything about God, but we
can at least minimally understand this idea of God as the greatest conceivable being. So moving to premise 2, whenever we understand something, that thing is, as we say, "in our minds." We can conclude then
(premise 3) that this conceivable God at least exists as a figment of our
imaginations.

The second stage of the argument is in the form of a *reductio ad
absurdum*. There are two ways to prove a conclusion. One can offer
positive reasons for holding the conclusion. Or one can show that the
opposite view is impossible or absurd. In the latter case, to show that
a proposition P is true, you consider not-P, show that *it* is impossible,
giving you not-(not-P), which is equivalent to P. You thereby prove that

---

◆

AN ONTOLOGICAL ARGUMENT FOR GOD'S EXISTENCE

1. A person can understand the idea of "a being than which nothing greater can be conceived."
2. Whatever is understood exists in the understanding.
3. Therefore this being exists in the understanding.
4. Suppose this being exists only in the understanding.
5. Now, this being can be conceived to exist in reality.
6. And it is greater to exist in reality than to exist merely in the understanding.
7. Therefore *if* this being did exist only in the understanding, it would be a being a greater than which *can* be conceived.
8. But it is impossible that the greatest conceivable being not be the greatest conceivable.
9. Therefore this being, the greatest conceivable, must exist in reality as well as in the understanding.

◆

---

it is indeed *P* which is true. This is a *reductio ad absurdum* (a reduction of the opposing view to absurdity). As Anselm argues, if you try to suppose that God only exists in our minds (premise 4), you will end up contradicting this supposition. For it is the case both that we can conceive of the greatest conceivable being as really existing and that it is greater to exist in reality than merely to exist in the imagination. Since what is meant by "God" is the greatest conceivable being, it follows that the hypothetical in premise 4 is false, and therefore God must exist in reality.

A number of objections have been raised against ontological arguments since Anselm developed this type of theistic proof, and a number of variations of ontological arguments have been formulated to deal with possible objections. Let us focus on two objections which do seem to raise doubts about ontological arguments and briefly consider one contemporary version of the argument.

To be successful, every deductive argument must meet four conditions. (1) It must be correctly constructed or *valid*. That is, it must have appropriate premises which, if they are true, will prove the conclusion. (2) It must be *sound*, which is to say it must be both valid and have true premises. (3) If it is sound, the conclusion it then actually proves must be the *intended* conclusion. (4) If it is sound and has the intended conclusion, the argument must be *convincing*. Point 4 is important (and also applies to inductive arguments) because the purpose of giving arguments is to convince one's audience of the conclusion. The most splendid, sound argument is worthless if no one understands it, or if no one believes that it *is* sound.

Anselm's Ontological Argument is valid. If true, its premises would prove the conclusion. It also has the correct conclusion – indeed, if successful, God's necessary existence would be proven. But is the argument sound, and is it convincing? The key to the argument is premise 6, the idea that it is greater to exist in reality than to exist merely in the understanding. Steps 1–3 just show that God at least exists as a figment of some people's imagination. Premises 4, 5, and 6 imply 7; 8 follows from 7; and 9 follows from 8. That brings us back to steps 4, 5, and 6. Premise 4 cannot be questioned, because it is a mere hypothetical, only setting out for consideration the opposite of what Anselm hopes to prove. Premise 5 certainly seems acceptable. Whether or not chimeras and unicorns, intelligent life on other planets, or the greatest conceivable being actually exist, it seems that each can be conceived to exist. So unless we question premise 5, the success of the argument rests on the truth of premise 6.

Now there are two difficulties with premise 6. Premise 6 involves a comparison between existence in reality and existence in the understanding, the former said to be greater than the latter. The first problem is this. Premise 6 says in effect that existence is a perfection: anything which has the property of existing is more perfect than it would otherwise be. But as Immanuel Kant observed against ontological arguments, is existence even a property so that it could be a perfection? (Sometimes this question is put linguistically by asking whether existence is even a predicate.)

Suppose the music director of a symphonic orchestra tells you that he has just hired the greatest violinist in the world. So you go to rehearsal to see this phenomenal young woman. The director describes her knowledge of the repertoire, her exquisite technique, her inspired tone. And then, he adds, "she exists." There is something amiss here. We have been told that something is great, and so we get a list of its properties – in this case, a violinist's knowledge, technique, and tone. But of course we *assumed* that she existed. In fact, nothing seems to be added when the director ends by announcing, "And she exists." Perhaps existence is an additional property and therefore a perfection. But it is not at all clear that it is. It certainly does not seem to fit into any normal list of properties: knowledge, skill, insight (or female, 5'6" tall, and Asian-American). Perhaps there is no knock-down argument that existence cannot be a property. But if it is even unclear that existence is a property, then it is unclear that existence is a perfection. Therefore it is not clear that premise 6 is true. So it is not clear that Anselm's argument is sound.

A second puzzle about premise 6 is related to the first. We are asked to compare the greatest conceivable being as existing "merely in the mind" versus existing "in reality." What are we supposed to be comparing here? It is not as if a god who is a figment of our imagination performs acts, thinks, or judges things any worse – or any better – than a God who really exists. Consider again our greatest violinist. Imagine two orchestras – the London Philharmonic and the Wish Fulfillment Orchestra. They both claim to have the greatest violinist. The London Philharmonic asks their violinist to perform a series of compositions. And she does. Then they ask the Wish Fulfillment Orchestra to have their violinist perform the same program. Nothing visible or auditory happens. Yet the director of Wish Fulfillment declares, "We have conceived of the greater violinist. Our violinist is more knowledgeable, more capable, more inspired. We can see her wondrous virtuosity in our mind's eye." How are we supposed to compare the playing ability of the two musicians? One plays a widely acclaimed performance. We are told the other can produce even greater performances "in the mind's eye." The problem is, they don't perform in the same arena.

In other words, we are trying to compare two different modes of existence. One musician exists in the mode we call reality; the other exists in the mode we call imaginary. This is like trying to compare the heinous crimes of real murderers and those of fictional murderers in books. Authors can provide fictional accounts of more heinous crimes than those of any real murderer. But it is hard to see how we could actually compare them. Only real people die – or perform real violin programs – in the real world. While things with the same mode of existence – whether imaginary, or fictional or real – are comparable, it is not clear that we can do what premise 6 asks of us: compare real existence (one mode) with imaginary existence (another mode). Once again, premise 6 is unclear, and so it is not clear whether Anselm's intriguing argument is sound.

Modern versions of the Ontological Argument, such as suggested by Alvin Plantinga, attempt to evade some of these problems with the Anselmian argument we have been assessing by appealing to the notion of a "possible world." The notion of a "possible world" was developed in modern philosophical thought by Gottfried Leibniz (1646–1716). Leibniz's idea was that at creation God had a choice among numerous, possible compositions for the universe. One such possible world is the actual world, our universe. Another would be a world without humans; another a world without any animate life, and so on.[16]

Now, a modern version of the ontological argument suggests that God should be thought of as "maximally perfect." That is, if God exists, God would be a being possessing the perfect set of properties which, taken together, would make a being great. If we grant that this idea of maximal perfection makes sense, then it is possible that God exists. In terms of possible worlds, this means that God exists in *some* possible world(s). But it would be more perfect to exist in all possible worlds, than only in some. Therefore, God exists necessarily, for there is no possible world –including the actual world – in which God would not exist. However, this line of reasoning hinges on the supposition that it is possible for a being to possess maximal perfection. Plantinga himself cautions that, while he believes that maximal perfection (or maximal greatness) could be instantiated:[17]

> We must ask whether this argument...*proves* the existence of God. And the answer must be, I think, that it does not...Not everyone who understands and reflects on its central premise...will accept it. Still, it is evident...that there is nothing *contrary to reason* or *irrational* in accepting this premise. What I claim for this argument, therefore, is that it establishes, not the *truth* of theism, but its rational acceptability.[18]

The stumbling block to accepting ontological arguments as proof of God's existence is that those already disinclined to believe in a Transcendent will probably not be convinced that a maximally perfect being makes sense – especially when they discover that they are thereby agreeing that there is a Transcendent. So even this modern version of the Ontological Argument is likely to be convincing only to those already convinced of God's existence, or those with no serious doubts about God's existence. But there is a further problem. Consider an ontological argument for Brahman which Stephen H. Phillips extracts from Hinduism in his book *Classical Indian Metaphysics*.[19] In Phillips' words, the argument is shown in the box on page 76.

Anselm and others have felt that ontological arguments show the "rational acceptability" (to use Plantinga's phrase) of Christian faith. But here we have a parallel argument purporting to show the rational

---◆---

AN ONTOLOGICAL ARGUMENT FOR BRAHMAN

1. Brahman is cognized (from scripture).
2. Brahman is cognized as self-conscious, all-inclusive, and non-differen-tiated.
3. What is cognized is to be accepted, unless the cognizing is (challenged and) defeated. (Every cognition is innocent until proven guilty.)
4. The logic of the content of teaching about Brahman (or the nature of Brahman) precludes any challenge or defeat.
5. Brahman is to be accepted.

---◆---

acceptability of Hindu faith and applicable to Advaita Vedanta as well as forms of Hindu theism. So even if one is inclined to think that there is a Transcendent, an ontological argument for the existence of God may not be the ontological argument for a Transcendent which one finds most convincing. Once again, Anselm's argument seems to be a proof only for those who are already convinced that God exists and for whom it demonstrates the rationality of their belief – and of course the same holds for this Ontological Argument for Brahman and whether one is already convinced that Brahman is real.

Where does this leave us? If an *a priori* argument like Anselm's for God's existence does not succeed, perhaps this is because the conclusion that God necessarily exists is too strong to prove, or prove in a way which convinces the skeptical. But what about *a posteriori* arguments for God's existence, arguments based on empirical evidence? *A posteriori arguments* try to demonstrate a weaker conclusion, that it is a fact that God exists, or that it is most probable that God exists. For this reason, they are more likely to be successful than *a priori* arguments. We will consider some *a posteriori* arguments in the next chapter.

THE ADVANTAGES OF THEISM

As we begin the twenty-first century, the idea of a transcendent God has come to seem irrelevant or absurd to the modern scientific and humanis-tic mind. But for those with Jewish or Christian or Muslim or *bhakti* Hindu or Sikh faith in God, the idea of God is inextricable from their worldview. The idea of God is not an expendable notion at the periphery of their worldview, for it is foundational to the monotheist's worldview.

One longstanding objection to theological realism since at least the nineteenth century is the charge that God has come to be viewed as so transcendent that the idea of God has become an abstraction without content. The theological realist has several possible lines of response. One is to give at least equal weight to the idea of the immanence of God as is given to that of the transcendence of God. Incarnational and embodiment theologies do this. We will discuss those theologies in chapter 7. Another possible response is to suggest a means of meaningfully speaking about God despite God's transcendence. These suggestions have traditionally centered on the notion of analogical predication (e.g. the work of Thomas Aquinas or Madhva); more recently they have centered on the use of models and metaphors (for example, the work of Sallie McFague and Janet Soskice). And still another possible response is to take primary theistic texts, symbols, images, and creedal statements as emphasizing an immanent God who confronts humans in their present lives (here we might place the Jewish thinker Martin Buber as well as embodiment theologies). But whatever lines of response are followed, to avoid postulating a God who is so transcendent as to be unavailable to humans, theological realism must understand God as a personal being with whom humans can interact in devotion, in love, and in moral outlook. We will return to this theme in the last chapter.

Further reading

INTRODUCTORY

Saint Anselm of Canterbury. *The Major Works*. Oxford, Oxford University Press, 1998

Barth, Karl. *The Humanity of God*. Atlanta, John Knox Press, 1960

Cohn-Sherbok, Lavinia and Dan. *Judaism*. Oxford, Oneworld, 1997

Cragg, Kenneth. *Jesus and the Muslim: An Exploration*. Oxford, Oneworld, 1999

Fakhry, Majid. *A Short Introduction to Islamic Philosophy, Theology, and Mysticism*. Oxford, Oneworld, 1997

Flood, Gavin. *An Introduction to Hinduism*. Cambridge, Cambridge University Press, 1996

Forward, Martin. *Jesus: A Short Biography*. Oxford, Oneworld, 1999

Hebblethwaite, Brian. *The Ocean of Truth: a Defense of Objective Theism*. Cambridge, Cambridge University Press, 1988

McLeod, Hew. *Sikhism*. London, Penguin, 1997

Parrinder, Geoffrey. *The Bhagavad Gita: A Verse Translation*. Oxford, Oneworld, 1996

Rahner, Karl. *Foundations of Christian Faith*. New York, Crossroads, 1978

Ramanujan, A.K., trans. *Hymns for the Drowning*. London, Penguin, 1973

Schleiermacher, Friedrich. *On Religion: Speeches to its Cultured Despisers*. New York, Harper and Row Publishers, 1958

Swinburne, Richard. *Is There A God?* Oxford, Clarendon Press, 1996

Tayob, Abdulkader. *Islam*. Oxford, Oneworld, 1999

Ward, Keith. *Christianity: A Short Introduction*. Oxford, Oneworld, 2000

IN-DEPTH

Barth, Karl. *The Epistle to the Romans*. Oxford, Oxford University Press, 1972

Hyman, Arthur and Walsh, James J., eds. *Philosophy in the Middle Ages*. Indianapolis, Hackett Publishing Company, 1973

Lipner, Julius. *The Face of Truth*. New York, State University of New York Press, 1986

Lipner, Julius. *Hindus: Their Religious Beliefs and Practices*. London, Routledge, 1994

Maimonides, Moses. *The Guide for the Perplexed*. New York, Dover Publications, 1956

Radhakrishnan, Sarvepalli and Moore, Charles A. eds. *A Sourcebook in Indian Philosophy*. Princeton, Princeton University Press, 1957

Runzo, Joseph, ed. *Is God Real?* London, Macmillan, 1993

Schleiermacher, Friedrich. *The Christian Faith*. New York, Charles Scribner's Sons, 1928

Swinburne, Richard. *The Christian God*. Oxford, Clarendon Press, 1994

Swinburne, Richard. *The Existence of God*. Oxford, Clarendon Press, 1979

Tillich, Paul. *Systematic Theology*, Volumes 1, 2, and 3. Chicago, The University of Chicago Press, 1957

Ward, Keith. *Religion and Creation*. Oxford, Clarendon Press, 1996

Watt, William Montgomery. *The Faith and Practice of Al-Ghazali*. Oxford, Oneworld, 1994

5 A POSTERIORI ARGUMENTS FOR GOD'S EXISTENCE

I supplicated, I demanded a sign, I sent messages to Heaven, no reply.
Heaven ignored my very name. Each minute I wondered what I could
be in the eyes of God. Now I know the   answer: nothing. God does not
see me, God does not hear me, God does not know me . . . I am going
to tell you a colossal joke: God doesn't exist.[1]

Jean-Paul Sartre (1905–1980)

There are four basic types of classic arguments which attempt to prove
God's existence. First there is the kind of argument which we assessed
in the last chapter, an "ontological argument" (from the Greek word
ontos, or "being"). These proofs argue from the purported nature, or
being, of God to God's necessary existence. They attempt to show *a
priori* that it is impossible that God not exist. A second type of classical argument for God's existence is a "cosmological argument" (from
the Greek word *cosmos*, or "universe"). These arguments start from
some particular, general feature of the physical universe and argue that
God's existence best explains why the universe has that feature. The
third sort of argument is a "teleological argument" (from the Greek
telos, meaning "end" or "goal"). These arguments suggest that there is
a pattern or purpose or design to the universe – its order, its beauty,
the ecological interdependence and interrelatedness of its parts – which
point to the likelihood that there is an intelligent designer, i.e. God,
behind that pattern or purpose. These arguments are often referred
to as "design arguments." In this chapter we will take up the latter
two types of *a posteriori* arguments, the cosmological and teleological

arguments. A fourth type of argument, also *a posteriori*, is less often employed, but may be the most important. These are axiological arguments, arguments from value(s) – such as considerations of morality or aesthetic or aretaic (virtue) values – to God's existence. We will discuss those kinds of *a posteriori* arguments in chapters 11 and 14.

THE NATURE OF PROOFS

In order to understand *a posteriori* attempts to prove God's existence, we need to understand certain things about the nature of proofs. First we need to distinguish between the kind of information used to prove something, and the way in which that information is used to arrive at the intended conclusion. There are two basic kinds of information which can be employed in a proof. Sometimes we offer a proof in terms of things we know on the basis of reason alone. This is typical of mathematical proofs and proofs in theoretical physics. We call such proofs *a priori* (meaning "prior to" or not involving empirical data). The other sort of information used for proving something is evidence acquired via the senses. This includes information acquired by direct perception as well as through the use of telescopes, microscopes, cyclotrons, and so on. Proofs which employ this type of information are *a posteriori* (meaning "after" or involving empirical evidence), though they might also employ some *a priori* considerations.

There are also two basic methods of proof, having to do with the kind of conclusion we wish to reach. Some proofs are *deductive*. Here we attempt to deduce a truth from a set of assumptions (or premises). A deductive proof is meant to be so constructed that by correctly combining an appropriate set of true premises, it will follow from those premises that the conclusion we hope to reach must be true. Anselm's Ontological Argument which we considered in the last chapter is a deductive argument. On the other hand, *inductive* proofs attempt to show that something is more probable than we might have thought apart from the proof. For example, an amateur bird watcher may wonder whether she is correctly identifying crows. Every large bird she has identified so far as a crow has been black. She goes to a roosting area known to have a large number of crows, talks to ornithologists about the other features of crows, and continues her field studies. Every bird that fits other criteria of being a crow continues to turn out to be black. As she increases the number of observations of black crows, she is implicitly developing an inductive argument in her own mind to the conclusion that there is a high probability that all crows are black.

COSMOLOGICAL ARGUMENTS

There are two basic types of cosmological arguments for God's existence. Both focus on a particular feature of the cosmos: the sequences of causes and effects in the natural order. They both deductively argue to the conclusion on *a posteriori* grounds that there must be a Divine Being to give the cosmos this particular feature. But the first type of argument asks how the causal sequences of our universe began; the second asks why the universe, with this causal structure, exists at all.

The first type is called a *kalam* cosmological argument. Initially, it was primarily proposed by Islamic philosophers, such as the great Al-Ghazzali (1058–1111), who drew on the work of Aristotle, but it has also been put forward by some Jewish philosophers and some Christians, such as Thomas Aquinas's rival Bonaventure (1221–1274). The general reasoning is shown in the box below.

---◆---

KALAM COSMOLOGICAL ARGUMENT

1. The universe exhibits a series of changes, or causal sequences.
2. Whatever changes must be caused to change by something else.
3. There cannot be an infinite regress of these causal sequences.
4. Therefore the universe itself must have a beginning.
5. Everything that begins to exist must have a cause for its beginning.
6. Therefore, there must be a First Cause of change, itself unchanging, which caused the universe to begin.

---◆---

Premise 1 is simply an empirical observation, that there is change in the universe (causes and effects). Premise 2 is the rather generally accepted idea that a thing cannot change unless something else (its cause) makes the change occur, and, likewise, premise 5 seems obvious: a thing cannot come into existence unless something else causes it to exist. Premise 4 follows from premise 3. Finally, the reason the First Cause of change must be unchanging (the conclusion, premise 6) is that otherwise – by premise 2 – the First Cause would itself have a cause, and the regress of causal sequences would continue, unexplained.

This leaves premise 3, the assumption that there can be no infinite regress of causes, as the key to this type of cosmological argument. Some feel that premise 3 is intuitively obvious. But others, such as David Hume, Immanuel Kant, and J.S. Mill, have argued that it is not obviously true, a view which Buddhism shares. For why could not the universe extend back infinitely in time: effects following from causes, which are themselves effects of other causes, and so on and so on? We seem to have reached an impasse here. The argument will only be convincing to those who find premise 3 acceptable, and they are likely to be those who already believe that there is a Creator.

There is, however, another problem with the *kalam* argument. Even for those who feel that the argument is sound and convincing, it does not appear to provide the conclusion which the monotheist hopes to prove. Suppose there is a First Cause of the universe. Why suppose it is God? The *kalam* argument primarily concerns power (and perhaps intelligence) sufficient to begin or create the universe, with its myriad causal laws and sequences of causes and effects. But God is perfectly good and loving, a personal God on the monotheist's view. And it does not follow from the considerations of this argument alone that the natural order was brought into existence by this personal God with those attributes.

Let us turn, then, to a second type of cosmological argument, cosmological arguments from contingency. Rather than focusing on the temporal beginning of the causal sequences of the universe, this argu-

---

◆

COSMOLOGICAL ARGUMENT FROM CONTINGENCY

1. Contingent things exist.
2. Every contingent thing has a cause of its existence.
3. The cause of its existence must be something other than itself.
4. The cause of its existence must provide a sufficient reason for its existence.
5. The sufficient reason for the existence of any contingent thing cannot be provided merely by other contingent things.
6. Therefore, what causes any contingent thing to exist must be a set of things, other than itself, that contains at least one noncontingent (necessary) being.
7. Therefore, a necessary being exists.

◆

ment considers the fact that the causal sequences of the universe as a whole might not have existed.

To see how this argument works, let us look at the famous mid-twentieth-century debate between Bertrand Russell and Father Frederick Copleston.[2] In the debate, Russell takes the position of an agnostic, although he was an atheist. Copleston, in the Roman Catholic tradition, represents a traditional theological realist position like Thomas Aquinas's, and defends what is basically a version of the third of Aquinas's five arguments for God's existence, the argument from contingency.[3]

In order to understand Copleston's position, consider the universe as a whole: things in the natural order – rocks, trees, penguins, quasars, etc. – are all contingent. They might not have existed. We ourselves are obviously contingent upon the fact that we had biological parents (cause and effect). We might not have existed. But like all natural things, as living beings we also remain contingent after we come into existence. Our continued life depends upon such things as good nutrition, the continual functioning of our immune system against disease, and so on. So too, inanimate objects are also doubly contingent: the existence of particular rocks is initially contingent on volcanic activity (cause and effect), but they remain contingent on the continuous operation of gravity, the strong and weak forces among their sub-atomic particles, and other causal relationships.

Now in Copleston's mind, if everything that exists or has existed is contingent, there would be no explanation for why anything at all happens to exist. As rational beings we look for a sufficient reason to explain the fact of the universe. That is, we look for a reason which would be adequate to explain the existence of the universe and the things in it.[4] Copleston suggests the following analogy. The universe of contingent things is like a box of chocolates. No matter how many of the chocolates in the box you analyze the composition of, or how many kinds or sizes you divide the chocolates into, you would not be able to explain why there are any chocolates in the first place. Likewise, if everything that exists or existed is contingent, such that you can only explain each thing in terms of other contingent things, you still end up with mere contingency (you remain "inside the box"). There might have been nothing, so why is there something, rather than nothing? Thus Copleston concludes that whatever adequately explains the universe with its contingent objects cannot itself be contingent. What we would be looking for then to explain everything is a necessary being, a being that has *aseity*, or self-existence. Hence, to explain the contingent existence of the natural order, one must ultimately hold that there is something (God) with necessary existence.[5]

In response to this, Bertrand Russell says that Copleston is asking for an explanation precisely where we cannot get an explanation. Copleston is clearly asking us to go outside the confines of scientific explanation, and to Russell this is not reasonable. Copleston suggests that the existence of the universe needs "a total explanation, to which nothing further can be added," to which Russell responds, "Then I can only say that you're looking for something which can't be got...I should say that the universe is just there, and that's all."[6] For Russell, it is just a brute fact that the universe exists, that each contingent object is here. We can give many interesting explanations of things from inside the realm of the natural order via physics, chemistry, etc. But to ask why anything is here at all is to attempt to go beyond the limits of explanation. (We shall consider further in chapter 10 this sort of position as espoused, for example, by the physicist Stephen Hawking.) Interestingly, Buddhism also assumes a similar zero point cosmology: the universe just is, and its existence (or cycle of existence) is our starting point.

Copleston has very different intuitions. While Russell thinks we must explain things as best we can with the material we have at hand through science, Copleston feels that as rational beings we are driven to find ultimate explanations and so it is more reasonable to hold that there is some necessary being, something which provides the sufficient reason or adequate explanation for the existence of the contingent universe.[7] However, Russell does not show that Copleston's argument is unsound. Nor does Copleston negate Russell's position. So what we have arrived at is another impasse.

Whenever such different attitudes or intuitions are held going into a debate – the intuition of a scientific humanist who feels that only scientific explanation is adequate and the intuition of a theist that there must be supra-cosmic explanations – then it is natural and expectable to get very different perspectives on the value of *a posteriori* theistic arguments. However, even if this impasse could be overcome, and we did find the cosmological argument from contingency convincing, we are still left with a problem for all cosmological arguments: even if they were to show that the universe has a First Cause or is grounded in a Necessary Being, they do not show that a *personal* God exists. This brings us to a third type of argument for God's existence.

TELEOLOGICAL ARGUMENTS

Teleological arguments are by far the most common and least technical of the traditional arguments for God's existence. Indeed they are a kind of "sidewalk argument" – the sort of proof of God's existence that someone might offer his or her neighbor in everyday conversation when asked "Why do you think God exists?" In brief, the teleological response goes, "Look around at the world. It is organized and orderly. The rain produces flowers; the flowers offer a profusion of color; the bees are attracted and pollinate the flowers; the flowers scatter their seeds. And so the cycles go. Surely there is design in nature. And surely there is a Designer behind the design."

Though teleological arguments have a long history, the eighteenth-century theologian William Paley developed a quintessential analogical form of the argument. Suppose you were walking across a desolate stretch of land and stumbled upon an unfamiliar object – a pocket watch. You notice the curious manner in which all the parts – gears and counter weights and springs – are so adapted and interconnected that each serves a function in producing an orderly result, namely the movement of the hands. Had you stumbled over a rock, you would not have particularly questioned its authorship. But the watch exhibits such an obvious design that you cannot but infer that it must have had a designer. So too, Paley suggests, the remarkable adaptation of the eye to its functions, animals to their environments, and the inner workings of whole ecological systems (which we are even more acutely aware of today), analogously point to a Designer of the universe. Unlike the cosmological forms of argument for God's existence, the conclusion reached in teleological arguments is that there is not just a Cause or Being, but a Divine Mind behind the universe.

The most penetrating analysis of teleological theistic arguments is found in David Hume's *Dialogues Concerning Natural Religion* (1779), which actually preceded Paley's own defense of the argument. Hume neatly lays out two variations of teleological arguments. If we formalize these,[8] the first variation is similar to Paley's, and is a more narrowly construed analogical argument.

---◆---

AN ANALOGICAL TELEOLOGICAL ARGUMENT

1. The universe resembles a mechanical system of parts (like a watch).
2. Whenever we investigate a mechanical system, we find it had a designer.
3. Similar effects have similar causes.
4. Therefore the universe has a Designer, similar to though proportionately greater than the designers of mechanical systems.

---◆---

The argument uses empirical data (premise 1) to suggest that the universe is analogous to certain artifacts; those artifacts have a designer (premise 2); therefore by analogy (premise 3) the universe has a Designer. Premise 2 is obviously true and premise 3 – similar causes have similar effects – articulates a straightforward principle: for example, if it typically rains in semi-arid southern California each January (similar effects), we assume that the same sorts of weather patterns (similar causes) bring about January rains each year. This leaves the key to the argument, premise 1.

People in the seventeenth and eighteenth centuries were particularly fascinated by mechanical systems, so they found it easy to envision the not very well understood inner workings of nature as being like a mechanical system of parts. But the universe is not really very much like a mechanical system. Indeed, as David Hume points out, with its rather organically interconnected parts, the universe resembles less a mechanical system than an organism like an animal or a vegetable.[9] So the purported analogy to a machine is weak. Consequently, we have

---◆---

PROBABILISTIC DESIGN ARGUMENT FOR GOD'S EXISTENCE

1. The universe exhibits an adaptation of means to ends.
2. For everything which exhibits an adaptation of means to ends, and of which we know whether or not it has been designed, it turns out that it was designed.
3. Therefore it is highly probable that the universe too was designed and has a Designer.

---◆---

been given no good reason to infer that the universe has a designer. The analogical teleological argument fails. (We will see other reasons why it fails in a moment.)

The second variation of teleological argument Hume addresses avoids analogies with mechanistic systems and is more general, and more promising (see box at foot of page 86).

Suppose you are confronted with a tall opaque container and told it contains 10,000 colored balls. You cannot see over the top into the container. You reach over the top and start removing the balls, one by one, and each one you remove is red. It means little that the first ten, then twenty in a row are red. But as the numbers increase – say you remove 1,000 balls, and they are all red – it becomes more probable that all the balls in the container are red. That is, based on the available evidence, the epistemic probability that all the balls are red increases, though this will not change the fact that if a few of the balls are green, they will remain so and would eventually be discovered by your slow extraction method. And, just as the repeated discovery of red balls in the container increases the epistemic probability that all the balls are red, the repeated discovery that things which show an adaptation of means to ends are indeed designed seems to increase the epistemic probability that *all* things – including the universe itself – which exhibit means-ends adaptation are designed. This is an inductive or probabilistic teleological argument.

The general structure of the probabilistic teleological argument is to set out a comparison of two classes of objects. Consider the class of all things that exhibit an adaptation of means to ends, a very large class. Within that class, consider a second class of objects: the subclass of objects for which we know whether or not they were designed. We have investigated these latter objects – watches, lawn mowers, computers – and in every case when we determine whether or not they had a designer, all had a designer. What about the remaining objects in the larger, original class of objects? What is the epistemic probability that they are all designed also? Well it appears to be rather high. And the universe is one of these objects. So, based on the available evidence, it seems probable that the universe was designed. However, there are at least four major objections to this line of reasoning.

To see the first objection, suppose someone presented the argument shown in the box on the next page.[10] This hypothetical argument follows the pattern of the Probabilistic Design Argument. There are two classes of objects to consider. The larger class is all the IBM computers plus

---

◆

A HYPOTHETICAL PROBABILISTIC
TELEOLOGICAL ARGUMENT

1. Consider the class of objects which includes all IBM computers plus the Universe.
2. Every member of this class of objects, such that we know whether it was designed, was designed.
3. The Universe is a member of this class of objects.
4. Therefore, it is highly probable that the Universe was designed.

◆

---

the universe, and the sub-class is everything in that group except the universe. Everything in the sub-class turns out to be designed. The suggested inference is that the one remaining object in the class – the universe – is itself most likely designed.

Clearly, something is wrong with this argument. To see this, go back to the argument about the colored balls in the container. You do not know the colors of any of the balls ahead of time. You start with 10,000 balls. You retrieve 1,000. If they are all red, it is highly probable, based on the available evidence, that the remaining balls will be red. Thus, you are genuinely discovering something through your method of inquiry. In contrast, the computers-and-universe argument is biased. You know before starting that all the computers are designed – designed by IBM. You have not learned anything new about their origin, and thus nothing by implication about the probability that the universe had a similar origin. And this tells us something about the proper way to construct probabilistic arguments. When putting together classes of objects to compare, you must make sure that you have not biased the manner in which the original collection of objects is constructed. You must not know ahead of time whether they will have the characteristics under investigation. Importantly, one needs to be able, at least in principle, to arrive at a negative answer, to discover that some of the objects do not have the characteristic in question. And this possibility is missing from the Probabilistic Design Argument for God's existence.

In the absurd IBM computers-universe argument we know ahead of time that we could never get a negative answer to whether any of the computers is designed. In contrast, when you begin to conclude after 1,000 retrievals that all the balls in the container are red, the situation is not biased because there is the possibility of a negative answer. It is always possible that we have a container of variously colored balls, and that at some point a white or green ball will show up. Thus the first objection to probabilistic design arguments for God's existence is that they are inherently biased since their construction rules out the possibility of a negative answer to the question of whether any of the objects to be compared to the Universe was designed.

Moreover, this problem is compounded by a point Hume makes against the defender of the teleological argument:

> Have you ever seen nature in any such situation as resembles the first arrangement of the elements? Have worlds ever been formed under your eye, and have you had leisure to observe the whole progress of the phenomenon, from the first appearance of order to its final consummation? If you have, then cite your experience and deliver your theory.[11]

Unlike the numerous colored balls in the container, we do not have a whole series of universes (and their origins) to look at. The defender of the Probabilistic Design Argument not only would need to come up with a class of objects, including the universe, where we do not know ahead of time whether the vast majority of the objects are designed or not; additionally the larger class of objects would need to contain objects equivalent to the universe for comparison. But there are no such objects. Consequently, it is hard to see how it could be shown *a posteriori* that it is probable the universe had a designer.

The second objection to probabilistic design arguments goes as follows. All design arguments have the general form, "there is a pattern to the universe, so there is a patterner," or, "there is a plan, so there is a planner," and so on. It is supposed that the structure of the universe indicates certain underlying intentions and goals of a Designer. But this supposition involves the fallacy of equivocation. An equivocation occurs when, in the middle of an argument, the meanings of key terms are changed, so that by the end of the argument you are talking about something entirely different than you began with. Since the conclusion of an equivocal argument is, then, unrelated to the initial premises, it remains unproven. If we look at the probabilistic design form of the teleological argument, this fallacy is evident.

The question is whether the universe was created purposely by a Mind. There are two senses of purpose. One sense of "purpose" is the notion of something having a function. You inspect a pocket watch and wonder what the purpose of this gear is – that is, its function – in the overall system. Design arguments all start with this sense of "purpose," by beginning with the observation that the universe has design – a pattern, a purpose – the parts all functioning in an interrelated manner like a watch. In another sense of "purpose," though, we ask why *someone* did something. Thus we ask whether you did something on purpose: did you have a reason for knocking over the lamp, or did you stumble and hit it accidentally? This second sense of "purpose" involves intention, and necessarily involves a mind, as only minds have intentions and do things on purpose. And this is the sense in which the universe might be said to have a purpose in premise 2 of the Probabilistic Design Argument. For the second premise basically says that whenever you discover a "purpose," there has to be someone – a mind – behind that "purpose." Thus, if you look at a Navajo rug, you can see that the intricate pattern was purposefully created. And so it might seem, the universe with its intricate design must have had a designer with a purpose.

Now, when design arguments begin by in effect observing that the universe exhibits "purpose," this is just an observation that things function in an interrelated manner. We can readily agree. This premise is neutral with respect to the question of whether there was a designer. However, the second premise of the argument we are considering introduces intentional design by suggesting that every design has a designer. But that is false. Navajo rugs have design, and it turns out they were produced on purpose. However, there are numerous examples of natural phenomena where there is a design (pattern) but not an intentional design.

A simple case: you go to the beach and notice that the sand at the water line has a ripple pattern. Yet you do not suppose right off, "Oh, someone planned this." Rather, you infer that the waves washed in in such a way as to cause the patterning. There is no obvious connection between the pattern in the sand and a conscious patterner. Another example: toothpicks accidentally spill out of a box and fall into a pattern spelling "Beethoven." It was not done on purpose. No intention was involved. No intelligent mind planned it. Yet the toothpicks form a precise pattern, however unlikely. This shows we can have perfectly natural occurrences where there is pattern and no designer. Thus, the second problem with design arguments is that they employ the notion of "purpose" in two different senses, leaving an unbridged gap in the argument. The Probabilistic Design Argument never does answer the question whether the universe has the kind of pattern (intended) that requires an intelligent mind.

A third objection to design arguments is related to the previous objection. As we have seen, these theistic arguments depend on the assumption that intelligent design best explains the present ordered structure of the universe. But there is an obvious alternative: our universe might have come about by chance, by the random collocation of elementary physical particles and energy. This is especially easy to see if we assume that the universe contains a finite, even if extremely large, amount of matter and energy. Given enough time, a finite number of objects subject to a structuring but random means of arrangement, will eventually develop every possible pattern. Thus, a successive set of chimpanzees randomly pressing a computer keyboard, with its finite number of keys, will eventually produce the Magna Carta or the Gettysberg Address or the United Nations' Universal Declaration of Human Rights. Now the finished product certainly looks like the result of intelligent contrivance. Yet the chimps' apparent political statement is just a set of letters in random sequences which looks like a product of intelligence. We can see then that we need some good reason to think that it is intelligence in particular, and not just the random, structured interaction of the physical elements of the universe, which is the best explanation of the current structure of the universe.

The fourth objection to teleological arguments brings us full circle back to our earlier discussion of cosmological arguments. For the teleological form of argument shares a failing with cosmological arguments: even if they were successful, teleological arguments do not show that God is the author of the universe. At best, they show that the universe is designed. This is an advantage over cosmological arguments, for if there is a designer of the universe, that designer would at least be an intelligence and more probably personal. But teleological arguments do not show that there can only be one designer; they do not rule out polytheism (could there be a committee of gods working together?). And if there is only one designer, teleological arguments do not show that the designer of the universe is infinite: as far as the argument goes, a finite though very powerful being could have created the universe. Importantly, teleological arguments tell us nothing of the moral character of the designer(s). After all, malicious but very clever and very powerful individuals create works of art and whole cities and govern the affairs of state. If we are arguing by analogy, might not the designer of the universe be smart, powerful, and a little mean? In short, the stronger the purported comparison between designers we know and the designer of the universe, the less the designer appears to be like God, whereas the weaker the comparison is granted to be, the less likely that any Divine Designer can be inferred from design arguments.

Indeed the problem of evil, to which we turn in the next chapter, poses a particular obstacle for all *a posteriori* arguments, including teleological arguments. While beauty and order are striking features of the universe, evil is another salient feature. If we truly use the data before us to determine that there is a Mind behind the structure of the universe, would not the best explanation be that the Designer is as much evil as good? Thus, the *a posteriori* arguments we have looked at not only fail to provide positive proof that God exists; they face the formidable negative data against the existence of a good and loving God. They face the problem of evil which we will address in the next chapter.

THE VALUE OF THEISTIC "PROOFS" AND CUMULATIVE ARGUMENTS

Despite an extraordinary tradition of attempted proofs of God's existence in the Western monotheisms, (a) it seems highly unlikely that a convincing proof of God's existence can be constructed, and (b) there are good religious reasons for thinking no proof of God's existence *could* be successful.[12] One sort of strong defense of (b), the rejection of arguments for and against God's existence on religious grounds, is offered by Søren Kierkegaard. For instance, in the *Concluding Unscientific Postscript* he argues that the most valuable feature of religiosity is infinite passion and that one cannot have infinite passion unless the object of one's passion is highly improbable. This may be too extreme. A more general line of objection to the attempted proofs would be that if one could prove God's existence, such a proof would be open only to the intellectual elite (a gnostic view) and God would not have set up creation in such a manner. We discussed this rejection of gnosticism in the Introduction and will return to it in chapter 14.

Another limitation of attempted proofs of God's existence is that they do not tell us how we ought to act, at best only telling us that God exists. The whole point of religious belief is to learn how to act, how to live the religious life. Hence, the majority of people who believe in God do not even worry about proofs for God's existence. In addition, traditional proofs of God's existence do not tell us which scriptural traditions or interpretations to follow. Suppose you believe Anselm's Ontological Argument is sound and convincing, and that therefore God exists. But is God trinitarian in nature? Did God become incarnate? And (as we shall investigate in chapter 7) is the world God's body?

This does not mean that the proofs for God's existence do not have value. If you have a proof that works for you, it would demonstrate the rationality of belief, thus further substantiating your religious worldview, and help you better understand what it is you believe. Still, it is probably a mistake for theists to look for a single proof for God's existence. It would be better to look for interconnections among the proofs. In other words, one might find elements of the cosmological argument or moral argument or teleological argument attractive, and one might derive some sense of God's providence from cosmological arguments, some sense of God's moral character from moral arguments, and some sense of God's rational mind from teleological arguments. This is a suggestion which Richard Swinburne has developed in detail as a "cumulative argument" for God's existence. Through the use of various proofs which have value as a collective set of considerations, belief in God may become more reasonable or rational. Proofs would then add to one's religious understanding rather than being the ground of or the sole form of understanding.

Further reading

Many anthologies in the philosophy of religion include good selections on these issues from the work of Western philosophers like Anselm, Aquinas, Hume, Kant, and Paley as well as contemporary presentation and analysis. Louis P. Pojman's anthology is excellent in this regard. Further references can be found under the suggested Further Reading of chapter 4.

Hume, David. *Dialogues Concerning Natural Religion*. New York, Hafner Publishing Company, 1966
Pojman, Louis P. *Philosophy of Religion: An Anthology*. New York, London; Wadsworth Publishing Company, 1998
Swinburne, Richard. *The Coherence of Theism*. Oxford, Clarendon Press, 1977

6 EVIL: AN ARGUMENT AGAINST MONOTHEISM

"Imagine that you are creating a fabric of human destiny with the last object of making [people] happy in the end, giving them peace and rest at last, but that it was essential and inevitable to torture to death only one tiny creature – that baby beating its breast with its fist, for instance – and to found that edifice on its unavenged tears, would you consent to be the architect on those conditions? Tell me, and tell the truth."

"No, I would not consent," said Alyosha softly.[1]

Fyodor Dostoevsky (1821–1881) from *The Brothers Karamazov*

THE PROBLEM OF EVIL

The strongest consideration against the existence of God is the so-called "problem of evil." How can this one innocent girl suffer in Dostoevsky's story and God not seem to care? And there is not just the problem of suffering of a single innocent; there is also the question of massive amounts of moral evil. How could God allow the systematic genocide of the Armenians from 1894–1915, or allow the horrific atomic destruction of the innocent civilian populations of Hiroshima and Nagasaki, or allow the starvation of thirty million Chinese in one year in 1960, and not intervene? However, there is a human tendency to absorb ourselves in the emotionalism of horrendous evils "out there" and so anesthetize ourselves to the root of evil in the small acts of egoity within ourselves. So I will not focus so much on the massive moral evils of human history as on the inner root of evil.

To face evil is to come to understand the aphorism "we have met the enemy and he is us." As we saw in the last chapter, Buddhism has been particularly astute at articulating this understanding. Despite horrendous moral evils across history, one might best put the problem of evil by asking "How could a good God have created *me* – and a whole human race like me?" Besides moral evils, there are additionally the horrific physical evils in the universe. And we can ask how a good God could allow the Black Plague to decimate medieval Europe or AIDS to develop and especially ravish sub-Saharan Africa, or allow the cancer to exist which kills your younger sister? But it will be as much as we can do here to address moral evil.

Since Hinduism and Buddhism have no Creator-God, there is no problem of evil in these traditions. Rather Hinduism and Buddhism face the problem of suffering. We especially considered the Buddhist response to the problem of suffering in chapter 3. The general form of the problem of evil is "How could God be good, and have both created and have providence over the universe, and yet allow evil to exist?" This raises serious questions about Western monotheisms. Following Dostoevsky's reasoning, we might put the problem by saying "surely we would not want to be responsible for the suffering of even one innocent, even to bring about a good world, for how could such a world then be good?" Even more so, how could God allow such a world? The problem of evil actually divides into two different formulations, a strong and a weak formulation. The strong formulation is an argument against God's existence, the weak formulation an argument against belief in God.

THE STRONG FORMULATION OF THE PROBLEM OF EVIL

The strong formulation of the problem of evil is an atheological argument which suggests that given the existence of evil, it is impossible that God could exist. The problem of evil arises for monotheism because God is thought to have three attributes in particular: omnipotence, omniscience, and perfect goodness. For surely a perfectly good being, if it existed, which had all power and all knowledge, would not allow the evils we find in our world. Even if one thought that *some* evils would be allowable, surely not all the evils or the magnitude of evil in our world would be allowed. So God must not exist. Thus, the strong formulation of the problem of evil is an atheological counterpart to Anselm's Ontological Argument (see page 72) which is an attempt to show that God must exist.

◆

STRONG FORMULATION OF THE PROBLEM OF EVIL

1. If God exists, then God is omnipotent (all-powerful), omniscient (all-knowing), and perfectly good.
2. An omnipotent, omniscient, and perfectly good being would have the power, the knowledge, and the desire to prevent evil.
3. Evil exists (or horrendous evil exists).
4. It is morally unacceptable not to prevent an evil, which one has the power and knowledge to prevent.
5. Therefore God, if God existed, would have no morally acceptable reason for not preventing evil.
6. Therefore, it is impossible that God exists.

◆

An obvious solution to the strong formulation would be to give up one of the three key divine attributes. The least likely attribute to give up is perfect goodness, for if "God" designates nothing else, the term designates a being which is perfect in its goodness. Consider then the other two attributes. If God is not omnipotent, it will be easy enough to explain why there is evil. For then when push comes to shove, so to speak, God does not have the power to prevent evil. However, this leaves us with the notion of a relatively minor deity: a god who works hard and gets the world created and in working order, yet when Hitler rises to power and starts the Second World War – in which Russia alone will lose twenty million people who will die from the Nazi scourge – even though this god would prefer to stop Hitler and the forces of Nazism, this god is not powerful enough to do so. Even if this story makes sense, this is not a story about God, a being than which no greater can be conceived. So the problem of evil has been solved by giving up monotheism. Likewise, if God is not omniscient, one can easily solve the problem of evil. On this scenario this god is perfectly good and has all power, but as an evil starts to occur, despite all this god's power and a desire to prevent that evil, this god does not know how to do so. Again, this is no solution for the monotheist – or rather, this is to concede that monotheism is false – because we are no longer talking about God, a being than which no more worthy of worship or loving devotion can be conceived.

Another solution is to deny premise 3, that evil exists. One might go about this in several ways. One might say that what we call evil is an illusion. God has created a perfectly good universe, and nothing is really evil; we are just misled into thinking there is evil. However, if upon hearing Dostoevsky's story of the abused child with which we began, you regard the suffering of this innocent child as a genuine evil, you will need to face the problem of the very real evil of child abuse. Another tack is to argue that what we call evil is simply a lack of something, a privation. In this scenario everything is good, and God is perfectly good, but some areas of the universe lack good, and we call this privation "evil". But then the problem for monotheism can be reformulated as the problem of privation: why would God create a universe with portions that lack good? Whatever the analysis, and whatever it is called, child abuse and other things we call evil must be faced by the monotheist. So it looks as if premise 3 will stand: there is evil.

Now, the strong formulation attempts to conclude that it is impossible that God can exist if evil exists. You can only show that something is impossible if you can show that there is no possible case imaginable in which the circumstances could occur. This means that theists can defeat the strong formulation if they can show that it is possible that God and evil co-exist. Normally when someone allows another person to suffer pain, we say it is wrong. If you stand idly by while one child maliciously beats up on another, you are morally culpable. So it seems that if God were to allow us to undergo pain by suffering at the hands of others, God would be wrong, which is to say, in effect, that God does not exist. However there are certain cases where we do not in fact hold someone accountable for allowing or even causing someone else pain.

Suppose you have a child with lymphoma. A very painful course of chemotherapy will most probably keep the cancer in remission. Do you subject your child to the chemotherapy? An evil is being produced, extreme pain, but it is being produced to prevent death. Therefore you have a morally sufficient reason for allowing your child to suffer great pain (and the physicians have a morally sufficient reason for causing the pain). Quite simply, it is possible that God likewise has a morally sufficient reason for allowing evil in the world. For all we know, if God exists, God has some reason for allowing evil to occur in the world such that some greater good is produced, a good which far outweighs the evil. We do not need to know what God's reason is; the theist does not even have to give a hint of what God's reason might be. Perhaps you think that all the reasons theists typically give for why God allows evil fail as morally sufficient reasons. Still, for all we know there is some other reason we have not yet thought of. So it is possible that God has a morally sufficient reason, and therefore it is possible that God and evil can co-exist. Premise 5 fails in the strong formulation, for it is insupportable. Hence, the intended conclusion, that God must not exist, is too strong to prove.

THE WEAK FORMULATION OF THE PROBLEM OF EVIL

The drawback with the foregoing defense of God's existence against the strong formulation is that even if it is possible that God and evil could co-exist, it may not seem plausible that God could exist in the face of evil. This is a much more severe problem for the theist. For suppose you are a theist and feel that you have an *a priori* argument for God's existence (like Anselm's argument), or like Kierkegaard you believe in God on the basis of faith apart from reason. In that case, all you may need is the hope that some solution to the problem of evil *could* be produced (by God, if not humans). But suppose, like those in the Islamic *kalam* tradition or William Paley or St. Thomas Aquinas, you think you can show by an *a posteriori* argument that God exists (see chapter 5). Or suppose you think that you know God exists because of personal religious experience which could constitute an *a posteriori* argument. Then as David Hume pointed out, the problem of evil is a much more serious problem than in the first case, where you believe on the basis of *a priori* argument or on the basis of faith. With *a posteriori* arguments the theist is collecting positive evidence to support belief in God. And the evidence includes malevolent people and nasty actions that inflict pain: not good evidence for the existence of a good God.

Suppose you go to a museum and see for the first time a painting, *Guernica*, by an artist previously unknown to you named Pablo Picasso. It is a painting of an event in the Spanish Civil War showing the mutilated bodies and the tortured faces of various people and animals. What can you conclude from the evidence before you? Well, that the artist feels compelled to paint pictures of the horrors of war. Unbeknownst to you the artist rarely took war as his subject. You can speculate about what sort of subjects he might have painted in works hanging in other museums, but for all you know, on the basis of the evidence available to you, he is primarily a painter of the horrors of war. Now consider the universe. Here we are, stuck off in an obscure corner of the uni-

EVIL: AN ARGUMENT AGAINST MONOTHEISM ◆ 99

verse on the planet Earth, where we find a considerable amount of evil. For all we know, the rest of the immense universe is mostly good, or perhaps there is no evil at all. It may very well be that God exists, and God hates evil and rarely allows it to exist. But on the basis of the empirical evidence, in our corner of the universe, it seems as if we would not do well to try to give an *a posteriori* argument for the existence of a perfectly good God.

THEODICIES AND THE FREE WILL DEFENSE

A theodicy is an attempt to provide a specific set of reasons why evil and God's existence are compatible. But first off, is there even any defense against the apparent evidence that God, if God exists, directly injects evil into the universe? Consider the story in the *Torah* of the Israelites making bricks under harsh conditions as slaves of the Egyptians. They are determined to leave, and rightly so. They flee and arrive at an impassable body of water, it miraculously rolls back on both sides, and they cross safely to the other side. But as the pursuing Egyptian chariots and foot soldiers start across, the water closes up "by God's act," and the Egyptians drown. Perhaps some of the Egyptians were themselves evil, but there must have been some Egyptians there who justifiably said "Hey, what did I do to deserve this?" – poor and innocent soldiers who had been pressed into service. Moreover, what about the horses that drowned? How could a good God wreak such pain on these people and their animals?

In the Western religious traditions, Zoroastrianism traditionally dealt with similar considerations about the power behind the evil in the world by distinguishing between Ahura Mazda, the god of Light, and Angra Mainya, the evil spirit who opposes Ahura Mazda, and with whom Ahura Mazda struggles. (Present day Parsis, the Zoroastrian community of India, have rejected the idea of Angra Mainya in favor of monotheism.) But the postulation of evil spirits and demons will not function as well for monotheism, though Christianity derived the idea of a devil, i.e. Satan, from the early Zoroastrian tradition. For an omnipotent God does not lack for power instantly to overcome evil spirits *if Godself so desired*. Nevertheless, another move is open to the theist here, and that is the traditional monotheistic rejoinder to the problem of evil that it is humans themselves, exercising their free will in misguided and evil ways, who are responsible for the evil which befalls them, even bringing evil to the rest of creation (e.g. the horses of the Egyptians). Humans, not God, are responsible for evil. This is the free will defense, which is an integral part of most theodicies.

There is an obvious immediate objection to the free will defense. If God was originally trying to create the best possible world, should not God have chosen to create a world which contains only people who do only good, a world with, for example, no greedy and evil Egyptian pharaohs? Why did God not create a universe like ours except that people are so constituted that they are not tempted by desire? Or perhaps God should have created a world in which, for example, whenever you and your neighbor begin to eye the same potential lover, God intervenes and causes one of you to lose all desire for the person (I suppose God would fix the one left out with another prospect). However, you cannot call someone good unless they are good for having in part not done something they might have done which would have been bad. To be morally good is to choose freely the good over what would be evil. You do not get moral credit for doing things about which you have no choice. So hypothesizing that God might create people who only do good or who can never do evil is to hypothesize a world in which there is no genuine free will for humans and nothing for which humans can be morally lauded.

The next obvious question is why give creatures free will in the first place? If it was inevitable, what could justify originally allowing humans the freedom which eventually produced such horrendous evils as Hitler

PROBABILISTIC FORMULATION OF THE PROBLEM OF EVIL

1. If God exists, then God is omnipotent (all-powerful), omniscient (all-knowing), and perfectly good.
2. An omnipotent, omniscient, and perfectly good being would have the power, the knowledge, and the desire to prevent evil.
3. A horrendous number (and types) of evils exist.
4. It is morally unacceptable not to prevent an evil which one has the power and knowledge to prevent, unless there are extenuating circumstances.
5. It is highly probable that God, if God existed, would have no morally acceptable reason for not preventing the evils which do occur.
6. Therefore, it is highly probable that God does not exist.

or Pol Pot wrought, or the massacre at Wounded Knee in 1890 or the so-called rape of Nanking in 1937? How do we account for such large-scale evil or such stupefying evil? The free will defense responds with the basic notion that evil is necessary as a means to good. If there is no evil, it is impossible to have certain sorts of goods in the universe, and those goods are so good that they would be integral to the best world which could be created.

This leads us to the "weak" (though more potent) probabilistic formulation of the problem of evil articulated in the box on page 100.

Theodicies are particularly important to the theist to combat the probabilistic formulation of the problem of evil. For while the conclusion of the argument is weak – that God probably does not exist – the argument could seriously threaten theistic faith because its conclusion is easier to prove than that of the strong formulation. So what is supposed to be the great good of free will which could give God a morally acceptable reason for allowing human free will for good and for evil?

Consider the following set of relationships between levels of good and evil. At the lowest level we have, in the simplest terms, the evil of pain and corresponding good of pleasure. Perhaps these goods and evils balance out. But even if they do, what higher good might God have created to justify the evil of pain? At a higher level of good than mere pleasures are positive character traits. That is, certain habitual ways of acting are morally better than others and constitute a great good. For example, a person who is sympathetic is better than someone who is unsympathetic. A person who is heroic – including moral heroism – or a person who is benevolent is better than a person who is not. And, the theist claims, the world is a better place for having sympathetic, morally heroic, and benevolent people. In effect theists feel that not only do these moral traits make people better, but it is so valuable to have these moral traits in the universe that it is permissible to have some pain in the universe so that these virtues can be present.

The key here is that you cannot have sympathy if there is no one in pain, just as you cannot be benevolent if everyone has everything they need, for to be benevolent is to be disposed to give the needy something they do not have, and so on. Hence God allows evil at the first level, namely pain, because the presence of pain allows humans to achieve a much higher level of good, namely the good character traits of sympathy, benevolence, heroism, etc. In short, a universe with persons with these character traits (even though it also has pain in it) is a better universe than a universe that did not have these qualities in it at all. It is better overall to have a universe with at least some good people, than to have no people at all in the universe.

But this has not yet solved the problem. For just as there is a second level of good – good character traits – which requires pain to exist, it is also true that the very presence of pain also makes possible the development of bad character traits – namely cruelty, cowardice, malevolence, and so on. Here is Dostoevsky's tale in more detail:

> I meant to speak of the suffering of [humankind] generally, but we had better confine ourselves to the sufferings of children...
> This poor child of five was subjected to every possible torture by [her] cultivated parents. They beat her, thrashed her, kicked her for no reason till her body was one bruise....Can you understand why a little creature, who cannot even understand what is done to her, should beat her little aching heart with her tiny fist in the dark and the cold, and weep her meek unresentful tears to dear, kind God to protect her? Do you understand that, friend and brother, you pious and humble novice [Aloysha is studying for the priesthood]? Do you understand why this infamy must be and is permitted? Without it, I am told, [we] could not have existed on earth, for [we] could not have known good and evil. Why should [we] know that diabolical good and evil when it costs so much? Why, the whole world of knowledge is not worth that child's prayer to "dear, kind God"! I say nothing of the sufferings of grown-up people...But these little ones!
> ...If all must suffer to pay for the eternal harmony, what have children to do with it, tell me, please? It is beyond all comprehension why they should suffer...It is not worth the tears of that one tortured child who beat itself on the breast with its little fist and prayed...with an unexpiated tear to "dear, kind God"!

True, without for example the pain of the child you cannot develop sympathy toward the child, and perhaps you cannot so begin to act as to develop the trait of compassion. However, the very fact that the child could undergo pain allows for the cruelty and malevolence of its tormentors. So when the theist points to a second level of good which is qualitatively more valuable than and thus supposed to outweigh that first level of evil, a second level of evil, such as the character trait of cruelty, also arises. And it seems that the cruelty and other evil traits thus produced could even outweigh the good character traits produced at this second level. The theist needs to show that there is an even higher level of good which would justify the rampant evil in the bad character traits of humans – in Hitler and Pol Pot, for example, as well as in ourselves.

The final, third level of good which the theist postulates is free, loving, and compassionate people. The result is shown below.

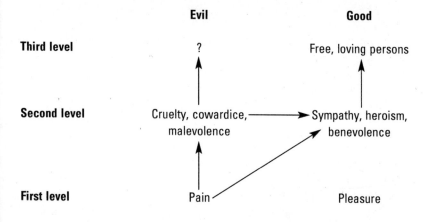

Once again, though, the theist seems to be in trouble. Yes, the trials and tribulations of life can produce loving and compassionate people – a great good exemplified by Mother Teresa of Calcutta or Bishop Desmond Tutu – but on the other side of the scale the very same kinds of trials and tribulations result in the Idi Amins and Pol Pots of the world.

THE AUGUSTINIAN THEODICY AND HELL

At this point the theist needs a detailed theodicy to deal with the fact of malevolent people. St. Augustine (354–430), the greatest of the early theologians ("church fathers") in the Christian tradition, produced a systematic theology in which, among other problems, he dealt with the problem of evil and offered a solution which might solve the problems raised thus far. The Augustinian theodicy is outlined on page 104.

The Augustinian theodicy offers two ways to give a morally sufficient reason for, and so justify, the evil which God allows. First, humans are directly responsible for the free acts of evil which they commit (the free will defense) and, second, God rectifies all evil in the end by judging "the quick and the dead" and giving malevolent persons their just deserts and good persons their just reward. This would provide an

---◆---

AUGUSTINIAN THEODICY

- Human beings were created in a paradise.
- Humans fell from their state of perfection by their own sinful free acts.
- Through their own free actions, human beings introduced moral evil into the world.
- Humans hope to regain the lost state of paradise, i.e. salvation.
- Death is a consequence of sin.
- At the eschaton God judges human free actions and on the basis of merit perfectly justly causes good persons to be saved and evil persons to be damned.

---◆---

explanation at the third level of good and evil – God does not ultimately let the truly malevolent person profit from his or her evil character. And it also accounts for the suffering of innocent and good people in this life – their reward is infinite, far outweighing the evil they endured in this life.

There are three standard objections to the Augustinian theodicy. First, if humans were initially created in a state of paradise (so that all God's creation was good), how did they manage to fall in the first place? There is no real explanation of how they fell, except to turn to the idea of Satan as deceiving humans. But this just pushes the problem back one step: if Satan (an angel) was originally part of God's all-good creation, how did Satan fall? Second, the Augustinian theodicy assumes that humans never really improve as a race in this life. But there seems to be some progress in human civilization – the development of civil law, notions of human rights, of *ahimsa*, etc. And third, how could a good God eternally torment people by condemning them to hell?

The notion of hell as a place of everlasting torment and punishment was first developed by Zoroaster (630–553 BCE). In traditional Zoroastrianism, what happens to each person after death is a direct consequence of his or her deeds in this life, each of which is recorded in a book of life. After death, those who were good (and this includes *humata*, good thoughts) cross safely over the Chinvat Bridge (Bridge of the Separator, or Accountant) into paradise. Next, those who have an overall balance of good and evil in their actions pass into an intermediate stage of existence until a final judgment. Finally, those whose evil thoughts and deeds outweigh their good thoughts and deeds lose their footing on the Chinvat Bridge and fall into hell. Christianity derived its notion of hell from Zoroastrianism from whence it influenced Islam (the *sheol* of Judaism is not a comparable doctrine). This doctrine of hell is vividly portrayed in its Christian form in the *Dies Irae*, the sung description in the Latin Mass of the day of final judgment:

Dies irae, dies illa,	Day of wrath, that day dismaying,
solvet saeculum in favilla,	shall fulfill the prophet's saying,
teste David cum Sibylla.	earth in smoldering ashes laying.
Quantus tremor est futurus,	Oh, how great the dread, the sighing,
quando Judex est venturus,	when the Judge, the All-descrying,
cuncta stricte discussurus!	shall appear, all secrets trying!
Tuba mirum spargens sonum,	Then shall the trumpet's weird knelling,
per sepulchra regionum,	through each tomb and charnel dwelling
coget omnes ante thronum.	all before the Throne compelling.
Mors stupebit et natura,	Death shall stand in consternation,
cum resurget creatura	nature quake, and all creation
judicanti responsura.	rise to answer the citation.
Liber scriptus proferetur,	From the book shall shine the writing,
in quo totum continetur,	all the bygone past reciting,
unde mundus judicetur.	and the world of sin indicting.
Judex ergo cum sedebit,	Then the Judge shall sit, revealing
quidquid latet apparebit,	hidden deed, word, thought and feeling,
nil inultum remanebit.	and to each just sentence dealing.

Hinduism and Buddhism have no corresponding idea of an eternal hell. For one thing, there is, of course, no God to be a final judge and no final judgment in these Asian traditions. But further, the Buddhist idea of "hell" is more like the Zoroastrian idea of an intermediate stage for those who have accumulated too much evil (bad *karma* in Buddhism) or like the Roman Catholic idea of purgatory. The Buddhist hells are part of the cycle of *samsara*, eventually dissolved in the release to *nirvana*. But the Augustinian hell is permanent. It seems difficult to reconcile eternal punishment with the idea of a loving God.

SOUL-MAKING THEODICIES

Another kind of theodicy which avoids some of these problematic issues for the Augustinian Theodicy are soul-making theodicies. The first church father, Irenaeus (125–202 CE), was not heavily influenced as

---
◆

IRENAEAN THEODICY

- God created humans in God's image: humans are free rational beings, capable of interpersonal relations with God.
- God did not create humans in God's exact likeness, for to be in God's exact likeness would mean that humans were perfect beings.
- God created the world not as a paradise, but rather as a proper environment for soul-making – an environment for humans to develop into better, good persons.
- Humans sin, but death is simply the finite limit on this life.
- Through their own free will acts of sin, humans produce evil.
- Through trials and tribulations humans can evolve into better persons, for one cannot develop good character unless there is the real possibility of pain and cruelty in the world, and of doing evil.
- The end result will be humans who become free, loving, and compassionate persons.

◆

Augustine was by Manicheanism (an offshoot of Zoroastrianism), and he developed a rather different, soul-making theodicy. The general points of an Irenaean theodicy, which was also later espoused, for example, by the German theologian Friedrich Schleiermacher and even more recently by John Hick, are set out above. In the Irenaean theodicy the emphasis is on God creating humans in the image but not the likeness of Godself, such that the purpose of life is to undergo soul-making, or character building, and the end goal of creation is free, loving, and compassionate persons. This is similar to the Hindu and Buddhist idea that the wise person knows that achieving good *karma* is an essential element of the path to liberation – though for Buddhism in particular there is no God who intends this world to be an environment for the improvement of character through good karmic action.

There are points of agreement between the Augustinian and the Irenaean theodicies. Both agree that God permits evil. However, in the Augustinian view it is better that there is good and evil in the world than that there were no evil at all, because if there were no evil at all, there could be no free creatures (free will defense). Irenaeus holds that God allows for there to be good and evil, not just to allow for human freedom but to make possible soul-making or character building. On the Augustinian view, evil comes into the world because of the Fall, whereas on the Irenaean view, pain is present in the world because it is part of the environment necessary for us fully to exercise our ability to become better creatures. Both Augustine and Irenaeus think God is just and loving. But while Augustine emphasizes God's justice, Irenaeus emphasizes God's love.

Soul-making theodicies postulate a third level of good: becoming a loving, compassionate person through transformation of the self. We will return to this at the end of the book in chapter 14. But where do soul-making theodicies leave us with respect to the third level of evil – evil persons? There are three alternatives with respect to evil persons. The Augustinian theodicy offers a first alternative, namely that evil persons receive just deserts, so justice triumphs over evil. Universalism offers a second alternative: all persons eventually become loving and compassionate through soul-making, so that love triumphs over evil. Some will object to the first alternative on the grounds that it makes God retributive, and some will object to the second alternative on the grounds that it does not seem as if the thoroughly evil person could achieve a state of loving kindness by his or her own free acts. This leaves a third option. Unlike Hinduism and Buddhism which are universalist, and more like Jainism, in which only the true *jina* (conqueror of *samsara*) achieves ascent to the *siddha loka* or celestial palace, some persons might freely choose even in the end to be evil, and a hell of their own making will be a hell of their own choice.

THE BEST POSSIBLE WORLD

Are these theodicies convincing? That probably depends on whether you are more inclined to see the world as good or more inclined to emphasize the amount of evil in the world. Gottleib Leibniz suggested that what God must have created is "the best of all possible worlds." That is, in effect God considered (perhaps atemporally) all the possibilities before creation. There are innumerable ways the world could have been created, i.e. a universe of water with no people, one with just one person, with different physical laws, etc. But when God considered the possibilities, God would have chosen to create the best of all these possible worlds. But how could this be the best universe, when there are such horrendous evils? Indeed, in his clever parody, *Candide*, Voltaire relates the adventures of a professor of philosophy, Pangloss, who is a Leibnizian. Pangloss expresses the theory that this is the best of all possible worlds even as, traveling together with a naive young man, terrible things happen: they are beaten, mugged, thieves fall upon them – a long litany of evils. What could possibly be the reason for allowing so much evil?

In response, consider an analogy which Nelson Pike has suggested. You have a set of blocks that can be fitted together. What you are trying to do is to produce the most aesthetically pleasing block arrangement. Among the blocks, some are beautiful, and some are ugly – and then there is this one *really* ugly, repugnant block. However, as you get ready to arrange the blocks, you discover that the most aesthetic arrangement requires that block than which an uglier can hardly be imagined. This scenario is perfectly plausible. For all we know, this parallels how God, in choosing which possible universe to create, knows that some ugly (or potentially ugly) blocks are needed for the best result. That ugliness, of course, is the moral evil of free creatures who misuse their freedom. Is God then culpable for allowing evil in the universe which God does create? Not if the universe could not have been better had it been created any other way.

For this to function as a successful theodicy against the probablistic problem of evil, it needs to be plausible that our world is one among the best possible worlds. (There may be no single best possible world, but equally good, best possible worlds.) To construct a successful theodicy, theists need to make a convincing case that there is one final level of good which plausibly outweighs all the levels of evil. And is it not better to have a universe with free persons, some of whom become free, loving and compassionate people, despite the inevitable presence of evil in such a universe? (Of course what most people mean when they suggest that God should have created a world with less evil is that someone else, not them, should have been left out of the created universe.) It certainly seems to be the case that whatever else is true of humans, we cannot be truly free, loving creatures unless there is a possibility that we will go wrong. And that makes it highly probable that there *is* going to be evil in the universe, even if it is the best possible universe in the sense that it is a universe no better than which could have been created.

Further reading

The Book of Job

Bowker, John. *Problems of Suffering in Religions of the World.* Cambridge, Cambridge University Press, 1970

Dostoevsky, Fyodor. *Brothers Karamazov.* Andrew McAndrew, trans. Toronto, Bantam, 1987

Hick, John. *Evil and the God of Love.* New York, Harper and Row, 1978

Ling, Trevor. *Buddhism and the Mythology of Evil: A Study in Theravada Buddhism.* Oxford, Oneworld, 1977

Peterson, Michael L., ed. *The Problem of Evil.* Notre Dame, University of Notre Dame Press, 1992

Swinburne, Richard. *Is There a God?* Oxford, Oxford University Press, 1996

Voltaire. *Candide.* Lowell Bain, trans. Toronto, Bantam Doubleday, 1981

Leibniz, Gottfried Wilhelm. *Theodicy.* Diogenes Allen, ed. Indianapolis, Bobbs-Merrill Company, 1966

7 EMBODIMENT, GENDER, AND GOD[1]

Chamunda of India is quite unlike the Holy Mother Mary of Europe...unlike Mary, she is not pure and refined, and she wears no fine apparel. Rather, she is ugly and worn with age, and she groans under the weight of the suffering she bears...the goddess who endured the bites of poisonous snakes and scorpions and, while afflicted with leprosy and hunger, offered her milk to swarms of children, which is the mother of India. An image not of a mother's plentitude and gentleness but of an old woman reduced to skin and bones grasping for breath. Despite it all, she was still a mother.[2]

Shusaku Endo (1923–1999) from *Deep River*

Leaving aside the question of the existence of God or a Transcendent, let us now take up an issue that faces all religious realists. How should one understand the relationship of this real Transcendent to the world and to human beings? A critical part of any answer to this question is the question of what language is appropriate for speaking about the Transcendent. As we saw in chapter 4, theological realism needs to avoid a too transcendent, too abstract idea of God. The antidote to the idea of a Transcendent Reality or a God removed from humans and of no human concern is an immanent God, a personal God with whom humans can interact. Embodiment theologies are directed toward this understanding of God. But if there is a Transcendent God who is also immanent, what kind of language is appropriate to talk about this immanent God?

INCARNATION AND EMBODIMENT

The notion that the Transcendent or God is not just transcendent but also immanent is reflected in the incarnation of various divine personae, such as Shiva and Krishna (Vishnu) and the Tibetan Dalai Lama, an incarnation of the *bodhisattva* Avalokiteshvara. Even Christians, though often reluctant to see the body as holy, proclaim that God so loved the world that God incarnated Godself (John 3:16; Rom. 5:8). Thus, it is a common theme in the World Religions that the Transcendent seeks embodiment. As the *Bhagavad Gita* puts it:

My self is changeless and unborn,
and I am Lord of beings,
but using Nature, which is Mine,
by My own power I come into being.

Whenever there appears on earth
decline of Righteousness,
uprising of Unrighteousness,
I send Myself to birth.

For protection of the good,
the wicked put to flight,
I come into being age by age
establishing the Right.[3]

And in early Indic thought, the entire world itself (that is, each *kalpa* in an endless cycle) is depicted as created by the sweat that falls from Shiva Nataraj's brow in the great cosmic dance.

Now, part of the logic of these incarnational metaphors is that creation or manifestation is the means by which God's love is expressed.[4] The body is essential for the expression of love. The body makes love affective – it gives love focus, and it makes love vivid. This is captured in the Hindu notion of *darshan*, the passionate reciprocity of physically both seeing the divine and being seen by the divine during, for example, a visit to a temple.

In religion, whenever the idea of the spirit is radically separated from the idea of the body, the result is an austere, intellectualist view of the Transcendent. We already saw this in the Introduction when we considered the work of the medieval Jewish theologian Moses Maimonides who equates learning metaphysics with being in the presence of God. Similarly in the Christian tradition in the West a dichotomy developed between the bad, which resides in the body, and the good, the mind and spirit, in part as a result of an increasing turn in Western theology toward an Aristotelian emphasis on the mind and the way of knowledge to God. However, as contemporary Christian feminist theology has demonstrated in the West, the notion of divine embodiment offers a richer understanding of the plenitude of the Transcendent.[5] And moving beyond the mind, embodiment theology confronts the person of faith with an inescapably immanent, interactive, loving God.

FEMININE DIVINE METAPHORS

Once God is envisioned as embodied, questions of gender and also of sexuality arise, questions which then bring philosophy of religion and philosophical theology closer to the lived life of religion itself. Human embodiment and human relations are fundamentally shaped by gender, which is a set of socially defined notions of masculinity and femininity. This leads to a natural inclination to speak about an embodied Transcendent in the gendered terms of one's culture. Thus, one striking feature of Asian traditions is the prominent place given to the female divine. In contrast, the model of male strength in herdsman/shepherd cultures which most influenced the great monotheisms of the West has traditionally given Western monotheism a patriarchal orientation. However, as feminist theology has made a strong case for the use of more organic female metaphors to refer to the Divine in order better to capture the lived religious life of humans in the West, Western conceptions have been brought closer to Asian conceptions. It should be emphasized, however, that gender language when applied to the Transcendent is being used metaphorically and analogically.

An excellent example of feminist theological reformulation is Sallie McFague's *Models of God: Theology for an Ecological, Nuclear Age* which challenges traditional Christian theological formulations and proposes an alternative account of the world as God's body, and of God as mother, God as lover, and God as friend. McFague argues that the classical Western monarchical model of God treats God as too uninvolved with the world (too transcendent). On her account this results in a hierarchical, dualistic way of thinking which can be used to support oppression (e.g. rich/poor, white/colored, male/female, and Christian versus non-Christian). Much like the non-realism of Don Cupitt which we discussed in chapter 3, McFague argues on the basis of moral considerations for a reinterpretation of Christian doctrine which emphasizes divine immanence, but unlike Cupitt she offers a realist interpretation of divine immanence.

In her embodiment theology, McFague first develops a model of "the world as God's body." Emphasizing God's immanence, this model centrally portrays a God in intimate and caring relation to the world. McFague suggests that this model supports an ethics directed toward responsibility and care – an ethics which she sees as more female, rather than the more traditional (male) concern with competing rights. This leads to three other models. She suggests the model of God as mother which emphasizes a nurturing divine closeness unlike the often disinterested God of father imagery. She suggests the model of God as lover which emphasizes the value of the other in the divine-human relationship. And she suggests the model of God as friend, which she describes as an "astounding" model, for this says that God *likes* you, desiring a "companionable sensibility."

What is the status of these new models *vis-à-vis* traditional models for God in the West? Initially McFague states that the models of the world as God's body, and God as mother, lover, and friend, are several among many possible valuable and instructive models for contemporary Christian faith. Yet McFague's later assessment of each suggests that these are superior models in an era of ecological awareness and nuclear threat. For example, she writes:

> All of us...have the womb as our first home, all of us are born from...[and] fed by our mothers. What better imagery could there be for expressing the most basic reality of existence: That we live and move and have our being in God?[6]

This is problematic. Not all people, given their personal psychological histories, will see mother as a positive model. (Consider, for example, the little child tortured by her parents in Dostoevsky's example in *The Brothers Karamazov* which we addressed in the last chapter.) Perhaps it would be better to say that for many people the models she proposes will be illuminating. For others, different models and metaphors may be equally insightful.

Turning to McFague's specific embodiment models, the model of the world as God's body is reminiscent of Ramanuja's Hindu view (see chapter 4). McFague attempts to explain the model of the world as God's body with an analogy: God is to the world as our self is to our bodies. At one point she suggests that God's body is the entire universe and God is a self whose intentions are expressed in the universe. However, at other times she states that God's body "is not matter or spirit but the matrix out of which everything that is evolves,"[7] and that "in some sense God is physical (as well as beyond the physical)."[8] But in what sense is God physical? This leaves her central body metaphor unclear. To explain her position, McFague also denies any mind-body dualism (though she partially retracts this by saying that humans are spirits that possess bodies). If the Godself/world relation is not a form of dualism, does this amount to some version of pantheism? The more pantheistic tendency in this view is expressed in the notion that God is "the matrix" of the body and spirit in the universe.

McFague draws certain geocentric and anthropocentric conclusions from this view of an embodied God. She says that we have "the responsibility to care for God's body, our world" and that humans, as "the only conscious ones among the beloved," have "ultimate power over good and evil" since in the throes of nuclear insanity we can be the "uncreators of life."[9] This raises a host of puzzles. Is God's body the whole universe, or is God's body only the earth? If the latter is proposed, it seems egocentric to identify our home planet with God's body. Moreover, it seems improbable that *homo sapiens* are the only conscious beings in the universe. Buddhists would certainly dispute this *vis-à-vis* our planet, as would Jains with their notion that *jivas* are found in every form of life. But going beyond our planet, if there are other life forms throughout the universe, it seems unlikely that we could be the uncreators of life. And if God's body is the whole universe, then how significant would the destruction of life on earth actually be in the cosmic scale?

These questions show us that, as important as they are, embodiment metaphors for the divine are especially difficult to clarify. The traditional Christian doctrine of the Incarnation and *bhakti* Hindu notions of Krishna or Shiva illustrate the difficulty of explaining where divinity leaves off and something other than the divine begins. Still, the models of the world as God's body, and God as mother, lover and friend offer a potent vision of the love and care of God, and of human interdependence and responsible action within and with the world. Even if McFague fails in her stated task to "unseat" traditional Christian monarchical language, the value of these metaphors lies in their exposition of incarnational faith in God as the belief that "The universe is neither malevolent nor indifferent but is on the side of life and its fulfillment."[10]

These feminine metaphors portray a God who is both transcendent and immanent, neither too distant from, nor too subsumed in, the world.

THE PROBLEM OF REFERENCE AND REPRESENTATION

Some theologies envision God through male metaphors, others through female metaphors. We might question the value of any given metaphor, but we cannot rid ourselves altogether of metaphor. The difficulties we have just seen with incarnational or embodiment metaphors for God are part of a larger problem with divine predication.

Human ideas and means of expression come from the natural order. There is no one-to-one correspondence between natural things and the supernatural or transcendent. So on the one hand, one cannot make univocal reference to the Transcendent. Terms which apply to the natural order cannot be applied – at least in the same way – to the transcendent order. For example, we cannot use terms for God in the same sense that we use them to refer to natural things. God is good and humans (can be) good, but God is not good in exactly the same sense as humans are good. However, on the other hand, if every attempt to communicate about God were a mere equivocation there would be no cognitive content to talk about God. God cannot be called good if God is supposed to be good in a way utterly unlike any way in which anything else we know about is good. So as Ramanuja and Thomas Aquinas suggested, attempts to refer to the Transcendent must fall in between these extremes – they must be analogical. That is, we can only refer to the Transcendent by analogy with things in this world.[11]

In order to express ideas about the Transcendent successfully, we must use elements of the natural order which have a partial likeness – for they cannot have a full likeness – to the Transcendent. Now, embodiment and gendered metaphors and models are analogical in their portrayal of an immanent God. Consequently, if one wishes to represent God as immanent, the question is not so much whether embodiment and gendered metaphors should be used to refer to God, but rather which embodiment metaphors are most felicitous.

SEXUAL METAPHORS

This brings us to what at first appears to be an odd way to refer to God, and that is the use of not just gendered metaphors but sexual metaphors. For example, consider the bride mystics of medieval

Christianity. St. Teresa of Avila relates this famous experience of hers:

> I saw an angel close by me, on my left side, in bodily form. He was not large, but small of stature, and most beautiful...I saw in his hand a long spear of gold, and at the iron's point there seemed to be a little fire. He appeared to me to be thrusting it at times into my heart, and to pierce my very entrails; when he drew it out, he seemed to draw them out also, and to leave me all on fire with a great love of God. The pain was so great, that it made me moan; yet so surpassing was the sweetness of this excessive pain, that I could not wish to be rid of it. The soul is satisfied now with nothing less than God.[12]

Here we have the explicit erotic imagery of sexual encounter employed to represent divine-human encounter. An instructional text for many classical Christian mystics like St. Teresa, St. John of the Cross, and St. Francis de Sales as they sought a deeper understanding of the divine-human relationship was found in the earlier Jewish tradition in the passionate eroticism of the *Song of Songs*:

> My beloved is to me a bag of
> myrrh,
> that lies between my breasts...
> My beloved is mine and I am his.[13]

This sexual imagery becomes transmuted in the Christian monastics and also in Hasidic strands of Judaism, into an erotic representation of the encounter of lover of God with God, the beloved.

Within the Jewish Kabbalistic tradition, while sexual imagery is not directly used to represent divine-human encounter as the eminent Jewish scholar Gershom Scholem points out, God is seen as the locus of sexuality: "in God there is a union of the active and the passive, procreation and conception, from which all mundane life and bliss is derived."[14] In the Islamic tradition, we find a similar use of erotic representation in Rumi, the greatest of all Persian mystic poets:

> For God hath mingled in the dusty earth
> A draught of Beauty from his choicest cup.
> Tis *that*, fond lover – not these lips of clay –
> Thou art kissing with a hundred ecstasies.[15]

Finally, another Western monotheistic way to understand divine-human relationship in erotic terms is found in the famous Jewish Kabbalistic mystical text the Zohar or Book of Splendor. While not directly eroticizing divine-human relationality, it does so indirectly by portraying the Torah itself as lover to the devoted reader of the *Torah*:

> What a multitude of humans there are who dwell in confusion, failing to perceive the way of truth that abides in Torah, and the Torah, in love, summons them day by day to her, but woe, they do not so much as turn their heads...
>
> She may be compared to a beautiful and stately maiden, who is secluded in an isolated chamber of a palace, and has a lover of whose existence she alone knows. For love of her he passes by her gate unceasingly, and turns his eyes in all directions to discover her...She thrusts open a small door in her secret chamber, for a moment reveals her face to her lover, then quickly withdraws it. He alone, none else, notices it; but he is aware it is from love of him that she has revealed herself to him for a moment, and his heart and his soul and everything within him are drawn to her.[16]

If we turn to the Asian traditions, we find even more common and salient uses of sexual imagery for divine predication. In the Hindu tradition, as we saw in chapter 4, the male gods have female counterparts or consorts. Parvati, the female consort of the great god Shiva, pursues him relentlessly, first outdoing Shiva in mediative practice to get his attention and then making endless love to win the Dark Lord. Parvati is a mother and also a lover, and their relationship of love is mirrored in the world. While Christianity and Islam have more typically understood God in Godself in non-sexual terms, not surprisingly a better comparison within monotheism to Hinduism is found in Jewish Kabbalism. Gershom Scholem points out that:

> Non-Jewish [Western] mysticism, which glorified and propagated asceticism, ended sometimes by transplanting eroticism into the relation of man to God. Kabbalism, on the other hand, was tempted to discover the mystery of sex within God himself....every true marriage is a symbolical realization of the union of God and the Shekhinah [the glory of God as it appears].[17]

This general global tendency to place the locus of sexuality in the Divine raises a number of philosophical questions about the significance and appropriateness of sexual symbolism.

First, gendered, and more especially sexual, symbolism will be in general appropriate to divine-human encounter if the term "God" is used to refer to the Transcendent conceived of as entering into personal relationships. This is the notion which Sallie McFague captures for Western Christianity when she says "the universe is neither indifferent nor malevolent but that there is a power (and a *personal* power at that) which is on the side of life and its fulfillment."

Second, without necessarily accepting a fully Jungian analysis of symbols, we can see that Carl Jung's foundational proposal that humans share archetypes helps explain this universality of sexual imagery for personalistic conceptions of the Transcendent: "like the instincts, the collective thought patterns of the human mind are innate and inherited. They function, when the occasion arises, in more or less the same way in all of us."[18] It is a common human frustration expressed in all the theistic traditions that the manifestation of God is more subtle than overt.[19] But if there is a Transcendent and if the Transcendent is personal, we would expect the hard wiring of the brain, as passed on from past human experience, to include dispositions to detect the personal Transcendent. As Jung says, "just as the human body represents a whole museum of organs, each with a long evolutionary history behind it, so we should expect to find that the mind is organized in a similar way."[20] The archetypes of sexual symbolism may be just such genetically based dispositions to express divine-human encounter.

Third, notice that sexual symbolism would be most appropriate for divine-human encounter if, even more fundamentally, sexual symbolism is appropriate for expressing the divine reality itself as experienced by humans. As the American philosopher Robert Nozick notes, "in sex one can also engage in metaphysical exploration, knowing the body and person of another as a map or microcosm of the very deepest reality, a clue to its nature and purpose."[21] Transferring this to the divine-human encounter, the use of sexual symbolism would indicate that there is at the deepest level, so to speak, a divine metaphysics of love. Widely diverse traditions express this. For example, this view is succinctly expressed in the Christian book of I John in a passage which could as well come from the *bhakti* Hindu tradition: "God is love, and he who abides in love abides in God, and God abides in him" (I John 4:16).

SYMBOLS, SEXUALITY, AND GOD

The use of sexual symbolism for divine predication does not imply that God is physical – that would be the mistake of univocal predication. But to avoid equivocation there must be some literal meaning to the symbolism. Sexual symbolism is both inextricably relational and inextricably gendered. So the use of sexual symbolism implies that in some measure God literally can be conceived of as both personal and gendered. Regarding the latter, it is important to keep in mind that gender is a fluid notion. Hence appropriately, symbolic representations of the Divine often include a co-mingling of gender: androgenous representations of Shiva, the male-female coupling of the *yab-yum* of Tibetan Buddhism and the Chinese *yin* and *yang*, as well as the notion of mystic, whether male or female, as bride of God within Western conceptions of divine-human encounter.

To better see how these sexual symbols function, consider Paul Tillich's suggestion that symbols in general have six characteristics: (1) symbols point beyond themselves; (2) they participate in that to which they point; (3) they open up new levels of reality; (4) symbols unlock dimensions of our spirits (Tillich uses the more Western term "souls") which correspond to the new levels of reality disclosed; (5) they cannot be produced intentionally; and (6) they live and die according to the situation in which they arise.[22] It will be helpful to consider each of these points in turn.

Taking points 1 and 3 together, symbols point beyond themselves and open up new levels of reality which could not otherwise be accessed.[23] Not only are our finitely limited concepts unable fully to express the transcendent and infinite, the religious person also wants to be able to express the non-intellectual affective aspects of encountering the Transcendent. Hence, those with a personalistic conception of the Transcendent need both the analogical and the emotive power of symbols, whether in language, action, or art, to enhance and expand a felt sensitivity to the personal Divine. Sexual symbols can provide this affective dimension. For instance, Mahadeviyakka, the Hindu *bhakti* saint of the twelfth century, sings of her love for Shiva, using the complete abandonment of sexual ecstasy as an analogy to the utter commitment of faith:

> He bartered my heart,
>> looted my flesh
>> claimed as tribute
>> my pleasure,
>> took over
>> all of me.
> I'm the woman of love
>> for my lord,
>> white as jasmine.[24]

Likewise, in the Vaishnava tradition, Krishna, eighth avatar of Vishnu, is the dark-skinned lover, playing his flute to entice devotees, who encircle him in the *rasamandala,* each facing inward toward Krishna and each passionately convinced that Lord Krishna loves him or her specially, while he loves all.

Perhaps theists could excise all sexual symbolism and replace it with another sort of symbolism. But the replacement symbolism could no more completely capture the divine-human encounter than does sexual symbolism. The use of sexual symbolism to convey a glimpse of the personal divine being is no different in kind than any other expression of divine-human encounter: expressing the Divine is, so to speak, *symbols all the way down.* (This does not mean that the Transcendent must itself be just symbols. Sometimes symbols do not point to anything beyond themselves – and this is the risk of using symbols – but symbols can sometimes successfully point beyond themselves. The ancient Israelites, for example, claimed that the golden calf failed, where the Ten Commandments succeeded, in pointing to the truly Transcendent.)

Now consider characteristics 2 and 4 of symbols: they participate in that to which they point, and they unlock dimensions of our spirits which correspond to the new dimensions of reality disclosed. Sexual symbolism is fundamentally relational. This means that the erotic representation of the experience of the Divine is meant not only to reflect the divine love but to indicate that humans can participate in the divine love. Indeed, the deepest relation between humans and the Divine would be a love relationship. Even as the expression "God is mind" is dispassionate, to say "God is Love" holds relational promise.

Finally, consider characteristics 5 and 6: the idea that symbols cannot be produced intentionally and that they live and die in the situation within which they are formed. Here I would disagree with Tillich – and also Jung – because sexual symbols, like all aesthetic symbols, can be produced intentionally. On this score, a better analysis is offered by Sallie McFague's notion of theology as constructive, as modeling God through the use of metaphor. McFague compares metaphorical theology to painting a picture and also describes the metaphorical theologian as part poet and part philosopher: constructing imaginative models for contemporary faith, yet needing to show the coherence, comprehensiveness, and systematic application of those models. However, we should note several difficulties with McFague's suggestion that the impetus for metaphorical theology is the recognition that our concepts cannot directly refer to God.

McFague claims that a "metaphor is a word or phrase used inappropriately" and that "God-language can refer only through the detour of a description that properly belongs elsewhere."[25] This is too strong, for it rests on a misunderstanding of the nature of metaphors. While a metaphor does not provide a direct description of its referent, a metaphor is only used properly and can only be successful if there are certain features which the intended referent, and the normal referent of the metaphor when it is taken literally, have in common. A related, epistemological problem is McFague's insistence that traditional divine predication properly refers "only to our existence, not God's,"[26] – e.g. knowledge properly refers to human capacities and not to God's. For even if we cannot know that theological constructions do successfully refer to God, we also cannot know that they do not, or could not, properly refer to God, if God exists. It may be that no names – mother or father, creator or lover, judge or friend – could successfully describe the divine nature, but it is part of the expectation of doing any theology that language will in some measure succeed in referring to and partially, however imperfectly, describing the Divine. Otherwise theology will not even be poetry, and silence would be the wisest course of action. This becomes especially apparent in McFague's claim that humans always see God through pictures and not directly. For if human pictures of the Divine never properly refer to God (whether we can know this or not), then all we will have is our pictures. This will reduce theological language to the language of religious non-realism, which we discussed in chapter 3.

Now as McFague notes, the use of metaphor in theology "encourages...novel ways of expressing the relation between God and the world," for they are "imaginative leaps across a distance – the best metaphors always give both a shock and a shock of recognition."[27] Sexual symbolism provides both a shock – suddenly seeing the Divine in unexpected ways – and more importantly a shock of recognition. For those who experience the passion of faith, encountering the Divine is so profound – the devout feels so vulnerable and yet so integrated, so desirous to be one with the beloved – that only the archetype of sexual experience seems to compare. This is beyond the rational. This is emotive and intuitional. As the twelfth-century *bhakti* saint Basavanna says of Shiva:

When
like a hailstone crystal
like a waxwork image
the flesh melts in pleasure
     how can I tell you?

The waters of joy
broke the banks
and ran out of my eyes.

I touched and joined
my lord of the meeting rivers.
How can I talk to anyone
of that?[28]

Metaphors are in part literal predications. As we say, Richard is "lion-hearted" or "life is a stage" because each member of the pair – Richard and a lion; life and theater – has certain characteristics in common. So too, God would be properly referred to as beloved and lover for the devout if the God-human relationship shares some characteristics of earthly lovers. Symbols point. What the embodied erotic symbolism of religion points to is the desire to be with the divine beloved, even a desire to *be* the divine beloved, for it is a desire to be of one will with the beloved. We will return to the way of love in chapter 14.

Further reading

INTRODUCTORY

Cabezon, Jose Ignacio. *Buddhism, Sexuality, and Gender.* New York, State University of New York Press, 1985

Hampson, Daphne. *Theology and Feminism.* Oxford, Basil Blackwell, 1990

Heyward, Carter. *Touching Our Strength: The Erotic as Power and the Love of God.* San Francisco, HarperSanFrancisco, 1984

O'Neill, Maura. *Women Speaking, Women Listening.* New York, Orbis Books, 1990

Parrinder, Geoffrey. *Avatar and Incarnation: The Divine in Human Form in the World Religions.* Oxford, Oneworld, 1997

Ruether, Rosemary Radford. *Sexism and God-Talk: Toward a Feminist Theology.* Boston, Beacon Press, 1983

Runzo, Joseph and Martin, Nancy M. eds. *Love, Sex, and Gender in the World Religions.* Oxford, Oneworld, 2000

IN-DEPTH

Alston, William P. *Divine Nature and Human Language: Essays in Philosophical Theology.* London, Cornell University Press, 1989

Cahill, Lisa Sowle. *Sex, Gender, and Christian Ethics.* Cambridge, Cambridge University Press, 1996

Fiorenza, Elisabeth Schussler. *In Memory of Her.* New York, Crossroad, 1983

Hawley, John Stratton and Donna Marie Wulff, eds. *Devi: Goddesses of India.* Berkeley, University of California Press, 1996

McFague, Sallie. *Models of God: Theology for an Ecological, Nuclear Age.* Philadelphia, Fortress Press, 1987

Scholem, Gershom G. *Zohar: The Book of Splendor.* New York, Schocken Books, 1949

Scholem, Gershom G. *Major Trends in Jewish Mysticism.* New York, Schocken Books, 1954

Sharma, Arvind, ed. *Today's Woman in World Religions.* New York, State University of New York Press, 1994

Sharma, Arvind, ed. *Women in World Religions.* New York, State University of New York Press, 1987

Sharma, Arvind and Young, Karen, eds. *Feminism and World Religions.* New York, State University of New York Press, 1999

Sharma, Arvind, ed. *Religion and Women.* New York, State University of New York Press, 1994

St. John of the Cross. *The Living Flame of Love.* E. Allison Peers, trans. New York, Image Books, 1962

St. John of the Cross. *Spiritual Canticle.* E. Allison Peers, trans. New York, Image Books, 1961

St. Teresa of Avila. *The Autobiography of St. Teresa of Avila.* E. Allison Peers, trans. New York, Image Books, 1960

St. Teresa of Avila. *Interior Castle.* E. Allison Peers, trans. New York, Image Books, 1961

8 LIFE AFTER DEATH

To die, to sleep –
No more, and by a sleep to say we end
The heart-ache and the thousand natural shocks
That flesh is heir to; 'tis a consummation
Devoutly to be wish'd. To die, to sleep –

...But that the dread of something after death,
The undiscover'd country, from whose bourn
No traveller returns, puzzles the will,
And makes us rather bear those ills we have,
Than fly to others that we know not of.[1]

William Shakespeare (1564–1616)

THE RELIGIOUS IMPORTANCE OF LIFE AFTER DEATH

Can there be life after death? This is one of the central philosophical
questions in the World Religions. All of the great World Religions postulate life after death. Indeed, the notion of life after death is part of
the glue, as it were, of the worldview of every World Religion, providing culmination for each religious path in either salvation or liberation,
explaining the consequences of sin or *karma*, and offering a final
realization of the true nature of the Transcendent. In the Western
monotheisms heaven (paradise for Islam) is the afterlife state of existence in the presence of God, the goal and end of human life; in
Hinduism *moksha* or enlightenment is the final realization of either oneness with Brahman (as in Advaita Vedanta) or union with Brahman

(such as we find in Ramanuja's Vishishtadvaita Vedanta or Madhva's Dvaita Vedanta); and in Buddhism the karmic cycle of *samsara* ends in the final enlightenment of *nirvana*.

It is easy to suppose that the question of life after death is more pressing in the Western monotheisms where the traditional view is that humans have only one life to live before the final determination of what each human's final state will be in the afterlife. After all, if Buddhism or Hinduism are correct and one has the prospect of a multitude of reincarnations, it would seem to matter less what one does in this life, for there are many lives in which to make up deficiencies of character. However this goes against Hindu and Buddhist teachings. Buddha Shakyamuni used an allegory to explain the significance of this life regarding the prospects of reincarnation as a human. Imagine, he suggests, an enormous ocean on which floats a yoke with a hole through the middle. In the depth of the ocean lives a blind turtle who only comes to the surface once every one hundred years. Our chance of being reborn in human form again after this life is similar to the chance of the blind turtle surfacing with his head through the hole in the yoke which floats upon that enormous ocean.

Consequently, the question of life after death is as pressing an issue in Hinduism and Buddhism as it is in the Western monotheisms. Since in both Hinduism and Buddhism one is tied to the wheel of *dharma* in the endless cycle of *samsara* by the state of one's character (*karma*), and since one can only significantly improve one's *karma* and can only break the bonds of ignorance when in human form, to be a human is a rare opportunity not to be squandered. For as the *Dhammapada* says "Like a fish which is thrown on dry land, taken from his home in the waters, the mind strives and struggles to get free from the power of Death."[2] And within Hinduism and Buddhism, life after death holds not only the potential for achieving final *moksha* or *nirvana*, even short of that, life after death offers the prospect for eventual reincarnation as a human and the opportunity to improve *karma*.

THE PROBLEM OF DEATH

The key philosophical issues regarding life after death are twofold: (1) is life after death even possible, and (2) if life after death is possible, which particular religious conception of life after death makes the most sense? We will primarily focus on question 1, leaving to the reader any detailed inquiry into question 2. There are three options regarding question 1 – that it is impossible that there can be life after death, that it is possible that there can be life after death, and that there is life after death.

Regarding the third option as to whether or not there *is* life after death, apart from an *a priori* argument that the soul, for example, is immortal, the fact of whether *you* will achieve life after death is an empirical issue which cannot be settled in this life. For even if someone else died and reappeared after "coming back from the dead" – and even if this is a divine figure like Jesus Christ – this would not provide evidence that *you* will survive your death, though it may lend credence to that possibility. On the other hand, *a priori* arguments for the immortality of the soul (such as Plato gave) do not seem to be any more successful as convincing proofs than the sort of *a priori* arguments for the existence of God or Brahman which we assessed in chapter 4. Generally *a priori* arguments for various elements of religious belief do not so much prove their conclusion as articulate the rationality of faith in God or Brahman or the immortality of the soul, etc., for the person who is already committed to these ideas.

This brings us to the other two options within question 1: the view that it is impossible that there could be life after death versus the view that it is possible that there is life after death. Any resolution of this dichotomy will rest on the answer to a further question, namely, the question of personal identity: what makes a person the person they are and not someone else? For life after death to be possible, there must exist before death a person who is identical to a person who exists after death. And this is important because if personal identity is not determined by an immortal soul or the like, then it is a serious question whether there can be any life after death at all.

CONCEPTIONS OF THE SELF

There are five basic conceptions of the self. One of the oldest and most prevalent views is dualism, the view that a human being consists of two substances, the body, on the one hand, and the mind or soul or spirit, on the other. A second view is materialism, the view that human beings are nothing more than material bodies either because a human being just is a human body or because a human mind is equivalent to a brain or central nervous system. A third view is the double-aspect theory (e.g.

as proposed by P.F. Strawson) that a person is a unique entity consisting of both physical and mental aspects but not reducible to either physical or mental aspects alone. A fourth type of view includes the various forms of idealism. Idealism holds that the body is merely an illusion and that a person is either solely a mental substance with ideas (the view of the British Empiricist George Berkeley), or that a person consists of a bundle of mental events – thoughts, emotions, perceptions, etc. – but that there is no underlying substance (a view held by the British Empiricist David Hume), or alternatively that a person consists of a bundle of mental and physical events all of which are ultimately illusory (the *anatman* view of Buddhism.) The fifth view is an evolutionary idea of the soul. On this view human beings begin life as physical entities, but the soul emerges or evolves from the physical and eventually becomes a separable mental entity.

Let us analyze each of these views in turn, beginning with dualism. Dualism comes in two variations: a two-substance composite view that a person is a mind (a substance) plus a body (a second substance), or the view that a person is simply the mind, which is a mental substance, and that this mental substance is associated with a physical substance, which is the body. The latter is more common and is the view espoused by such prominent Western philosophers as Plato and René Descartes, as well as constituting the principal view which has been held in Christianity and Islam. Hinduism has generally held a mind-body dualism within the cycle of rebirth, though at the level of *moksha* this distinction dissolves, particularly in Advaita Vedanta. In Hinduism, the self or *atman* migrates from incarnation to incarnation in the endless cycle of *samsara* until *moksha* is reached. Thus as the *Bhagavad Gita* says:

> A man his worn-out garments laying by
> some different and newer clothes will try;
> and thus the bodied soul takes other forms
> when it discards the worn-out ones that die.[3]

The most significant problem for dualism is the relation between the mental and the physical. You cut your finger, feel pain, and retract your hand from the sharp object which you have encountered. On a dualist analysis, the physical event of your finger being cut is followed by the mental event of the felt pain, which is followed by another mental event of will to retract your hand, which is finally followed by the physical event of retracting your hand. Most dualists hold interactionism, which is the view that the mental substance, the mind, interacts with the physical substance, the body. Traditional problems raised with this are the question of where this interaction takes place (Descartes had hypothesized that mind-body interaction occurs in the pineal gland at the base of the brain because he could find no other function for this bit of physical matter) and the problem of how this interaction occurs.

Obviously, the greater problem is the question of how this interaction occurs, for no matter where mind-body interaction might occur, this leaves unresolved the question of how a mental event, which has no physical dimensions, could affect a physical event, which has the physical dimensions of energy and mass. Two attempted solutions to this problem reject mind-body interaction. One is epiphenomenalism, the view that there is only one-way causation: physical events cause mental events but not *vice versa*. Thus on this view, held for example by the French philosopher Nicolas Malebranche (1638–1715), mental events are like the sparks given off from the smoke stack of a steam engine and the steam engine itself is like the body. All of the significant physical actions of the steam engine (the body) are caused by the steam engine itself, and while the sparks are caused by and accompany the physical actions of the steam engine, they are mere epiphenomena and do not themselves affect the actions of the engine.

Another alternative to interactionism is parallelism, which is proposed for instance by Gottfried Leibniz (1646–1716). Leibniz conceives of minds as self-contained monads each reflecting within itself the whole of the universe from its own perspective yet not directly interacting with other monads. On this view, monads are associated with bodies, but there is no causal connection whatsoever between the physical and the mental. Instead there is a predetermined harmony – predetermined by God in Leibniz's view – between physical events and mental events. The cut on your hand is followed by the pain event and the "will to move your hand" event which is followed by the event of moving your hand from danger, but this sequence of events unfolds in a predetermined manner at two causally unrelated levels – the mental and the physical – such that it only appears that mental events cause physical events and *vice versa*. In fact all that is happening is that physical events precede mental events which precede physical events in an harmonious order that looks as if there is causal interaction.

Epiphenomenalism and parallelism have attracted few adherents primarily because those who are dualists do not usually find these views convincing alternatives, and for those who are not dualists these views appear to be attempts to save an already unsavable dualism with improbable causal theories. For dualism faces other difficulties beyond the problem of mind-body interaction. One is whether the notion of a non-material substance (in Descartes's terms a "thinking thing") even makes sense. How can we tell, on this view, whether we are in the presence of another mind? You can tell that you are in the presence of your best friend because of his or her various physical actions including actions of speech. But then the body would seem to be the criterion for personal identity, not the elusive Cartesian mind. This objection against Cartesian dualism is developed by Gilbert Ryle as the notion of "the ghost in the machine." The machine (the body) explains everything that needs explanation. Talk of the mind (the ghost) as a mental substance seems irrelevant, and Cartesian dualism seems to collapse. A similar problem is the problem of individuation: what makes two minds distinct? Again, you can tell you are in the presence of your best friend and your worst enemy because of the way the two bodies in front of you act. Once again, the body appears to be the criterion of personal identity, talk of mental substances seems irrelevant to personal identity, and Cartesian dualism seems to collapse.

In short, the fundamental objection to Cartesian dualism is that it is unnecessarily complex. It is a theory which posits two kinds of substances, mental and physical, when only one kind of substance or state of affairs – either just the physical or just the mental – is needed to explain personal identity, individuation, and action. The most obvious alternative to Cartesian dualism is materialism, the view that a person just is his or her body or, alternatively, just is his or her brain and central nervous system. As we have already seen, we do emphasize physical properties when we identify persons. So is it not more parsimonious and conceptually elegant to eliminate talk of the mental as if it were a separate category? Materialist views are reductionist, reducing mental state to physical states, and materialism has become a prominent view with the rise of modern science and a better understanding of the complexity of physical states, especially through such studies as neurophysiology and artificial intelligence.

In psychology, reductionist materialism can be expressed as behaviorism. This view, promoted by B. F. Skinner and others, holds that mental terms simply stand for dispositions to behave. So to say "I am in pain" just means that I am in a physical state such that I am disposed to act in certain ways – namely to cry out, to writhe, to express disapproval of the object or persons who have impinged unpleasantly on my bodily space, etc. However, a first objection to behaviorism is that it eliminates the felt *qualia* of mental events, the interiority of our mental states. We normally think of the idea of "being in pain" as pointing to a certain subjective interior mental state which is not, as in pain behavior, publicly shared. And second, if behaviorism is right, then pain just is pain behavior, or the disposition thereof, yet we can easily imagine the behavior apart from the mental state, and therefore they do not seem to be in fact the same.

Stage actors and computer-generated cybernetic constructions of human faces are successful precisely because they can imitate or simulate the behavior which is associated with various mental states – such as pain, hate, fear, and being in love. The actors are not in those states (usually), for they are after all just acting, and there is no real person whose face exists in cyberspace. This alone shows that mental states are not reducible to states of behavior. Moreover, states of behavior can be caused by external sources which have nothing to do with the mental state in question. We can imagine a diabolical psychologist who, unbeknownst to you, hooks a little black box up at the base of your brain which causes you erratically to exhibit all sorts of bizarre behavior which is as puzzling to you as it is to those around you. While you persist in exclaiming "but I do not hate you," you continue to snarl, spit, grimace, and scowl at them. Hating and hate behavior are not identical, and in general mental states are not reducible to states of behavior.

This brings us to the most prominent contemporary form of materialism, the identity theory. This is the view that mental events are identical with physical processes of the brain and central nervous system. This view has gained prominence as we have come to understand more about the physiology of the brain and more about the apparent intelligence which computers seem to exhibit and/or replicate. On the identity theory, while mental events are identical with physical processes, terms for mental states do not mean the same thing as terms for physical states. On this view, just as water is identical to H_2O but the term "water" is not identical in meaning to the term "H_2O," the mind is the brain but the term "mind" has a different meaning than the term "brain." "H_2O" is an explicit description of the chemical composition of water, and water a more general descriptive term; "brain state" is an explicitly neuro-physiological description while "the mind" is a more general descriptive term.

However, the identity theory itself faces serious problems. First, what exactly is supposed to be this difference between physical and mental terms? Notice that the idea that one is an outer description (brain) and one is an inner description (mind) of the same thing is unworkable. For a sophisticated neurosurgeon can in some sense see inside my own brain better than I can see inside my own thoughts, if my thoughts are just brain states. Another problem is this: in our ordinary way of thinking, mental and physical states do not both co-exist in the same time and space. (We should be generally wary of any philosophical theory which is *prima facie* strongly counter-intuitive.) It would be odd to say that our thoughts occur at just such and such a point in the brain. We think of our thoughts as having no size and weight, yet brain states have size and weight. We could of course change the way we talk about our thoughts and start referring to them as having physical location, size and weight, but at the least this would be a radical change, and at the most it would be to change the topic.

However, the most significant problem faced by the identity theory is a problem of meaning. Minds give significance or meaning to things and states of affairs. So on a humanistic view, humans give the only meaning there is to things which have meaning, and on a theistic view God, and God together with other conscious beings, gives meaning to what has meaning. Therefore a key question about the identity theory is this: if the mind is the brain, can brains and/or central nervous systems give meaning to things?

One way to see the significance of this problem is the philosopher John Searle's analysis of whether a computer could be a mind. If computers are or can be minds, as is often held in artificial intelligence circles, then since computers are purely physical objects, minds can be purely physical objects. In *Minds, Brains and Science* Searle attacks the strong artificial intelligence thesis that an appropriately programmed computer is (or will be in the near future) a mind, i.e. the thesis that an appropriately programmed computer could understand things. He uses an analogy to explain why this thesis is false. Imagine a person who is in a room which contains several baskets full of Chinese symbols. The person in the room does not understand Chinese but has been given a rule book in English for manipulating Chinese symbols. Searle says, "The rules specify the manipulation of the symbols purely formally, in terms of their syntax, not their semantics. So a rule might say: 'Take a squiggle-squiggle sign out of basket number one and put it next to a squaggle-squaggle sign from basket number two.'"[4] Now, additional Chinese symbols are passed into the room from the outside by a group of people, called the programmers, and there is a second set of rules for taking Chinese symbols out of the baskets and passing them outside whenever new symbols are passed inside.

Unknown to the person in the room, the symbols passed into the room are called questions by those on the outside, and the symbols passed back out are called answers to the questions. Finally, suppose that the "programmers" on the outside are so good at asking questions, and the person in the room gets so good at manipulating the symbols by the rules, that a third party watching the exchange of symbols from the outside of the room to the inside and back out again would not be able to distinguish the "answers" to the "questions" from the answers which a native speaker of Mandarin Chinese would give to questions in Mandarin.

Notice that the person in the room learns absolutely nothing about Mandarin Chinese by manipulating the symbols in front of her. A computer functions like the person in the room. A computer performs "computational operations on formally specified elements." By doing so, in Searle's words, "the computer is unable to *duplicate* however powerful may be its ability to *simulate*" consciousness, thoughts, feelings, emotions, and so on.[5] To the third party it may look like the person in the room comprehends and expresses various emotional reactions to the "questions" passed in to her, just as it may look like a computer can understand the questions it is asked, but this is not so. While the computer and the person in the room are competent at syntax, what their operations lack is semantics, or meaning. Thus, computers might simulate the operations of minds, but computers do not duplicate the operations of minds. Therefore, the proposed inference that because computers are minds, since computers are physical, a mind can be physical and so a mind can be identical to the brain, is a fallacious inference. Computers are not minds, and brains might not be minds.

As we call into question whether a purely physical object could bring semantic meaning to things, even more so this raises doubts whether a purely physical object, the brain, could bring moral or aesthetic or religious significance to things. Persons are moral agents, persons have aesthetic outlooks, and persons are potentially religious beings. Hence the identity theory, because it does not seem to account adequately for these features of personhood, seems unable to account for personal identity.

Now, one way this last objection might be handled is the proposal which is sometimes called the person theory or double-aspect theory. The mental and spiritual aspects of personhood do not seem to be adequately accounted for on a purely physical understanding of what a person is. The double aspect theory denies dualism but proposes that a human person is a different kind of entity than either a purely physical being or (if there are any) a purely mental being like Descartes's "thinking thing." Thus a person on this view is an entity with dual aspects, both physical aspects and mental aspects. Few though have subscribed to the person theory. This theory, like dualism, seems to multiply entities beyond necessity, adding as it does "persons" as an additional category beyond the physical (and perhaps also the mental). Moreover, we are still left with the problem of how persons relate to physical bodies, for at the least it seems as if the laws of physics would not apply to persons on the person theory, since persons are not bodies.

BUDDHIST REINCARNATION

So far we have not yet found a satisfactory conception of the self to which we could apply the question of whether life after death is possible. A very different sort of view of the self than those we have addressed thus far is found in the Buddhist literature, where we find an idealist conception of self. So far we have been concerned with the problem of personal identity because it certainly seems as though the person who exists before death must be identical to the person in the next life if there really is to be a next life. Buddhism effectively denies this. For example, the Fourteenth Dalai Lama argues as follows:

> There is a fault in this way of thinking, because it tends to see the person you are now and the person you will be in the future as one. Of course, the continuity is the same, but they are two separate persons. The person accumulating the cause is not the same person who experiences the result. You think of these two different continuities, the continuum of your past life and the continuity of your next life, as your previous and future continuums. They are labeled as such on the basis of the collection of your physical and mental constituents. These designations are made on the basis of different collections and different continuities. Therefore, they have no intrinsic existence.

A rosary or an army is similarly false and has no intrinsic existence. When many parts such as arms and legs are assembled together, we designate or call them a body. When beads are strung together, we call them a rosary. When many soldiers are gathered together, we call them an army. The person who possesses suffering is also a designation and has no intrinsic existence. There is no substantially existent owner who experiences suffering.[6]

Buddhism would want to avoid saying that it is the same person who exists before and after death, not just because Shakyamuni Buddha himself explicitly avoided this question (see chapter 3), but because the fundamental Buddhist view of the true self as *anatman* makes it impossible that the same person exist after death. On the Buddhist view everything is impermanent (*annica*). This parallels the Western philosophical view of Heraclitus (c.500 BCE) who worked in the same period as the Buddha, that all is in universal flux. Heraclitus was noted for observing that "one cannot step in the same river twice" to which one of his students – in fine Buddhist fashion – is reputed to have replied "one cannot even step into the *same* river."

Now, to explain the idea of *anatman*, the no-self doctrine of Buddhism, the monk Nagasena gives the following analogy as he talks to the Greek King of northwest India whom he would convert to Buddhism (recorded in the *Questions of King Menander* of the *Pali Canon*):

"What is the chariot? Is the pole the chariot?"
"No, your Reverence."
"Or the axle, wheels, frame, reins, yoke, spokes or goad?"
"None of these things is the chariot."
"Then all these separate parts taken together are the chariot?"
"No, your Reverence."
"Then is the chariot something other than the separate parts?"
"No, your Reverence."
"Then for all my asking, your Majesty, I can find no chariot. The chariot is a mere sound...You know what the word 'chariot' means! And it is just the same with me. It is on account of the various components of my being that I am known by the generally understood term, the practical designation Nagasena."[7]

Since everything is impermanent, Buddhism denies a substance ontology. That is, there are no underlying substances above and beyond the constituent elements of what we characterize as "things." Where, for example, Descartes defines the person as a "thing which thinks," a substance which has mental properties (he defined physical objects as "spatially extended" substances), Buddhism holds that what we call a person just is the mental and physical events which we ascribe to the person. Nagasena thinks, feels, perceives, kicks his legs, sits down and so on. But there is not a Nagasena behind, so to speak, these mental and physical events. Nagasena just *is* this collection of mental and physical events. This is a bundle view of what constitutes a person, which in the West is also espoused (though in purely mental or idealist terms) by David Hume.

So, if a human being is just a bundle of events, then does the same person even exist through a single lifespan? The answer is no:

"Reverend Nagasena," said the King, "when a man is born does he remain the same [being] or become another?"

"He neither remains the same nor becomes another."

"Give me an example!"

"What do you think your Majesty? You were once a baby lying on your back, tender and small and weak. Was that baby you, who are now grown up?'

"No, your Reverence, the baby was one being and I am another."

"If that's the case, your Majesty, you had no mother or father, and no teachers in learning, manners, or wisdom...is the boy who goes to school one [being] and the young man who has finished his education another? Does one person commit a crime and another suffer mutilation for it?"...

"Suppose a man were to light a lamp, would it burn all through the night?"

"Yes, it might."

"Now is the flame which burns in the middle watch the same as that which burned in the first?"

"No, your Reverence."

"Or is that which burns in the last watch the same that burned in the middle?"

"No, your Reverence."

"So is there one lamp in the first watch, another in the middle, and yet another in the last?"

"No. The same lamp gives light all through the night."

"Similarly, your Majesty, the continuity of phenomena is kept up. One person comes into existence, another passes away, and the sequence runs continuously without self-conscious existence, neither the same nor yet another."

"Well said, Reverend Nagasena!"[8]

This Buddhist answer to the puzzle of personal identity in this life raises the question: if there is no substance which is a person, how is life *after* death possible? Nagasena gives this analogy in answer to this puzzle:

> "Reverend Nagasena," said the King, "is it true that nothing transmigrates, and yet there is rebirth?"
> "Yes, your Majesty."
> "How can this be?...Give me an illustration."
> "Suppose, your majesty, a man lights one lamp from another – does the one lamp transmigrate to the other?"
> "No, your Reverence."
> "So there is rebirth without anything transmigrating!"[9]

Since reincarnation is like this process of passing on a flame, the image used in Buddhism for the cessation of transmigration and the realization of *nirvana* is that of the blowing out of a flame. Thus when all is said and done, Buddhism actually accepts the principle that if the person on this side of death is not identical with a person on the other side of death, then there is no life after death. In a restricted sense there is life after death, but this is within the realm of *samsara*, and it is not a personal life after death. But in Buddhism there is no life after death in any sense, even in some restricted sense, when final *nirvana* (*parinirvana*) is realized. Along with the dissolution of personhood, Buddhism accepts the dissolution of any ultimate distinction between life and death.

THE EVOLVING SOUL

For those who are dissatisfied with this notion of the extinction of self which is envisioned by Buddhism, and yet want to find a way to understand life after death without incurring some of the problems which dualism encounters, we now come to a fifth alternative. The notion of an evolving soul offers an alternative between extremes, for on this view the mental life of a person evolves from the physical, and so is connected to the physical, yet it becomes separable from the physical and so is not itself reducible to the physical. This avoids, at the one extreme, views which conceive of a person as a purely mental entity. For instance, this avoids Descartes's notion that a person is a thinking thing, where mind-body interaction is difficult to explain. And it also avoids the extreme Buddhist idea that a person is just a bundle of events leading to the inevitable dissolution of the self. At the other extreme, the notion of the evolving soul avoids the reductionist views of materialism.

When it comes to the question of life after death, materialism offers no hope. If you just are your brain and/or central nervous system, then when your brain disintegrates at your biological death you will cease to exist. Physical objects only retain their identity if they retain continuity in their physical existence. If you own a Ming Dynasty vase, pulverize it, drop the grains of porcelain in the ocean, leave them there for a year, come back with an extraordinarily sophisticated porcelain collecting device, manage to recollect all the pulverized grains of the original, and then manage further to reassemble a vase with each grain of porcelain in the precise relative location to the others of the original vase, you would not thereby have regained *your* original Ming vase. At best you would have *a* reassembled Ming vase, as any good auction house could tell you. In the same way even if God, say, were to reassemble all of the constituent parts of your brain exactly as it was during some point in your life, the result would not be *your* brain. In like manner, physical copies of physical objects are not originals, and even God could not make a copy of your brain which would be your brain – it would simply be a copy of your brain.

In short, though as we have noted we often use bodily criteria for personal identity, if we only have bodily criteria for personal identity, there can be no life after death. However, we also use mental criteria for personal identity. If a suspect in a murder has massively altered his features through plastic surgery, grown much older, and even undergone a sex change operation, he could still be convicted of the crime if he confessed to the murder and were able to provide convincing remembrances of sufficient detail to demonstrate that he committed the crime and is neither a pathological liar nor an innocent person bent on self-destruction. The mental criteria would suffice to determine the identity of the murderer.

We can also see this in the old story about the two crash victims, a man and a woman. The woman's body is irreparably damaged, and the man's brain suffers a massive hemorrhage. If a group of unusually talented surgeons quickly replaces the brain of the man with the brain of the woman so that there remains one fully functional body, whose body would it be? The body looks like the man's, but all the thoughts, emotions, desires, interests, and character traits are the woman's. Most of us would answer that the person before us now is the woman and not the man. This is not too different from the plausible supposition that you could be reincarnated as a person of a different sex than you now are. The plausibility of these scenarios strongly supports, though it does not prove, that mental criteria of personal identity supersede physical criteria.

Now, if continuity of personal identity could be retained across the transition from life to death to a possible new life, life after death would be possible. Only mental criteria could serve this function. One philosopher who addressed this problem is Thomas Reid (1710–1796), who holds that the identity of something presupposes the uninterrupted continuity of the existence of that thing. He critiqued John Locke's view that the mental criterion of memory could itself provide personal identity, for as Reid pointed out we often do not have a remembrance of previous parts of our lives. As we saw, the Fourteenth Dalai Lama uses just such considerations to conclude that the person who existed when we were young is in fact not the same person whom we are now. Against this Buddhist conclusion, however, Reid would argue that there is continuity of personal identity in this life and thus that continuity must be provided by an underlying mental substance, the soul. Taking this observation of Reid's into consideration, how might we conceive of the soul so that we avoid falling back into the problems of Cartesian dualism?

One religious problem for Cartesian dualism which we have not yet addressed is the issue of when an individual's soul first becomes associated with an individual's body. For instance, one can say that God implants a new soul in each new body, perhaps at the time of initial development of the zygote. But this tends to produce a notion of radical distinction between the body and the implanted soul, a distinction which leads to the problem of interaction. A more integrated conception of the body/soul relationship is offered by the idea of an evolving soul wherein human beings begin as purely physical beings. Rather than a distinct soul then being super-added to the body, there are dispositions in the central nervous system of the developing human to acquire various mental abilities – to acquire the logical process of reasoning, the notion of object permanence and of self as separate from others, as well as language skills, self-reflection, and moral agency. It is as these mental traits and abilities are acquired that a soul develops. This parallels the notion of human existence as a vale for soul-making which we addressed in our discussion of theodicies in chapter 6. Much as a soul-making theodicy offers an evolutionary conception of human salvation, the concept of an evolutionary soul suggests another evolutionary facet to human destiny.

What then is a soul if it is not a Cartesian "thinking thing"? What matters about a soul is not so much what it is but what it does. As Descartes says in the second of his *Meditations*, a soul is "a being which doubts, which understands, which conceives, which affirms, which denies, which wills, which rejects, which imagines also, and which perceives." Thus souls are identified in terms of mental activities which, in the broad sense, include character traits, moral outlooks, and religious propensities. Now as Keith Ward points out:

> The most important characteristic of the soul is its capacity for transcendence. It has the capacity to "exist", to stand outside the physical processes that generate it, and of which it is a part. We might see the soul, the subject of awareness, deliberation and intention, as one part of a vast web of interacting processes, at various degrees of complexity, coming to the conscious perception of the actions of other forces upon it; and realizing its own capacities in accordance with more or less clearly formulated principles. It is distinguished, not by being quite different in kind from its material environment, but by reflecting and acting in that environment in a more conscious, goal-oriented way.[10]

One does not have to think of the soul as some sort of blank receptacle to which mental properties inhere. Rather the notion of an evolving soul is a logical construct designating certain emergent properties of the complex physical object we call a brain.

True, as Buddhism points out, to talk about persons or souls is to give a name to or conceptualize the bundle of various physical and/or mental events, faculties and dispositions as being a person or soul. But we use logical constructs like "university," "army," or "religious tradition" because they are expedient for the explanation of various phenomena. Universities, armies, religious traditions and souls are composite phenomena. If all phenomena are illusory, then these composite phenomena are also illusory. However, if one does not hold, as Buddhists do, that all phenomena are illusory, then as monotheists and Hindu *bhaktas* will hold, our logical constructs make sense. Then our worldviews can be understood as pragmatic cognitive maps of the world, and logical constructs like "soul" conveniences in the integrative map of our web of concepts. We can even call that which is designated by the logical construct of an evolving soul a "substance," as long as this is not confused with the Cartesian concept of something which does *not* evolve from or originate in the physical.

Once again, life after death will be possible if there are mental criteria which can be applied to identify a person in the afterlife as being identical to a person in this life. The notion of an evolving soul as a logical construct will provide an understanding of the kind of uninterrupted continuity of existence which Reid argues is the basis of identity. For as Ward points out, once a set of mental properties emerge from the biological basis of a particular human body, the logical construct of the "soul" can be applied to the resultant collective phenomena of mental processes, concepts, character traits, beliefs, inclination, and desires of the person quite apart from his or her body. This transcendent designation could thus be applied again in the next life to designate the same person – i.e. the identical soul associated with a new means of manifestation, a new body.

WILL *YOU* BE THERE?

We have been assessing whether or not life after death is even possible. But there is another question we might ask, namely "is it *plausible* that there is life after death?" For even if it is possible that there could be life after death, say on an evolutionary conception of the soul, this may still seem like an unreasonable possibility. As a way to get at the question of plausibility, imagine the following. You have arrived in the afterlife. Or rather, it seems to you that you have arrived in the afterlife. Or rather, it seems to someone who thinks he or she is you that he or she has arrived in the afterlife. Is it you?

Suppose someone – let's call her Rose – is having a set of experiences that seem very much like afterlife experiences. Put yourself in Rose's place. Afterlife Rose seems to remember having been a particular person in life before death, the earthly Rose. The afterlife or heavenly Rose meets other people who exclaim "it seems as if we have survived death together." (It does not especially matter how these persons are embodied – the afterlife community might all look on the outside like R2D2 wheeled canisters.) Those other people listen to Rose's words, consider her thoughts and her expressions of character, and say, "Aren't you Rose? I knew you in the life before death." And the heavenly Rose interacts with various people in this apparently new place and seems to remember having met them before. She seems to remember having told them in a life before death about her deepest concerns and interests. Rose and her heavenly companions even seem to remember having discussed religion and the possibility of life after death. Is the heavenly Rose identically the same person as the remembered earthly Rose who lived in the previous life?

There is no way to give a completely impregnable answer to this question, but we can give a definitive answer. Quite literally, whoever the heavenly Rose is, she will have to decide whether she takes herself to be the same person as the apparently remembered earthly Rose of the apparent past life. The heavenly Rose could, of course, suspend judgment and simply try to avoid answering this question, but that would be most awkward, especially in the face of the repeated insistence by her heavenly companions that they are positive that they remember her from the previous life. This is much like the problem we face if, after we wake up in the morning, we ask ourselves in this life if we are the same person today that we remember being yesterday. All sorts of interesting scenarios can be developed to explain why we only think we remember being the same person, but that in fact our apparent memories are false. However, for most of us it is utterly impractical to persist in wondering whether or not we are the same person who existed the night before we went to sleep and whom we seem to remember being. We go on with our lives confident of our personal identity because this is the pragmatic course of action. In the same way the heavenly Rose would want to come to a pragmatic resolution, and despite the abruptness of appearing in a heavenly space, presumably the heavenly Rose would conclude and remain confident that she is indeed the Rose who remembers and who is remembered.

Of course on an Advaita Vedanta or Buddhist perspective, this pragmatic resolution of personal identity leaves us caught in the deceptive webs of *maya*. On these views, there will be no you who could exist after *moksha* or final *nirvana*, and there certainly would be no scenario which fits the heavenly story just sketched. But on a monotheistic perspective our story denotes a real possibility. If it turns out that this possibility becomes an actuality – and it seems to someone who thinks that he or she is you that he or she has arrived in the afterlife – then *you* will be present in the afterlife heavenly state in the sense that you would come to the resolution that you are there. Perhaps the fact that heavenly you is indeed you is something that only an omniscient mind, like God, could be completely certain about. Well, perhaps likewise only an omniscient mind could be completely certain that you are the same person you were last night. But just as we lose little sleep over this, afterlife persons – if there are any – would surely lose little sleep over this extreme epistemological concern.

Further reading

INTRODUCTORY

Perry, John. *A Dialogue of Personal Identity and Immortality.* Indianapolis, Hackett Publishing Company, 1978

Plato. *Phaedo.* G.M.A. Grube, trans. Indianapolis, Hackett Publishing, 1997

Sartre, Jean-Paul. *The Transcendence of the Ego.* New York, The Noonday Press, 1957

Searle, John. *Minds, Brains and Science.* London, British Broadcasting Corporation, 1984

Ward, Keith. *In Defence of the Soul.* Oxford, Oneworld, 1998

ADVANCED

D'Costa, Gavin, ed. *Resurrection Reconsidered.* Oxford, Oneworld, 1996

Hick, John H. *Death and Eternal Life.* New York, Harper and Row, 1976

Perry, John, ed. *Personal Identity.* Berkeley, University of California Press, 1975

Swinburne, Richard. *The Evolution of the Soul.* Oxford, Clarendon Press, 1986

Ward, Keith. *Religion and Human Nature.* Oxford, Clarendon Press, 1998

9 RELIGIOUS EXPERIENCE

Even if God were to make an immediate appearance, I would still need rational theology as a presupposition. For how am I to be certain that it is God himself who has appeared to me, or only another powerful being?[1]

Immanuel Kant (1724–1804)

RELIGIOUS EXPERIENCE AND SCRIPTURAL AUTHORITY

In chapters 4 and 5 we assessed various arguments for the existence of God (and also Brahman). Perhaps no argument will successfully prove that there is a God, or Brahman. But there is another obvious way in which religious truth-claims might seem provable. This is the belief that religious truth is authoritatively revealed in scriptural texts which convey the paradigmatic experiences of the traditions. Those religious texts, then, could serve as "proof texts."

Moses encountered God in his experience of the burning bush in the Sinai desert, Buddha achieved enlightenment at Bodh Gaya, and the cognitive content of their experiences is related respectively in Exodus 4 chapter 3 verse 4 and in the Buddha's first sermon on the Four Noble Truths which he gave in the Deer Park near Benares. And what could have more authority in one's life than knowledge through sacred texts of the Tao or of Brahman, or of the Buddhist way through the sutras, or of Akal Purakh through the Adi Granth, or of God through the Torah or the New Testament or the Qur'an? It is not just that one can learn about the Transcendent and human destiny by, for instance, reading the Sermon on the Mount or the Four Noble Truths, but that one can appropriate the experience of the Transcendent, in the person of Jesus or Buddha, in these instances, for oneself. And of course, if authoritative religious experiential knowledge is conveyed through scripture, that experiential knowledge in turn confers authority on scripture, or specific religious authorities, or special religious institutions.

Usually, people do not just get it into their heads one day to be devoted to Krishna, or to follow the Four Noble Truths or to believe in Akal Purakh or YHWH or Allah or the Trinity. Most people grow up in, or become associated with, a religious tradition and a community of faith. They listen to and read the scriptures of the community, have their own religious experiences, and come to believe in the experiential authority of those scriptures, in the authority of the seminal religious experiences of the community, and in the authority of experiences which are conveyed through the authoritative representatives and rituals of the temple, the mosque, the church, and so on. We will need to determine more precisely what the epistemological status (from the Greek *episteme* for knowledge) of this authority amounts to. But whatever else we conclude about the justification of religious belief, the experiential manifestation of the Transcendent is as authoritative for Jews in the *Torah* and the *Talmud*,[2] as it is authoritative for Christians in the Bible, for Muslims in the *Qur'an* and the *Bible*, for Sikhs in the *Adi Granth*, for monotheistic Hindus in the *Vedas*, *Upanishads*, *Bhagavad Gita* and the *Brahma Sutras*, and for Buddhists in the *Pali Canon*. In addition, there are also institutional religious authorities: the *magisterium* of the church in the Roman Catholic tradition, the *halakah* within Judaism, the ten Gurus in Sikhism, Zen Masters (*roshi*) in the Zen traditions and the Dalai Lama in the Tibetan traditions of Buddhism, as well as priests, theologians, saints, *imams*, rabbis, *arhats*, *bhikkhus*, and others. And each such institutional authority ultimately derives its religious authority from fundamental authoritative religious experiences.

Now if scripture is self-authenticating, then the question of the justification of religious belief is settled. As the message of salvation is succinctly put in the Christian New Testament: "If you continue in my word [Jesus is given as the speaker], you are truly my disciples, and you will know the truth, and the truth will make you free."[3] However, statements of this type are equally at home in, for example, the Judaic, Islamic, Buddhist, and *bhakti* Hindu traditions. Since the sacred scriptures of all traditions similarly claim unique authority, how could we determine which is correct? This very question encapsulates the new religious perspective of the modern mind. For with our global perspective, we can no longer ignore alternative religious (and secular) traditions.

In chapter 2 we addressed the range of possible responses to the problem of religious pluralism. Whatever position one does take on this issue, at the least, the fact of religious plurality should make the globally aware religious person cautious about too quickly claiming sole authoritative truth for his or her own scriptural tradition. Acknowledging the global religious pluralism of our world should form part of the "doubting faith" which Paul Tillich identifies as the genuine faith of the modern mind, with its awareness of the inherent risk of being misdirected (the risk of what he calls "idolatry"). For awareness of the problem of religious pluralism and of conflicting religious truth-claims inexorably raises the question for any believer: "What justifies one in following the particular scripture of my own tradition and not that of another tradition?"

Yet even if this question can be answered, as I hope to show it can, a second problem arises with appealing to the scripture of one's own tradition as authoritatively self-justifying, as one does for example by referring to the text of one's own tradition as the "word of God." This second problem is enunciated by St. Paul for those specifically in the Christian tradition:

> The word of the cross is folly to those who are perishing, but to us who are being saved, it is the power of God...in the wisdom of God, the world did not know God through wisdom, it pleased God through the folly of what we preach to save those who believe.[4]

To those outside a religious tradition and its scriptures, and so outside the worldview of the religious community, the claims of salvation or liberation held within the faith community's worldview can appear foolish. Further, in the World Religions the outsider does not achieve the saving knowledge, or *gnosis*, of the community merely through an intellectual comprehension of the various truth-claims of the tradition. Rather, one must both believe in or have faith in the Transcendent and have a fundamental commitment to the worldview of the community, in order to achieve religious insight and eventually derive a mature religious understanding from the scriptures of any tradition.

The fact that faith or commitment to a divine reality or Transcendent is a prerequisite for understanding scripture is actually built into the very notion of scripture. What makes the Hebrew law of the Pentateuch different from the law Code of Hammurabi, the canonical books of the New Testament different from the works of Plato, the *Qur'an* different from the works of Aristotle, and the *Bhagavad Gita* different from the legal systems of the feudal kingdoms of India is that, in the mind of the religious, the spirit of God is felt to be present in the religious but not the secular writings. But then to appeal to one's scripture to validate, for example, belief in God is patently circular reasoning about whether one should believe in God. More generally, philosophical, legal, and literary sources only count as scripture on the assumption that they convey the manifestation of the Transcendent. That of course presupposes the Transcendent, and one cannot use what is presupposed as a proof of the thing presupposed. The logical structure of the sort of argument that might be implicitly used to support the authority of a body of writings, W, as scripture has the general form outlined in the box below.

ARGUMENT FOR SCRIPTURAL AUTHORITY

1. Our community has faith that certain writings, W, make the Transcendent manifest.
2. Therefore these writings, W, are scriptural.
3. Through these scriptures, W, we learn about religious experiences which reveal the true nature of the Transcendent and what truly gives meaning to life.
4. Therefore, these scriptures, W, are authoritative.
5. Therefore, these scriptures justify our belief in the Transcendent.

In this hopelessly circular reasoning we have learned nothing new in the conclusion (premise 5), because we already assumed the reality of the Transcendent in the commitment of faith expressed in premise 1. So scriptures are not, in themselves, a self-validating authority.

JUSTIFICATION AND RELIGIOUS KNOWLEDGE

Suppose one does trust that the Bible, say, manifests God. What justifies that trust? How does one *know* that God is manifest in the Bible?

After all, some people trust that the secret of their destiny can be found in a close study of the stars (astrology), others may trust scriptures but believe in the *Upanishads* perhaps and not the Bible, and still others (like the French existentialists Albert Camus and Jean-Paul Sartre) believe we must trust solely in ourselves since there is no divine reality to which to appeal. Of course, it may be true that just as Christians believe that the Bible conveys truths about God, the Bible does convey truths about God. Then Christians would hold true opinions about God via their understanding of the Bible. Yet to have knowledge is more than having true opinions. Otherwise, unfounded guesses which turn out to be true would be the same as knowledge of the truth.

A four-year-old who guesses, despite the visual evidence to the contrary, that the sun is bigger than the moon does not know this, the way you or I or an astronomer know this. The difference is that we and the astronomer are justified in our beliefs: we have good grounds for believing that the sun is larger than the moon. Unlike the four-year-old, we have thought about the earlier, geocentric model of the universe, considered modern heliocentric maps of the solar system, think of the moon as a satellite of the earth and the sun as a star, and so on. In short, knowledge is basically justified true belief, whether about stellar objects or religious matters. Thus, there is the problem of not just whether it is true that, but how one is justified in believing that, any particular set of scriptures can be trusted, a problem magnified in our pluralistic age by the sheer multitude of alternatives we have become aware of, secular as well as religious.

Moreover, even if one believed that God's revelation, for example, is complete and final in a particular scriptural tradition, *what* is revealed there to the believer about God is inescapably structured by the worldview which the individual brings to the text(s). A worldview just consists in that total web of concepts and beliefs, interconnected by past reasoning and our present processes of reasoning, which the mind brings to all experience. Any authority which a scripture has is doubly affected by human worldviews. Each individual brings his or her own religious conceptions to the scriptural texts of a tradition, and human worldviews are embedded in the texts themselves. So the authoritativeness of scripture depends on one's willingness to accept (given one's own worldview) the worldview(s) expressed in the text.

INEFFABILITY AND MYSTICAL EXPERIENCES

Given the inevitable failure of an appeal to the authority of scripture alone to provide a general justification for religious commitment, another common type of appeal might be made. This appeal, not to authority but rather *against* authority, is the notion that one's religious commitment does not need to be justified, and indeed is not subject to rational checking procedures, because the object of religious belief is either ineffable or beyond our comprehension. Thus, it is often suggested that religious belief is validated by religious experience, and religious experience is ineffable. Regarding the ineffability of religious experience, Rudolf Otto says that the experience of the Transcendent, which he calls the "numinous," is:

> *Sui generis* and irreducible to any other; and therefore, like every absolutely primary and elementary datum, while it admits of being discussed, it cannot be strictly defined...[This experience] cannot, strictly speaking, be taught, it can only be evoked, awakened in the mind.[5]

In this sense of ineffability, the experience of the Transcendent is understandable to the one who has it, though the experience is so unlike other sorts of experience that it cannot be adequately explained, and certainly not defined, to those who have not themselves had the experience.

Now as Otto is himself aware, this is no different than numerous instances of ordinary experience. The taste of chocolate and the sound of bagpipes are experiences of this sort, not fully expressible to those who have not had the relevant experience. However, those who have not themselves had the experience can understand the idea of hearing bagpipes and the taste of chocolate insofar as they understand the terms "wind instrument," "high pitch," "a food," "tasting bitter," and so forth. Similarly, if an adamant atheist can come to experience God, for instance, then in Otto's terms he or she will have come to understand the various elements which Otto delineates within the experience of the numinous: e.g. a "creature-feeling," the feeling of "*mysterium tremendum*," and so on. Perhaps religious experiences, then, are like certain ordinary experiences which are only fully understandable to those who have had them, yet those who have not had the experience can partially understand the experiences if they have the relevant concepts. All these "ineffable" experiences of bagpipes and chocolate, Brahman and God are intrinsically conceptualized. Consequently, the experience of the Transcendent is not really ineffable. And just as we might be asked to

justify our claim that we once heard Margaret Thatcher playing the bagpipes, mystics can be appropriately asked to justify their claim that they
experience, for example, God or Brahman.

Walter Stace classically proposed a very different sort of ineffability
for religious experiences. He suggests that for both Eastern and Western
mystical experiences of God or of Brahman, "*no* concepts apply to
[them]" because "the mystic *himself*...finds his vision ineffable and unut-
terable. It is he who experiences the difficulty, not we."[6] But first, the
difficulty of communicating mystical experiences does not show that
they are conceptually contentless for the mystic. Consider an indefinable primitive like red. We can provide a physiological explanation of
what causes us to see objects as being red, and we can pick out objects
which are red – this tomato, that rose – but we cannot *define* red.
Consequently, Stace's idea of ineffability that "no concepts apply" might
just reflect the commonplace that direct experience of an entity denoted
by a primitive, like redness, cannot be communicated except by saying,
in effect, "I see redness," or "I experienced (the indefinable) Godhead
or Brahman." Furthermore, it is not at all clear that the mystic's experience is incomprehensible to the mystic. Meister Eckhart, the important
thirteenth-century Christian mystic to whom Stace often refers, says that
in mystical union it is necessary for God to enter the soul apart from
"all his [commonly attributed] divine names and personlike properties."[7]
But this just means that one must give up all usual conceptions of God
when speaking of the experience of God.

Third, and importantly, any mystic who like Eckhart claims that his
or her experience conveys knowledge, by that very fact employs some
set of concepts or other. As Anton Poulain says, speaking for the
Western monotheisms, "...we give the name of *mystic* to supernatural
states containing a *knowledge* of a kind that our own efforts and our
own exertions could never succeed in producing."[8] Presumably the mystics themselves understand the concepts they are using, and think they
are using the right concepts to refer to the object of their experiences.
Indeed, claiming that the Transcendent is utterly ineffable or unknow-
able gives rise to the danger which the eighteenth-century Scottish
philosopher, David Hume, so succinctly pointed out with respect to
belief in God:

> The Deity, I can readily allow, possesses many powers and attributes of
> which we can have no comprehension; but, if our ideas, so far as they

go, be not just and adequate and correspondent to [God's] real nature, I know not what there is in this subject worth insisting on. Is the name, without any meaning, of such mighty importance? Or how do you *mystics*, who maintain the absolute incomprehensibility of the Deity, differ from skeptics or atheists, who assert that the first cause of all is unknown and unintelligible?[9]

THE PROBLEM OF PRIVACY

It is often suggested by the religious that they are justified in holding their religious worldview because of their personal religious experiences. We already saw one problem with this in chapter 4: even within the same tradition, such as Hinduism, different conclusions about the Transcendent are reached on the basis of authoritative experiences which purport to be veridical. To use R.C. Zaehner's terms, there are "monistic" experiences such as Shankara's Advaita experience in which all distinctions pass away, and there are "theistic" experiences such as Ramanuja's Vishishtadvaita experiences which involve a loving union with the divine. This dichotomy of monistic and theistic experiences also, of course, pertains not just within but also between the World Religions: on the one side Japanese Buddhist *satori* is monistic (though even here the Rinzai tradition of Eisai says that *satori* is instantaneous, whereas the Soto tradition of Dogen holds that *satori* is a process), while on the other side the Hebrew prophet Isaiah and the Christian St. Teresa of Avila had theistic experiences. We will not try to determine here whether there is a hierarchy of types of mystical experiences (a point of dispute between, for example, R.C. Zaehner and Walter Stace over whether theistic or monistic experiences are superior), or whether these different sorts of mystical experiences have equivalent value (a view held by John Hick). There are, of course, shared characteristics among mystical experiences. As Rudolf Otto points out, "A characteristic common to all types of mysticism is the Identification, in different degrees of completeness, of the personal self with the transcendent Reality,"[10] though it must be added that for Buddhism and Advaita Vedanta there is ultimately no personal self. However, even with shared characteristics, suffice it to say that the differences among mystical experiences reflect the fact that the worldview which each mystic brings to his or her experience determines the characteristics of the experience as well as the way the experience is characterized.

Besides the comparative problem of differences in mystical experience stemming from differences in worldview, there is an even more fundamental problem regarding each experience in itself which is raised by the privacy of the experience. Normally we accept the experiences of another person as veridical – and we often only accept our own experiences as veridical – if they are either public or repeatable. If you go into the woods and think you unexpectedly see a bear, you quite naturally either ask a companion or check more carefully for yourself before deciding it really is a bear and not just a bush which you see. If a contemporary claims that Jesus or the Virgin Mary or Krishna or the Bodhisattva Kannon, etc., appears to them, we would expect some verifying evidence – otherwise the religious charlatan would have the same moral and religious status as the saint. But how could there be public checks on the vast majority of religious experience which is private?

William James suggests in *The Varieties of Religious Experience* that the value of religious experience is that it can be properly convincing for the person who has the experience but that there is no reason why it should be convincing to someone who does not have the experience. However, every World Religion is interested in showing that certain private religious experiences should be convincing to others on public grounds. Buddhism hopes that Shakyamuni Buddha's private enlightenment experience at Bodh Gaya will be widely accepted as veridical. Christianity hopes that St. Paul's theophany on the road to Damascus will be publicly credible, and the Gospels even provide the overlapping testimony of numerous witnesses to show that the resurrected Jesus was seen. Moreover, every World Religion actually has stringent public tests for the veridicality of private religious experience. The two basic tests are (1) whether the experience corresponds to sacred text and tradition; and (2) the moral worth of the experience.

Regarding criterion (1), no purported religious experience will be accounted veridical in any World Religion if it contravenes scripture or the accepted creedal and philosophical orthodoxy. Of course, interpretations of scripture vary widely as we see *vis-à-vis* the Buddhist *Pali Canon*, with its Theravada versus Mahayana interpretations, and *vis-à-vis* the Christian New Testament with its Roman Catholic, Protestant, and Orthodox interpretations. But still, within any particular strand of a World Religion, canonical texts and philosophical orthodoxy set the parameters for the acceptability of mystical experiences. However, the obvious problem with this criterion is the already noted fact that mystics tend to experience what their religious worldviews would predispose them to experience – that is, their experiences are structured or conceptualized by their worldviews. Hence, while criterion (1) will work as a sort of public test, it is only a test within the tradition or strand of the tradition of the mystic himself or herself.

Criterion (2) is more promising as a general public check on the veridicality of mystical experience. Purported mystical experiences have historically been routinely rejected within the World Religions whenever the mystic himself or herself acts in an immoral manner, either as a consequence of or despite his or her claimed religious experience. But it is also the case that those outside a religious tradition will use this same criterion of moral rectitude to judge the trustworthiness of mystical experiences in the tradition. The notoriously salacious or morally incontinent or hypocritical guru or television preacher is discounted by both those inside and outside the tradition which they pretend to represent, because of their blatant egoity and evident greed for power, fame, and fortune. In the Christian tradition, for example, criterion (2) is used when judgments are made about religious experience in terms of the ensuing "fruits of the spirit," particularly love; in Buddhism the same idea is expressed, though not in terms of the "spirit," where the fundamental character trait used to judge appropriate action is compassion (*karuna*). But even if the mystic meets these public criteria of moral worthiness, there would still remain the problem that mystics tend to experience what mystics expect to experience. Is this an insuperable difficulty for accepting religious truth-claims based on religious experience?

KANT'S ATTEMPTED SOLUTION[11]

As an explanation of why we tend to experience what we expect to experience, and in order to provide a firm foundation for doing metaphysics, Immanuel Kant proposed two revolutionary theses – one in metaphysics and one in epistemology. First he distinguishes between two different senses of reality, namely between the phenomenal world and the noumenal world. Phenomena are "things-as-they-appear-to-us." In contradiction, noumena are "things-in-themselves," things as they are independent of our perception. Second, Kant holds that all experiencing is conceptualized. We do not perceive noumena, the world in itself, directly and unmediated. Rather, we perceive the world in terms of, or as structured by, our worldviews. The world that we ordinarily think of as reality is the phenomenal world, a world determined in part by our concepts. If since birth you had continuously gazed through a fine wire grid, you might not be aware that the grid is there. But in fact the wire grid actually structures and shapes what you see. The world in itself – i.e. noumena – is on the other side, so to speak, of the wire grid of our concepts. Phenomena are on this side of our grid of concepts.

How can we be justified in our beliefs about the noumenal Transcendent on the basis of religious experience if all experience is conceptualized by our conceptual grids? How could we derive concepts which properly apply to the Transcendent? Kant suggests that we can derive positive content for the terms we apply to the Divine by means of a three-stage reasoning process.[12] We must initially employ negative predication to eliminate imperfect conceptions. Second, we must maximize each term we will apply to the Divine, for God does not, for instance, possess just power and knowledge, but *infinite* power and knowledge. Third, we must fill out the details of the infinite attributes which we have thus arrived at by using analogical predication (the view which, as we saw, is also proposed by, for example, Thomas Aquinas and Ramanuja). Thus we must consider "the whole world as a consequence of its ground *in* God."[13] How are we going to do this?

Overall on Kant's view, we should be striving for enlightenment in order to break the bondage of intellectual "tutelage" to religious authority and act as free, rational, beings.[14] Thus Kant argues for the principle of "thinking for oneself." This is the idea that one is only justified in a belief if one arrives at that belief on the basis of one's own, uncoerced reasoning.[15] So far this would seem to support all sincere religion. However at the beginning of Book IV of *Religion Within the Limits of Reason Alone*, Kant defines genuine religion as "the recognition of all duties as divine commands." This, of course, already rules out Advaita Vedanta and Buddhism, not to mention Confucianism and Taoism, as genuine religion. Further though, Kant divides genuine religion into revealed and rational religion. In revealed religion, after first coming to know (by revelation) that something is a divine command, one then recognizes it as a duty. In rational religion the reverse process is followed – one must first know (by reason) what one's obligations are, and then one can infer that those duties are divine commands.[16]

Kant concludes that only rational religion is warranted because it alone enables us to recognize our duties as divine commands. Kant's

---

◆

KANT'S ARGUMENT FOR RATIONAL RELIGION

1. There are only two types of religion – revealed religion and rational religion.
2. It is impossible for revealed religion to provide sufficient epistemic justification for religious truth-claims.
3. It is possible for rational religion to provide sufficient epistemic justification for religious truth-claims.
4. Therefore only rational religion can provide sufficient epistemic justification for religious truth-claims.
5. It is the practical vocation of every rational person to think for oneself.
6. Rational religion encourages thinking for oneself.
7. Therefore rational religion is the only epistemically justifiable form of religion, and it promotes the proper vocation of any rational person.

◆
---

argument[17] to this conclusion can be formulated as shown in the box above.

As we saw in the opening quote of this chapter, Kant holds that the problem with revealed religion is that even if someone were in the best possible position to comprehend a revelatory experience – he or she was able to consider the evidence thoughtfully and was not distracted by emotionalism or misled by dogmatic ideology which he or she had accepted solely upon authority – that person still *could not know* that his or her experiences were genuinely revelatory. Kant goes on to distinguish this sort of external revelation from *internal* revelation. Internal revelation is "God's revelation to us through our own reason."[18] On Kant's account, internal revelation provides us with the concept of God as most perfect being, which should be used to judge external revelation. This conclusion is reminiscent of Moses Maimonides' reasoning in the *Guide for the Perplexed* which we addressed in the Introduction, where reasoned metaphysics is preeminent over religious practice. The value of external revelation, for Kant, is that it can give humans the opportunity to search internally for pure concepts for God.

There are certain advantages of Kant's appeal to reason and his defense of rational religion. The first advantage, which lends support to premise 3 of the argument, is Kant's idea that *all* humans have access to God, for in contrast to Maimonides, Kant thinks it is dangerous to suppose that genuine religion is restricted to the cultured or those who are specially educated. On Maimonides' view:

> The true perfection of man [is] the possession of the highest intellectual faculties; the possession of such notions which lead to true metaphysical opinions as regards God. With this perfection man has obtained his final object; it gives him true human perfection; it remains to him alone; it gives him immortality, and on its account he is called man.[19]

Kant is concerned that the truth of revealed religion is limited either to those who have themselves directly received the revelation or to those who possess the requisite critical understanding of the historical record of the experience of those who had the revelatory experiences. Therefore he argues in support of what he thinks any rational being could arrive at, not, as Maimonides does, in support of what only the intellectual elite can understand.

A second and a third advantage both support premise 2. On the view Kant presents, true piety does not require a detailed historical-critical knowledge of text, as if all that really mattered was the historical facts, the sort of flawed view held by the Jesus Seminar which we addressed in the Introduction. Otherwise:

> The small body of textual scholars (the clerics)...would drag along behind itself the long train of the unlearned (the laity) who, of themselves, are ignorant of the Scripture...But if this, in turn, is to be prevented from happening, recognition and respect must be accorded, in Christian dogmatic, to universal human reason as the supremely commanding principle in a natural religion, and the revealed doctrine...must be cherished and cultivated as merely a means, but a most precious means, of making this doctrine comprehensible, even to the ignorant.[20]

Kant concludes that:

> Faith needs merely *the idea of God*, to which all morally earnest (and therefore confident) endeavor for the good must inevitably lead; it need not presume that it can certify the objective reality of this idea through theoretical apprehension. Indeed, the *minimum* of knowledge (it is possible that there may be a God) must suffice, subjectively, for whatever can be made the duty of every man.[21]

Still, while faith does not require a thorough knowledge of God, we can still properly ascribe attributes to God by analogy. In particular, we can ascribe to God the maximal form of those attributes which derive from the notion of personhood – for example, that God wills and knows.

The fourth strength of Kant's position is the central emphasis which he places on the role of reason in the religious life. Without the world-view to understand and experience God or Akal Purakh or Brahman or *Nirvana*, and without the framework for disciplined religious practice which a religious person's worldview provides, it is not possible to engage in an explicitly religious life. However, on Kant's view one can be religious as long as one is aware of one's moral duties and that awareness includes the idea that if God exists, God commands those moral duties. Thus in the *Prolegomena to Any Future Metaphysics* he says that:

> We are compelled to consider the world *as if* it were the work of a Supreme Understanding and Will...[but however] By means of this anal-ogy...there remains a concept of the Supreme Being sufficiently deter-mined *for us*, though we have left out everything that could determine it absolutely or *in itself*; for we determine it as regards the world and hence as regards ourselves, and more do we not require.[22]

This conception of monotheism does run the risk of reducing theology to ethics and the religious life to the moral life. But that aside, is Kant justified in inferring God on the basis of pure reason?

HISTORICITY, PLURALISM, AND FAITH

Kant assumes that there is a universally valid basic conception of God which is trans-historically and cross-culturally comprehensible by any-one who honestly pursues rational thought. This seems highly doubt-ful, especially now with our global pluralistic understanding of the great World Religions as well as the contemporary recognition of the enor-mous variety of worldviews in general, non-religious as well as religious. If anything, we have better grounds for supposing that all rational people will not come to hold the same pure concept of the Transcendent. However, at the least it is safe to say that even if it is true that all rational beings would, given the opportunity and time, come to the same concept of the Transcendent, we cannot know this to be true.

Kant argues that on his epistemology of religion one "will no longer be in danger of forming an incomplete concept of God from mere nature," for "I have already received from my reason a thoroughly determinate concept; and by means of this concept I can judge all God's works in this world insofar as He has revealed Himself in them." But as the theologian Karl Barth, with a more global understanding, notes two hundred years after Kant:

> We dispose ourselves upon our appropriate shelf in the emporium of religion and ethics, ticketed and labeled with this or that philosophy of life...from time to time we change our position; but this only suggests to those gifted with acute powers of observation the triviality of any particular position.[23]

It is not a trivial matter which worldview we do hold. But the fact that we hold the views we do primarily because of our historical place, the fact that we change our views, and the fact that there is a plethora of alternative views which we might hold, indicates the historical conditioning of, and so the plasticity of, the notion of what is obvious, what is reasonable, and what is epistemically warranted.

Kant's argument 1–7 fails because premise 2 is false and premise 3 is overstated and hence misleading. We will consider this further in chapter 13, but in short, reason alone is insufficient to ground religious belief. In order to achieve a more positive account of revelatory religious experience, what is needed is a different account of revelation. In this regard, consider an alternative in Christian thought offered in the neo-Reformed tradition. Karl Barth suggests that "Religion brings us to the place where we must wait, in order that God may *confront* us,"[24] and Paul Tillich defines revelation as "the experience in which an ultimate concern *grasps* the human mind."[25] In the same vein, Rudolph Bultmann talks about God "confronting us" in a "demand for decision." On this view, revelation is not the delivery of truths about God; revelation is the *self*-manifestation of God. Kant is right to emphasize the importance of reason for religion. Apart from the conceptual content of a religious worldview, the experience of the Transcendent would be incoherent, faith contentless, and the life of the religious person chaotic. Yet it is faith that must bring the religious person to the Transcendent because it is faith that the Transcendent is indeed revealed in or manifest in religious experiences, which can take humans beyond the limits of reason alone. We will return to this in chapter 13.

Further reading

Kant, Immanuel. *Immanuel Kant's Critique of Pure Reason.* Norman Kemp Smith, trans. London, Macmillan, 1933

Kant, Immanuel. *Lectures on Philosophical Theology.* Allen W. Wood and Gertrude M. Clark, trans. London, Cornell University Press, 1978

Kant, Immanuel. *Religion Within the Limits of Reason Alone.* New York, Harper and Row, 1960

Katz, Steven T., ed. *Mysticism and Religious Traditions.* Oxford, Oxford University Press, 1983

Otto, Rudolf. *The Idea of the Holy.* New York, Oxford University Press, 1923

Otto, Rudolf. *Mysticism: East and West.* New York, Macmillan, 1960

Pike, Nelson. *Mystic Union: An Essay in the Phenomenology of Mysticism.* Ithaca and London, Cornell University Press, 1992

Rossi, Philip J., S.J. "Conflict, Community, and Human Destiny: Religious Ethics and the Public Construction of Morality" in Joseph Runzo, ed., *Ethics, Religion, and the Good Society: New Directions in a Pluralistic World.* Louisville, Westminster/John Knox Press, 1992, pp. 114–125

Rossi, Philip J., S.J. and Michael Wreen, ed. *Kant's Philosophy of Religion Reconsidered.* Bloomington, Indiana University Press, 1991

Runzo, Joseph. *World Views and Perceiving God.* New York, St. Martin's Press, 1993

Stace, W.T. *Mysticism and Philosophy.* London, Macmillan, 1961

Strong, John S. *The Experience of Buddhism.* Belmont, Wadsworth Publishing, 1995

Ward, Keith. *Religion and Revelation.* Oxford, Clarendon Press, 1994.

Zaehner, R.C. *Hindu and Muslim Mysticism.* Oxford, Oneworld, 1994

Zaehner, R.C. *Mysticism: Sacred and Profane.* Oxford, Oxford University Press, 1967

10 USING SCIENCE TO ARGUE AGAINST RELIGION

Consider the idea of God...Why does it have such high survival value?...The survival value...results from its great psychological appeal. It provides a superficially plausible answer to deep and troubling questions about existence. It suggests that injustices in this world may be rectified in the next. The (divine) "everlasting arms" hold out a cushion against our own inadequacies which, like a doctor's placebo, is none-the-less effective for being imaginary. These are some of the reasons why the idea of God is copied so readily by successive generations of brains.[1]

Richard Dawkins (1941–) from *The Selfish Gene*

The beginning of the twenty-first century is witness to a sharp debate between science and religion. In the twentieth century, there was less a debate and more a critique carried out in the West, largely from the side of science and largely as a dismissal of religion. In philosophy at mid-century the logical positivists attempted to demolish metaphysics – including theistic metaphysics – while in theology the field was given up to the more powerful arguments of the philosophers and the scientists. Religion has begun to respond powerfully: sometimes the response comes from religious scientists – such as Paul Davies – but more often now from an invigorated community in religion, particularly among philosophers. These debates are often over questions about the compatibility of God and science since they are frequently carried out within Western monotheism. Here we will address the debate between science and religion from the global twenty-first-century point of view of the World Religions.

Against religion, materials to support a scientific humanist view of the sufficiency of science to explain everything can be drawn from three different areas: the physical sciences, the biological sciences, and the social sciences. In order to address the somewhat different types of objections to religion which can be raised on the basis of science, for the physical sciences let us consider in particular the work of Stephen Hawking, for the biological sciences that of Richard Dawkins, and for the social sciences that of the sociologist Ludwig Feuerbach, the anthropologist Marvin Harris, and the psychologist Sigmund Freud.

DOES PHYSICS EXPLAIN EVERYTHING?

In *A Brief History of Time*, Stephen Hawking tries to subsume both theology and philosophy under science in order to explain everything. As Carl Sagan puts it, when Hawking is done, there is "nothing for a creator to do."[2] Hawking ends *A Brief History of Time* with the bold assertion that if humans (read "physicists") ever came up with a complete theory of the universe which explained why the universe, as he puts it, "bothers to exist," "it would be the ultimate triumph of the human reason – for then we would know the mind of God." There are three problems with this assertion: (1) the virtual impossibility of the human mind achieving such a theory, if for no other reason than the Heisenberg Uncertainty Principle; (2) the impossibility of ever knowing that we *had* achieved such a theory even if it could be so; and (3) the inherent inevitable failure of such a theory to explain the mind of God.

Regarding the last point we can, of course, change our use of the term "God" *à la* Hawking to denote nothing more than a naturalistic explanation of the natural order. We might call this view "God As Ultimate Physicist." But the creator God of the Western monotheisms and the Fullness of Being that is Brahman are the source of all value, not just the source of all being. And that which has *derived* value cannot encompass that which *confers* value. So neither God nor Brahman is included in or exhausted by the derivative natural order. As even Einstein (who was only vaguely religious) says, the truly religious attitude is:

A knowledge of the existence of something we cannot penetrate, of the manifestations of the profoundest reason and the most radiant beauty, which are only accessible to our reason in their most elementary forms.[3]

And in what could be almost a forward projecting rebuke of Hawking, Einstein adds, regarding whether it is worthwhile to ask if life has a meaning, that "to answer this question at all implies a religion," and that the reason to take a truly religious attitude is that "the man who regards his own life and that of his fellow creatures as meaningless is not merely unfortunate but also disqualified for life."[4]

Hawking has made the mistake of supposing that the only question of meaning is the "what" question, not the ultimate "why" question. As he speculates at one point in *A Brief History of Time*:

> The quantum theory of gravity has opened up a new possibility, in which there would be no boundary to space-time and so there would be no need to specify the behavior at the boundary. There would be no singularities at which the laws of science broke down and no edge of space-time at which one would have to appeal to God or some new law to set the boundary conditions for space-time. One could say: "The boundary condition of the universe is that it has no boundary." The universe would be completely self-contained and not affected by anything outside itself. It would neither be created nor destroyed. It would just BE.[5]

This is just to rule out *a priori* the question of why the laws of quantum mechanics apply to the universe. However, even if we accept this dictate, at best Hawking would be undermining the traditional cosmological and teleological arguments for God's existence (see chapter 5 above). His line of reasoning simply does not address the kinds of considerations we find in arguments for God from Perfection or Goodness or Morality (such as Thomas Aquinas's Fourth Way, or fourth argument for God, and Kant's transcendental argument). The problem is that the extremely narrow focus of physics – its very strength – is its limitation.

Modern science, and physics in particular, is successful precisely because it is an abstraction. Quantifiable features of the universe are abstracted into probabilistic laws. The uniqueness of individuals is ignored in order to see better the general ways in which individuals fit into groups and patterns of group relationships. Fred the electron is no more significant than Fred the mailman in this grand scheme. In fact nothing is intrinsically valuable; everything just *is*. This mathematical approach to the universe is highly successful as a means to understand and control physical features of our environment, but why suppose that mathematical features of the universe are the most significant, much less the *only* or the *only significant* features of the universe? Naturally, if one presupposes a mathematical model of what counts as proof and truth, one will only glean mathematical truths. But this is not even mildly close to the empirical data of human experience.

We live at the level of friendships and parenting and love relationships, at the level of the pleasures of music and food and art and the pains of war and child abuse and oppression. This is the human condition, and religion addresses these features of our humanity. To suppose that the universe is reducible to quantifiable, mathematical, humanly constructed models is to take the abstraction for the thing of which it is an abstraction. Furthermore, we would expect rather different epistemologies to be applicable to our lived lives as opposed to the narrow mathematical considerations of science. Scientific method requires dispassion; human life invites passion. Science is analytical; human life often evolves through story, is maddeningly indefinite, and is often edged with mystery – much like the Hindu epic the *Mahabharata,* the sermons of the Buddha, or the parables of Jesus. Indeed, why would we expect anything less than the *Mahabharata's* complex narrative, the Four Noble Truths, or the Gospel story of the Good Samaritan if we wish to pursue the moral life and religious values? Physics is simply too limited methodologically to ask, much less answer, questions of morals, of ultimate metaphysics, and of ultimate values.

WHAT DOES EVOLUTIONARY BIOLOGY TELL US ABOUT RELIGION?

Still we must wonder, could the issue here be only one about physics, which simply provides the wrong level of explanation to account plausibly for certain "why" features of the universe? Perhaps we need to conceive of the sciences more broadly. Let us turn then to the life sciences, for they seem closer to our real lived existence.

Consider the view developed by the biologist Richard Dawkins in *The Selfish Gene* that "We, and all other animals, are machines created by our genes....[and] a predominant quality to be expected in a successful gene is ruthless selfishness."[6] On Dawkins' view, genes are "replicators", while organisms such as our bodies are vehicles carrying the replicators. Consequently he says:

> The essential quality that an entity needs, if it is to become an effective gene vehicle, is this. It must have an impartial exit channel into the

future, for all the genes inside it...Genes have something to gain from selfishly promoting the welfare of their own individual bodies at the expense of other genes [in the bodies of others in the group].[7]

Given this radical sociobiological worldview, Dawkins concludes his book with the assertion that "the only kind of entity that has to exist for life to arise, anywhere in the universe, is the immortal replicator."[8] This may be all well and good for the *what* of replicators, ceaselessly replicating themselves into the future, but what about the *why* and the origins of the replicators? Do we not need an explanation of *why* genes *qua* replicators work the way they do?

As Dawkins admits "the success that a replicator has in the world will depend on what kind of a world it is – the pre-existing conditions."[9] But Dawkins' answer to the question of origins is again sociobiological: "among the most important of these conditions will be other replicators and their consequences."[10] This raises the specter of an infinite regress of explanation. But putting that aside, more importantly his answer in terms of a history of selfish genes seems to leave no room for the origin of values such as love. Dawkins does not see this as problematic, concluding: "Much as we might wish to believe otherwise, universal love and the welfare of the species as a whole are concepts that simply do not make evolutionary sense."[11] This presents a cold, hard view of the universe and a rather pessimistic view of human life. In Charles Darwin's words in *The Origin of the Species by Natural Selection*, "There is one general law, leading to the advancement of all organic beings, namely multiply, vary, let the strongest live and the weakest die."[12]

Dawkins' only mitigating move to (so to speak) "make the world safe for values" is to invest the natural order with intentionality. Because he does not allow for the possibility that intentionality is brought about or manifest in the natural order by a Transcendent, he must locate intentionality in the physical world at the genetic level. So he talks about genes "*cooperating* with one another" and "*discovering* a way of spreading themselves" and "*happily collaborating* in manufacturing efficient survival machines" [such as our bodies], and he refers to genes as "*ingenious* replicators."[13]

This anthropomorphic view of genes is obviously fraught with difficulties, but even if we grant Dawkins considerable poetic license, how did the idea of God arise among us, vehicles as we are for the immortal replicators? Dawkins has a ready answer which opened this chapter. The idea of God has a high survival value because it:

> Provides a superficially plausible answer to deep and troubling questions about existence. It suggests that injustices in this world may be rectified in the next. The (divine) "everlasting arms" hold out a cushion against our own inadequacies which, like a doctor's placebo, is none-the-less effective for being imaginary.[14]

The view which he is attempting to discredit here we might call "God as Anti-Depressant." However, though he tries to explain everything, Dawkins' argument fails in two senses of being a total explanation. It fails as a total explanation of the physical universe, and it fails as a total explanation of everything which would include the idea of God. As we saw in chapter 5, even Bertrand Russell does not try to propose a total physical explanation when he objects to cosmological arguments for God's existence.

Regarding the first failure, Dawkins' view of the immortal replicator is like saying that a total explanation of why you get a steady stream of copies out of a xerox machine is that there is plenty of paper and ink, there is a mechanism for producing copies, and there is a memory in the microprocessor which patterns each copy in the same way. But this does not address the question of the origin of these original conditions. Why is there a specific memory in the microprocessor in the first place? Cosmological and teleological arguments for God's existence, even if they fail as knock-down proofs, are one attempt to answer such "why" questions *vis-à-vis* the universe.

The second failure in Dawkins' argument is intimated by the physicist Paul Davies' observation that:

> It is certainly a surprise, and a deep mystery, that the human brain has evolved its extraordinary mathematical ability. It is very hard to see how abstract mathematics has any survival value. Similar comments apply to musical ability.[15]

In a clearly biased manner Dawkins is comfortable proclaiming "mysteries" in sociobiology, while disowning the mysteries of religion. But value – including aesthetic value – is created by intentionality. For Dawkins' view to offer a complete explanation of values, we would need to be able to explain values as something that we, the vehicles of genetic replicators, would intend for their contribution to our survival. But aesthetic values and – even more damaging for Dawkins' view as well as Stephen Hawking's view as a physicist – mathematical values cannot be accounted for in this manner.

This deficiency of Dawkins' radical sociobiological worldview in accounting for values does not end with mathematics or music. Religious insight – a kind of genius which surely amazes and moves people as much as any mathematical or musical achievement – has been a constant of humanity. Jesus of Nazareth and Siddhartha Gautama, Isaiah and Muhammad, Mahavira and Lao Tzu and Dogen are surely as illustrious as Mozart and Beethoven, Newton and Einstein, Euclid or those who first invented numbers in India before Arabs brought them to the West. Further, the issue here is not just about genius. The recalcitrant data that sociobiology cannot account for includes data about quite ordinary aspects of human life, such as morality and love.

IS RELIGION JUST A CULTURAL PHENOMENON?

Perhaps again the only reason science seems unable to account for values is that with sociobiology – as with physics – we are working at the wrong level of explanation. Perhaps we need to move to an even more macro level – i.e. that of culture. So what sort of cultural analyses might explain the rise of religious notions?

At the beginnings of the development of sociology, Ludwig Feuerbach argued in *The Essence of Christianity* that ordinary sense perception is very different than religious perception, for we gain knowledge about the nature of reality through sense perception, but on his view we do not gain knowledge about the nature of reality through religion. Key to Feuerbach's conclusion is the notion, which follows Kant, that in sense perception (which for him is a model for all knowledge acquisition) it is essential that there is a clear distinction between the perceiving self, or the perceiver, and the object perceived. That is, one of the conditions for the proper acquisition of knowledge is that one be aware of the fact that one is different from what is being perceived. However, in religion (Feuerbach addresses monotheism) the object turns out to coincide with the perceiving self. Talk about God is talk about a supreme being, a comparative idea. The very language of the monotheist assumes that there is a distinction between the divine and the non-divine, between creation and creator, and between God and humans. Compared to human beings, God is the supreme being. But on Feuerbach's view, this is an infantile way of thinking, a view that Freud took up again in the twentieth century. Our human ancestors projected an idealization of themselves into the world and called that projection "God." Feuerbach therefore considers the divine versus non-divine dichotomy an illusion. We might call this cultural critique the idea of "God as Super-Me."

Feuerbach calls the divine the "human purified," that is, an idealized humanity. So according to Feuerbach, to talk about God is to talk anthropomorphically. To support this he suggests that an object is nothing more than its attributes or qualities. Humans ascribe to God a set of attributes also held by human beings: goodness, knowledge, etc. If we ascribe human attributes to God, then we are saying that God is a human-like object, though an idealized form of humanness. But this is just an anthropomorphic conception – "God as Super-Me." Hence, it is better to say that there is no God.

Feuerbach's projection argument will not, of course, apply to those World Religions which do not conceive of the Transcendent in personalistic terms. But even with respect to monotheism and henotheism Feuerbach's argument fails. For one thing, metaphysical attributes, like omnipotence, omnipresence, etc., are traditionally ascribed to God. If Feuerbach's argument were correct, since these attributes have a human counterpart, it would follow that anything that humans claim has power, knowledge, and so on, is just a projection of ourselves onto the world. But surely that is not the case. When we say Niagara Falls is powerful, we are not being anthropomorphic. Moreover, we can even see this with regard to personalistic terms like "loving" which are applied to God. We apply terms like loving also to puppy dogs, and in the future we might travel to Alpha Centauri, the nearest star, and extend our use of this term, finding that the beings we met on Alpha Centauri also love. But this does not make these features of dogs or Alpha Centaurians mere anthropomorphic projections of our minds. Feuerbach would have to show that the terms we apply both to God and to ourselves can only be applied to human beings, and he has not shown that.

Feuerbach also tries to argue that the dichotomy between humanity and God as the supreme being diminishes humanity. It is true that sometimes in the history of religion, human beings have thought of themselves as worthless compared to God (the Calvinist "I am but a worm").

However, one way in which monotheism and henotheism potentially increase the sense of the value of humanity is to enjoin faith in a divine being who cares enough about human beings to see them as valuable. We will return to this in chapter 14.

IS RELIGION JUST A PSYCHOLOGICAL PHENOMENON?

Another sort of cultural analysis of religion is offered by psychology. As psychology first developed and then became prominent in the twentieth century, a psychological critique of religion became prominent. The cultural anthropologist Marvin Harris suggests in Our Kind that cultural selection "works by preserving and propagating behavior and thoughts that more effectively satisfy the biological and psychological demands and potentials of individuals in a given group or subgroup"[16] How then would the development of religion be explained purely psychologically?

> Our kind has always wanted gods and other spirit beings to provide us with certain kinds of benefits...the basis of all that is distinctly religious in human thought is animism, the belief that humans share the world with a population of extraordinary, extracorporeal, and mostly invisible beings, ranging from souls and ghosts to saints and fairies, angels and cherubim, demons, jinni, devils, and gods.[17]

Initially humans supplicated the gods, Harris suggests, for improved health, wealth, and victory in war. Compared to these requests, requests "for immortality, resurrection and eternal bliss in heaven may seem less crass, but they nonetheless also involve the gods in the delivery of goods and services."[18] Indeed the World Religions, he says, "could not have achieved their eminence as world religions were it not for their capacity to sponsor and encourage military conquest and to aid and abet harsh forms of political repression and control."[19]

We might call Harris's Darwinian anthropological view of God "God as Divine Welfare System." It is true that many people *are* only superficially religious and/or manipulate religion to their own selfish ends. But it is an empirical defect of Harris's view that he does not consider the evidence of the religions themselves to understand their own *raison d'être*. Harris's view of religion deals only with the abuse of religion, not its intended use as encapsulated in Jesus' words, "if any man would come after me, let him deny himself" (Matt. 17:24) and the *Dhammapada* saying, "death, the end of all, makes an end of the man who, ever thirsty for desires, gathers the flowers of sensuous passion" (4:48).

Another psychological critique of religion is developed by Sigmund Freud, a scientific humanist who recommends scientific accomplishment in place of religion. This optimistic view of the value of human scientific accomplishment is encapsulated in Freud's *The Future of an Illusion*. Freud ends his book with the proclamation that "our science is no illusion. But an illusion it would be to suppose that what science cannot give us we can get elsewhere."[20] Freud argues that we have civilizations because we need them to do two things – to protect us from the forces of nature and to protect us from each other. If everyone ran rampant and followed whatever desires they had at the moment, life would be "nasty, brutish and short" (to quote the philosopher Hobbes.) On Freud's analysis, since civilization regulates our desires or interests, what we want is to have the good effects of civilization, namely protection from nature and from each other, without an undue amount of regulation. He argues that religion can now be totally eliminated from human civilization because whatever benefits may accrue from religion in the current age, those benefits are nowhere near sufficient to balance out the enormous amount of regulation that religion brings into our lives. And science can now do for us what we had once hoped as a species that religion could do.

Moreover, Freud suggests that religion has a psychological basis which actually makes religion an illusion, where science is not an illusion. He holds that religious beliefs are illusions because they are based on certain hopes or wishes: we wish there were a father protector figure for us; we wish that the forces of nature were controlled by an outside force; we wish there were something outside of ourselves to give us direction. Because of those psychological needs we project an idea of a God on the universe, and we come to believe in God. We might call this the view of "God as Neurosis."

Freud's argument may seem plausible at first, but he commits the fallacy of equivocation. He initially defines an "illusion" by saying that "We call a belief an illusion when a wish-fulfillment is a prominent factor in its motivation, and in doing so, we *disregard* its relations to reality, just as the illusion itself sets no store by verification."[21] Thus, a young girl who today dreams of marrying Elvis, the young prince Siddhartha Gautama who dreamed of reaching enlightenment, and the young Einstein who dreamt of developing the theory of relativity all had "illusions" in this sense. And clearly illusions are not necessarily false in this sense. Elvis is not available for the young girl, but Einstein fulfilled his dream, and Siddhartha became the Buddha. In Freud's words, "an illusion is not the same thing as an error; nor is it necessarily an error...What is characteristic of illusions is that they are derived from human wishes."[22] However, toward the end of *The Future of an Illusion,* Freud switches to a different meaning of "illusion," claiming that while religion *is* an illusion, "science has given us evidence by its numerous and important successes that it is no illusion."[23] In this latter use, "illusion" means a false belief, one that does not correspond to reality. Hence, Freud plays off our initial acceptance of naming religion an illusion on the grounds that it has an element of wish-fulfillment, and then attempts to claim that religion is false because illusions are false. But why should we accept the bare claim that religion is a false view of reality?

Freud's line of reasoning also commits the fallacy of begging the question. He argues that "an illusion it would be to suppose that what science cannot give us we can get elsewhere."[24] Of course, if we restrict ourselves to scientific explanation, we obviate the possibility of explaining anything not amenable to that methodology. But why should we suppose *a priori* that science *could* offer a complete explanation of the universe? If religion can tell us something about reality, then it has some value. And Freud offers no argument to show that religion cannot tell us about reality, merely the assertion that only science can tell us about reality, but that begs the question.

THE COMPATIBILITY OF SCIENCE AND RELIGION

Science is directed toward self and world. As we saw in the representative quotes from Jesus and the *Dhammapada,* religion is directed beyond the self. Hence, religious worldviews have a completely different directedness than a scientific humanist worldview. Religious worldviews are *other* directed. In this vein, Einstein identifies what he calls the "cosmic religious feeling":

> The individual feels the nothingness of human desires and aims and the sublimity and marvelous order which reveal themselves both in nature and in the world of thought. He looks upon human existence as a sort of prison and wants to experience the universe as a single significant whole.[25]

While religion is a quest for meaning and value in life through relation with the Transcendent, pure scientific explanation not only cannot explain religion (for it has a different purview), but the reliance on scientific reason alone as a total explanation is *a*-religious in the most fundamental sense. The religious impulse which informs religious world-views is an impulse to look for meaning and value beyond the transient natural order, i.e., beyond the order of scientific explanation. Hence, the sort of attitudes addressed by Hawking and Dawkins and Feuerbach and Harris and Freud in the views we designated as "God as Great Physicist," "God as Anti-Depressant," "God as Super Me," "God as Divine Welfare System," and "God as Neurosis" are not representative of genuine religion, for they are self-aggrandizing views of religion.

As the thoroughly scientific but more than merely scientific Albert Einstein says, *"The true value of a human being* is determined primarily by the measure and the sense in which he has attained to liberation from the self."[26] This corresponds to the New Testament injunction that "whoever seeks to gain his life will lose it, but whoever loses his life will preserve it;"[27] it corresponds to the Islamic notion of "surrender" and becoming a servant of Allah; and it corresponds to the Indic idea that to be obsessed with this world is to be trapped in *maya* or illusion. The last is expressed in Buddhism as the notion that in order to eliminate cravings for the impermanent things of this world, one needs to align oneself with the true underlying structure of things, the *Dharma* or law of the universe, and come to a realization of *anatman*, no-self.

This fundamental difference between science and religion does not entail that they must be in conflict. While scientific humanism does preclude religion, religion does not preclude a scientific understanding of the physical world. Any choice among worldviews has to be settled on the basis of which view is the epistemically most powerful for acting in the world, which accounts for the most significant and the greatest variety of relevant experience, and which solves what are taken to be the most significant problems. It is the latter, of course, which most importantly adjudicates between purely scientific and religious worldviews. The religious claim is the double claim that the most significant problem facing humans is how to explain meaning and value and that meaning and value can only be explained by reference to a Transcendent beyond the self.

We hold the worldview we do because of our values. Scientific method presupposes faith in the regularity of nature and faith that human reason can continue to comprehend the workings of the physical universe. Scientific method values regularity and reason. Religion, on the other hand, values relationship to other persons and relationship to the Transcendent. Scientific humanists offer faith in science alone. But science has inherent limitations. While a religious person with a global outlook in our contemporary world will value science, the remainder of this book addresses those things that religion additionally promises to deliver that science cannot.

Further reading

INTRODUCTORY

Berry, R.J. *God and the Biologist*. England, Apollos, 1996

Davies, Paul. *The Mind of God: the Scientific Basis for a Rational World*. New York, Simon and Schuster, 1992

Einstein, Albert. *The World As I See It*. New York, Carol Publishing, 1998

Freud, Sigmund. *The Future of An Illusion*. New York, W.W. Norton and Company, 1961

Peacocke, Arthur. *Intimations of Reality*. Notre Dame, University of Notre Dame Press, 1984

Polkinghorne, John. *Science and Providence: God's Interaction with the World*. London, Longdunn Press, 1989

Ward, Keith. *God, Faith, and the New Millennium*. Oxford, Oneworld, 1998

IN-DEPTH

Barbour, Ian G. *Myths, Models, and Paradigms*. New York, Harper and Row, 1974

Dawkins, Richard. *The Selfish Gene*. Oxford, Oxford University Press, 1989

Feuerbach, Ludwig. *The Essence of Christianity*. George Eliot, trans. New York, Harper and Row, 1957

Hawking, Stephen. *A Brief History of Time: From the Big Bang to Black Holes*. New York, Bantam, 1988

Kuhn, Thomas S. *The Structure of Scientific Revolutions*. Chicago, University of Chicago Press, 1970

Murphy, Nancey. *Theology in the Age of Scientific Reasoning*. London, Cornell University Press, 1990

Ward, Keith. *God, Chance, & Necessity*. Oxford, Oneworld, 1996

11 MORALITY, ETHICS, AND RELIGION

Is what is holy holy because the gods approve it,
or do the gods approve it because it is holy?

Plato (427–347 BCE) from the *Euthyphro*

MORALITY AND ETHICS

Within all the World Religions, to be genuinely religious is to be moral. But is morality necessarily tied to religion? And is there any difference between morality and ethics? Let us consider the nature of morality first.

Morality is a set of norms about what is right and wrong, good and bad. For example, we often ask such questions as: "Do you think suicide is moral?"; "Do you think animals have rights?"; "Do you think it is right to have an abortion?" Answers to these and similar questions are part of one's morality. But further, morality is systematic. It is a set of interrelated principles and imperatives about right and wrong, good and bad, which a society holds as true and normative of the relations between members of that society. So to speak as some do as if one could literally have one's own personal morality is tantamount to saying that one just acts in one's own self-interest. Any genuine morality is the shared morality of a society. Many societies are religious societies, and they share a religious morality.

Importantly, a shared morality may also be thought to extend to persons outside the immediate society. For example, consider several religious moralities. Within Judaism the seven moral imperatives of the Law of Noah in the *Torah* are held to apply equally to Jew and non-

Jew alike. However, only Jews are obligated to follow the more than six hundred imperatives of the Law of Sinai. Likewise, only traditional Hindus are obligated to follow the specific imperatives of the ancient Laws of Manu, even though non-Hindus are thought to be subject to the laws of *karma*, if not the specific karmic laws of caste. In Jainism, strands of Buddhism, and Hinduism, the moral laws of *karma* extend beyond persons to animals, and even to all life forms, whereas in the Western monotheisms morality is usually thought to extend only to humans.

Now when we discuss or assess a morality, there are three different kinds of things we might be doing. First, we could be engaged in a strictly descriptive investigation. Sociologists, anthropologists, and psychologists do this when they ask such questions as "what do Americans think?" or "what do people in another culture think?" or "what do eight-year-olds think?" about issues that we consider to be moral issues. These are descriptive questions in the social sciences. We hope to determine what various groups of people think is moral, or we want to know – in sociological, historical, or anthropological terms – why they think that way. In these scientific approaches we are not asking whether the people being studied are right or wrong to think about morality as they do. In contrast, the other two ways to discuss or assess morality, "normative ethics" and "metaethics," are not purely descriptive.

There is a tendency to use the terms "morality" and "ethics" interchangeably, but when used more precisely, they are not, in fact, interchangeable terms. While morality is a set of norms about what is right and wrong, good and bad, ethics is *reasoning* about morality. We do ethics when we want to determine what is right and wrong so as to guide our behavior accordingly. So to do ethics is to propose a systematic approach, or to give systematic reasons, or to offer fundamental principles, as to why you give the answers you do to moral questions. Insofar as one systematically lists what one is committed to holding as right and wrong, good and bad, one is implicitly engaged in a simple sort of ethics, since that is already to categorize actions or character traits into types. But ethics is more than this.

The foundational level of ethics is normative ethics which is a system of reasoning about morality. A normative ethical system is intended to do two things: explain why things are right and wrong and good and bad, and on the basis of that provide a systematic way of deciding moral issues when we face a moral choice. Moral issues arise in the context of a conflict. For example, you might mention something about abortion or animal rights, and I might voice disagreement with you. This would bring us into ethical conflict and could lead us to begin working out our own reasons for our moral stance on abortion or animal rights. Or you might want something which is not in my self-interest. Is there an ethical way to decide whose self-interest, mine or yours, ought to be protected in this situation? In a like manner, there are cross-cultural conflicts over moral stands. And sometimes there are conflicts within our own views. These conflicts also occasion reflection and analysis. In short, conflicts over questions of morality usually initiate the reasoning about morality which is ethics. And since normative ethical systems are intended to give answers in times of moral conflict, they do not merely give an answer to what is moral but provide a principled justification for why it is moral.

The second, even deeper level of ethics is metaethics. Metaethical questions are questions about or across normative ethical systems. Thus one might ask: "What does it mean in general to say that something is moral?"; or "what does it mean to say that there is a moral point of view?"; or "how are morality and ethics different from other action guides like the legal system?" We will first look at some of the major normative ethical systems which have been proposed before we turn to our original metaethical question of the relation of religion to morality.

SECULAR ETHICS

While most humans are religious and most have a religious ethics, secular normative ethical theories have become increasingly significant in the contemporary world. Normative ethical theories, whether religious or non-religious, subdivide into two types: deontological theories and consequentialist theories. Deontological theories are duty-based theories. Religious ethics is most often deontological, based in some way on religious duties. We will return to deontological views shortly. In contrast, a consequentialist is someone who says that the moral rightness or wrongness, good or bad, of an action is determined solely by the consequences of the action. Secular ethics tends to be consequentialist.

In order to understand consequentialism, we need to understand two different senses of "good" – a moral sense and a nonmoral sense. If I say that I have a good computer, I have not made any sort of moral comment about my computer, but rather a nonmoral comment about the value of my computer as a means of calculation, communication, graphics production, etc. Generally, inanimate things are only good in a nonmoral sense and not in a moral sense. (Jains would dispute this because of the presence of *jiva* in all things.) However, for some things we attribute another type of goodness, moral goodness. Timothy may be a superb athlete, and so when we see him on the athletic field, we may say "Timothy is good." This, too, is a nonmoral comment: those of us who are not so athletic are certainly not therefore morally deficient. But we could also make moral comments concerning Timothy, for unlike my computer he is a moral agent: "Tim is a good man" and "Tim did the right thing" said when he helps out at a charity.

Now, a consequentialist is anyone who defines moral notions strictly in terms of nonmoral value. So a consequentialist in ethics is someone who defines what is morally right and wrong and morally good and bad in terms of the nonmoral good produced. A consequentialist would say that if Timothy is morally good, he is morally good *because* his actions produce certain nonmoral goods. In contradistinction, the deontologist is anyone who denies this. A deontologist might say that morality is *not at all* dependent on producing nonmoral good, or a deontologist might say that morality is not *solely* dependent on the consequences of actions although consequences do matter to some extent. But more about the deontologist later.

The most extreme form of consequentialism is Ethical Egoism. Ethical Egoism is a secular ethics which holds that the standard of moral rightness and wrongness is what will produce one's own greatest nonmoral good. Typically, ethical egoists develop their view on the basis of the empirical view called psychological egoism. A psychological egoist is one who thinks that we humans are so constructed psychologically that we always act only in our own self-interest. Often psychological egoists are also psychological hedonists, holding that we human beings are so constructed that we always act for our own pleasure. Ethical Egoism is inherently opposed to the religious point of view, but is it a reasonable normative ethics in its own right?

We should first note that even if psychological egoism is true, this does not in and of itself entail Ethical Egoism. The ethical egoist is making a claim about what is morally right, about what really ought to be done; the psychological egoist is making a claim about what we in fact do, or try to do, as we are driven to seek our own good. So it might turn out that psychological egoism is true, but this does not tell us that what we do is what we ought to do. A more fundamental deficiency, though, with Ethical Egoism has to do with its validity as an ethical theory. Ethical Egoism really just amounts to a theory about prudence or self-interestedness. When we think about what it means to take the moral point of view as opposed to the self-interested or prudential point of view, we realize that taking the moral point of view must involve some consideration of the effects of our actions on the well-being of others. Hence, Ethical Egoism fails to be an ethical theory because it fails to take others into account.

Utilitarianism, the most prominent consequentialist secular ethics, is not susceptible to this criticism. A utilitarian holds the Principle of Utility which states that the ultimate standard of morality is the production of the greatest possible balance of nonmoral good over evil. Often Utilitarianism is explained in terms of the "utile," an arbitrary unit of nonmoral good. Suppose action A would produce ten units of good, or ten positive utiles, and another action B would produce twenty positive utiles but also five negative utiles. In this case, the moral thing to do would be to choose B because, even though it has certain bad consequences, B has the greater balance – fifteen utiles versus only ten utiles for A – of good over evil.[1]

Clearly, the utilitarian needs to define what is meant by "nonmoral good" since he or she has defined the moral good in terms of the nonmoral good. A utilitarian might be a metaphysical hedonist, holding that pleasure is the only nonmoral good. In his classic book *Utilitarianism,* John Stuart Mill offers the following sort of inference from psychological hedonism to metaphysical hedonism: (1) it is a psychological fact about us that we only desire pleasure (psychological hedonism); (2) the only test of what is desirable is what people in fact desire; (3) therefore, pleasure is the only thing that is desirable (metaphysical hedonism). Premise 2 trades on two different senses of "desire" (the valuable or desirable versus the wanted or desired), and so the argument fails. But if, apart from his argument, Mill's conclusion is itself true, and one is both a utilitarian and a metaphysical hedonist, then the relative morality of alternative actions can be assessed in terms of which action produces the greatest possible balance of pleasure over pain. Positive utiles then turn out to be pleasure utiles, and negative utiles are pain utiles.

This sort of hedonistic calculus, or more generally utility calculus, is illustrated by Dorothy Sayers in her short story "Dilemma":

I have no idea who started the imbecile discussion. I think it must have been Timpany. At any rate, it is just the futile and irritating sort of topic that Timpany *would* start at the end of a long day's fishing. By the time I had settled with the landlord about a boat for the next morning and had come back to the smoking room, they were at it, and had got to the problem about the Chinaman.

You know that one. If you could get a million pounds, without any evil consequences to yourself, by merely pressing a button which would electrocute a single unknown Chinese ten thousand miles away – would you press the button? Everybody seemed to have an opinion on the point.

The Colonel said Woof! of course he'd press the button. Too many damned Chinamen in the world anyway – too many damned people altogether.

And I said most people would do a lot for a million pounds.

And then Padre said (as of course he had to) that nothing could justify taking the life of a fellow-creature. And Timpany said, Think of the good one could do with a million pounds, and the old Popper said it all depended on the character of the Chinaman – he might have lived to be another Confucius – and from that talk drifted to still sillier problems, such as, if you had the choice between rescuing a diseased tramp or the *Codex Sinaiticus*, which would you save?[2]

The utilitarian notion of the greatest good for the greatest number seems equitable on the surface, but what prevents this notion from supporting the sort of slide into moral decay which Sayers illustrates when actual utilitarian calculations are made?

Arbitrary units of good supposedly produced by calculating on the basis of "the good one could do with a million pounds" can lead to grave injustices against individual persons. Precisely such considerations about all the good one could do led Raskolnikov to murder the pawnbroker and her sister on the basis of his "extraordinary man theory" in *Crime and Punishment*:

On one side we have a stupid, senseless, worthless, spiteful, alien, horrid old woman, not simply useless but doing actual mischief...a hundred thousand good deeds could be done and helped, on that old woman's money which will be buried in a monastery! For one life thousands would be saved from corruption and decay. One death. And a hundred lives in exchange – it's simply arithmetic.[3]

If lives are reduced to utiles, what value do we place on a human life, or on personhood, and what value would we place on the lives of non-human living beings for the sake of a substantial utilitarian payoff? Is not the subjective determination of utiles an invitation to overemphasize the value of what is in the interest of one's own group, or even in one's self interest? (We will look at a Buddhist utilitarian argument in chapter 12 when we discuss prudential arguments for religious commitment.)

MORAL DUTY AND RELIGION

The Padre in Sayers' story is a deontologist. He introduces a consideration often used against Utilitarianism, namely our duty to other persons simply because they are persons. This is encapsulated in Kant's famous deontological dictum that "we should never treat people merely as a means to an end, but as ends in themselves." Deontologists reject the reduction of morality to considerations of consequences, for a deontologist typically thinks that we should act instead on the basis of conscience, or out of a sense of duty toward other persons. (*Deon*, the root of "deontological," is the Greek term for that which is binding or proper.) Kant himself is a monistic rule deontologist. As we shall see, to determine moral duty he appeals to a single, foundational, generative rule for all morality.

Kant begins with a distinction between two different types of imperatives or commands. Hypothetical imperatives have the form "if you want X, then you should do Y." While hypothetical imperatives command you to do something, they are conditional upon whether you want what the action will produce. A second sort of imperative, a categorical imperative, is one that holds no matter what you may want or what is in your self-interest. On Kant's view, morality does not depend on what you want; rather moral claims on us are categorical, and morality is unconditional. While for a utilitarian like Mill what makes an action morally right is the consequence, for Kant an act is morally right if, first, your motive is morally good. Second, your motive is morally good if you act out of a sense of duty. Third, every action involves a maxim (or general rule). And fourth, you are acting out of duty only if you are willing to make the maxim under which your act falls into a universal law. Thus, you will be acting out of a sense of duty only if what you are doing is what anyone ought to do under the same relevant circumstances. So Kant comes to the monistic deontological conclusion that what is morally right is what fits a universalizable maxim or law.

Since for Kant all moral questions are categorical questions – and not dependent on what you as an individual want or do not want – what is moral is what any rational person can consistently say should be universally followed without exception by all persons irrespective of their individual desires. This completely rationalistic ethics of Kant's corresponds to Kant's notion of genuine religion. As we saw in chapter 9, Kant also argues that the only justifiable kind of religion is what he calls "rational religion," where we first rationally determine our moral duties (using the deontological principle he has identified) and then go on to infer that those duties are divine commands. So Kant's deontological ethics would suggest a strong connection between morality and religion.

However, there are a number of potential difficulties with this Kantian view. One objection might be that Kant's view is too broad, encompassing too much. According to Kant, if we can consistently will to universalize the maxim under which an action falls, that action would be morally right. The trouble with this, however, is that there are all sorts of maxims or rules that we can, in the rational sense, consistently will to be universal maxims and yet which are not moral at all. For example, we can consistently will that everyone should always put on their pants right leg first – which is surely not a moral maxim. Hence, Kant's system needs more restrictions on what will count as moral. However, another objection might be that Kant's view of what is consistently rational to will is too restrictive. For example, he feels that it is always morally wrong for one to commit suicide. But what is irrational about having a rule that says suicide is acceptable under special circumstances (for example, Japanese ritual suicide)? The same is true of another of Kant's suggested moral maxims, the maxim that one should never lie. What is irrational about having a rule that one can lie to save a life, as many did during World War II to save Jews from Nazi extermination?

This brings us to what has often been considered the most serious internal defect in Kant's ethics: since all moral maxims derive their status from the same, single principle, there seems to be no mechanism for dealing with the possibility of a conflict of moral maxims. When faced with a choice of either lying or not lying, perhaps we must never lie, or when faced with either committing suicide or not committing suicide, perhaps we should never commit suicide. But one point of a normative ethics is to have a system such that when we confront moral conflicts, we are already equipped with a systematic way of arriving at a timely decision. For example, to modernize an example from Aristotle, suppose a friend comes knocking at your door and with great agitation asks you to return the gun you have borrowed so that he can shoot his obnoxious landlady: "You do have the gun, don't you?" You remember full well that the gun is in the back room where you placed it, promising to return it soon. Do you keep your promise and not lie, or do you break your promise and lie in order to protect a life? Kant does not provide a clear way to resolve this conflict between moral maxims.

Before we turn to a resolution of this difficulty, we need to note the strengths of Kant's ethics. Salient among those strengths is Kant's universalizability principle, which is an important formal principle for any normative ethics. Universalizability is the idea that if an action is morally right for you, then it is morally right or permissible for anyone else who finds himself or herself in circumstances similar to those you are confronting. By itself this principle is too broad to identify *only* moral maxims, but the significance of the principle is that it enjoins taking other people seriously; it mitigates against thinking of ourselves as always being the exception to the rule. The principle of universalizability is a way to defeat Ethical Egoism.

Now, the British ethicist W.D. Ross takes up the strengths of Kant's view and presents a modified version of Kantian deontological ethics which is explicitly structured to deal with conflicts among moral maxims. Ross suggests that there are two senses of having a duty. Some duties are what he calls *prima facie* duties and others are actual duties. *Prima facie* duties are the initial general set of duties which we bring to any situation, such as the duty to keep promises or look out for the welfare of others. For Ross, one of our *prima facie* duties is utility, or producing the greatest happiness, though he argues against Mill's Utilitarianism on the grounds that it is insufficient as a complete normative theory. If when we face an actual situation, only one *prima facie* duty is involved, this is our actual duty, and we should adhere to it. But suppose we are confronted with a situation in which two (or more) *prima facie* duties (maxims) are in conflict? We should then determine our actual duty by deciding which of the conflicting *prima facie* duties is the duty to be followed in *this* case. That duty then becomes our *actual* duty. Ross provides a way to resolve the weapon-returning case: it is our *actual* duty to protect the sanctity of life and not to return the weapon, although we have a *prima facie* duty to tell the truth and to keep our promises.

In his assessment of Utilitarianism, Ross argues that Utilitarianism is insufficient as a normative theory because it does not take account of the effect that relations between persons have on morality, a criticism which also applies to Kant's deontological theory.[4] Utilitarianism only considers people apart from any personal qualities, and in fact Mill proudly endorses Jeremy Bentham's saying that "all must count for one and no one to count for more than one." But suppose you are a mother who brings one sandwich to school for her daughter. You arrive to find ten hungry kids. You could divide the sandwich into ten equal parts so that each child gets a tenth, and each is then less hungry though not quite satisfied. Or because of your parental relation with your child, you could – indeed this is likely to be your actual duty – give the whole sandwich to your daughter, even if her enjoyment is not ten times as great as each individual child's enjoyment would have been had you divided the sandwich among all ten. As the example shows, personal relationships are one consideration in deciding moral matters, one which both Kant and Mill fail to account for.

However, making moral decisions where we have to factor in our relationships with others will not always be easy, as Ross admits. Both Kant and Mill hope to produce a system where the answers to moral issues are rational and clear. To do so Kant calls for absolute, exceptionless moral maxims, while Mill is trusting that if we are just smart enough and have enough information, we can calculate the right answer to moral questions. Ross recognizes that the moral life is often messy, unsure, and difficult: often we face conflicts of duties; often the issues we face are subtle; and often it is not obvious what the answer is to our moral questions. A deontological ethics which takes account of real relationships and real situations, as well as the importance of the consequences of our actions, is more promising than one that does not.

In this vein consider Jainism, which, like its Indic counterpart Hinduism, offers a deontological normative ethics. To be moral is to follow the *Dharma* – the universal law of nature – out of a sense of duty, especially the duty of *ahimsa* (non-violence). Perhaps more than any other major religious tradition, Jainism has recognized the difficulty of applying moral duties to our real-life situations. Jainism has consequently developed the notion of *anekantavada*, an explicit recognition that knowledge is always from a particular perspective and that no single person has a perspective which is the whole truth. Utilizing both this principle of *anekantavada* as well as the distinction between *prima facie* and actual duties would lend great flexibility to the application of the notion of moral (and religious) duty, making more attractive the notion of following one's duty which can often sound formidable, inflexible and insensitive.

Hinduism has itself developed a religious deontological ethics around the notion of *karma-yoga*. Eliot Deutsch explicates the idea of *karma-yoga* in the *Bhagavad Gita* by focusing on verses III.9 and III.19:

> This world is in bondage to *karma*, unless *karma* is performed for the sake of sacrifice. For the sake of that, O son of Kunti, perform thy action free from attachment. (III.9)
> ...man attains the Supreme by performing work without attachment. (III.19)[5]

As Deutsch notes:

> *Karma*, in its widest traditional sense...means acts performed with the motive of attaining some end or fruit (*phala*), such acts binding one to future action. It is further assumed that this "law" of action implies a series of rebirths in the actor, with his respective place in the social order dependent upon the moral quality of his acts. *Karma* thus produces bondage to the world.[6]

But given this traditional view of *karma*, the *Bhagavad Gita* verse "This world is in bondage to *karma*, unless *karma* is performed for the sake of sacrifice..." is at first puzzling. For here the *Gita* denies that *karma* is bondage – or more accurately, holds that *karma* under the circumstances of sacrifice is not bondage. Deutsch suggests this explanation to resolve the puzzle:

> But what, one may ask, does it mean to perform action as a sacrifice? What is being sacrificed? to whom? [*Yajna* (sacrifice)] means rather the redirecting of one's being away from an involvement with the fruit of one's action to an eternal Spirit which is at one in and beyond the phenomenal world. *Yajna* means the turning away from our lower self (of desires, attachments) for the sake of our higher spiritual self.
> ...one must fill one's consciousness with the power of loving devotion. Implicit in the whole teaching scheme of the *Gita* is the belief that there is no other way to establish non-attachment than through a new attachment to that which is greater, in quality and power, than that to

which one was previously attached. One overcomes the narrow clinging to results, the passionate involvement with the consequences of one's own action, only when that passion is replaced by one directed to the Divine. *Bhakti* or devotion is thus in no way excluded from *karma yoga*, but it, on the contrary, is a necessary condition for it.

...*Yajna*, as applied to all actions, means then a self-surrender to the Divine, not in simple resignation or quietistic withdrawal, but rather in an active state of *nishkama karma*, action without desire for the fruits.[7]

Nishkama karma is moral action out of a sense of duty which is motivated by love of God. This devotion to God (*bhakti*) does not undermine personal responsibility and autonomy – in fact it is necessary for autonomy. As Deutsch says "success is possible only when the self unselfconsciously cooperates with Nature; that freedom is possible only where there is law and order." A precondition of autonomy is an underlying order – i.e. *Dharma* – within which our actions can have reliable and expectable results, enabling us to act with foresight and purpose. And the *bhakti-yoga* idea is that only through devotion to God can one successfully align oneself with the *Dharma*, and so achieve true freedom. Here an inextricable connection is postulated between the religious life and the moral life, offering a clear example of the manner in which the metaphysics of one's worldview drives the ethics of one's worldview.

ARE MORALITY AND RELIGION LOGICALLY CONNECTED?

We can now turn to the metaethical question of the relationship between morality and religion. The Hindu *bhakti* deontological ethics of *karma-yoga* in the *Bhagavad Gita* which we just looked at holds that the Divine makes true morality possible. But are morality and religion logically connected? Suppose you think that your totally non-religious neighbor is at least as moral if not more moral than you and more moral than the typical religious person. Plausible cases like this suggest that even if morality and religion are in fact connected, there is no necessary connection between being religious and being moral.

The Hindu *bhakti* tradition suggests one sort of possible connection between religious metaphysics and ethics; the divine command theory of Western monotheism suggests another possible connection. The divine command theory of ethics holds that what is right and wrong, good and bad, is what God commands. In assessing this view, William Frankena argues that:

> When one accepts a definition of any term that can be called ethical, one has already in effect accepted an ethical standard. For example, when one agrees to take "right" to mean "commanded by God," and at the same time to use it as a key term in one's speech, thought, and action, this is tantamount to accepting the moral principle "We ought to do what God commands" as a guide in life.
>
> ...when a theological definition is offered us, we may always ask why we should adopt this definition, and to answer us the theologian in question must provide us with a justification of the corresponding moral principle. And the point is that he cannot claim that either it or the definition follows logically from any religious or theological belief (which is not itself a disguised ethical judgment).[8]

In other words, once one accepts a religious definition of morality, one has already accepted the relevant religious form of life. Consequently, it will not be convincing to offer theological considerations for morality to those who are not already committed to the relevant religious form of life. The divine command theory only works internally to monotheistic worldviews. This same point holds for the *bhakti* view of *karma-yoga*. Unless one is already committed to a *bhakti* religious metaphysics, one will not accept the notion that only devotion to God makes following one's moral duty fully possible. Thus divine command theory, *bhakti karma-yoga*, and so on for other religious ethics, only serve as explications of morality and exhortations to morality for those already committed to the religious life. They do not provide a basis for convincing those outside the religious worldview of the suggested connection between morality and religion.

Yet even if there is no necessary logical connection between morality and religion, another possible sort of connection between the two is the idea that morality might imply a Transcendent. For instance, moral arguments for God's existence have become more common in the modern period as the limitations of traditional metaphysical arguments (see chapters 4 and 5) have become more evident. Immanuel Kant proposed a moral argument for God, a line of reasoning which was then recast in a more global version by C.S. Lewis in *Mere Christianity*. Lewis's basic line of reasoning is this: We assume that there are some sort of objective standards by which we can pass moral judgments on human conduct even if we do not know exactly what those standards are. Thus we say things like "that is not fair" when we feel that (by some objective standard) we have been mistreated. Now those objective standards do not seem to come from humans, because even with our dearest friends

---

◆

A MORAL ARGUMENT FOR GOD'S EXISTENCE

1. Our behaviour presupposes a standard of morality.
2. The standard of morality is not an instinct.
3. The standard of morality is not a matter of mere opinion.
4. Morality is basically the same trans-historically and cross-culturally.
5. We all believe some moral codes are better than others.
6. Therefore, the standard of morality is like the laws of mathematics – i.e. independent of the human mind.
7. We often fail to follow the standard of morality.
8. Therefore, the standard of morality is not a set of regularities about human behavior.
9. Therefore, the standard of morality is a reality above and beyond the mere facts of the natural order.
10. The standard of morality is like a set of directions or commands (imperatives) expressing intense interest in morality.
11. Only minds can give commands.
12. Therefore there is a mind-like being beyond the natural order which is intensely interested in morality.

◆

---

we have disagreements, and the standards of morality stand outside our human disagreements. Thus, there must be some other source which is the source of the objective standards of morality, one outside the natural order. And the source of those moral standards must be a divine mind, namely God. Thus, when people are trying to figure out the answers to moral questions, they are, knowingly or unknowingly, appealing to objective standards which come from God. The details of Lewis's argument are set out above.

Most of Lewis's line of reasoning is an attempt to combat naturalistic explanations of morality (premises 2, 3, and 8). For monotheism to posit a God outside of the natural order, there must be things in the natural order which are not explicable purely in naturalistic terms, since exactly what naturalists hold, and how naturalists defend their position, is to claim that everything is explainable within the natural order. Overall what the monotheist is proposing is that a sufficient explanation for morality needs to be given; morality needs to be undergirded by something apart from us. Perhaps Lewis's argument does show that morality is not, for example, merely a social contract. But there are three problems with his argument.

186 . Global Philosophy of Religion A SHORT INTRODUCTION

First, Lewis's argument depends on a series of qualified observations: "morality is *basically* the same trans-historically and cross-culturally;" "the standard of morality is *like* the laws of mathematics;" "the structure of morality is *like* a set of commands." This leads to a qualified conclusion: "there is a mind-*like* being beyond the natural order." Consequently, the strength of the conclusion depends on the degree of qualification. The less one thinks morality is indeed globally basically the same, or that morality is like the laws of mathematics, or like a set of commands, the less one will think that whatever is behind the standard of morality is like a Divine Mind.

The second and third problems have to do with whether the considerations which Lewis adduces would be sufficiently convincing to indicate that there must be something behind the natural order. For, second, one could just hold that humans are as a simple matter of fact either moral or immoral or nonmoral, and morality is itself simply a brute fact about our world (or the way we are). One either "gets it" and so acts morally, or one does not get it, and there is nothing further to say about these brute facts. Third, moral arguments for God's existence will be unconvincing to those with a worldview other than that of monotheism (this is Frankena's point but now applied across religious traditions.) Thus, Bhikku Chao Chu says that from a Buddhist perspective:

> Knowledge of moral values is considered to be like knowledge of other natural laws. Relations of cause and effect observed throughout the natural world are understood to extend into the realm of human violation and action. All normal human beings agree that happiness is preferable to suffering. The Buddhist ethical system is based on this universal understanding. No commandments are made, but suggestions are offered, based on the knowledge of the natural laws of moral cause and effect that lead away from suffering to the greatest possible happiness for all beings...
> A human being who has reached full spiritual perfection has direct knowledge and insight into the impermanence and subtle interconnectedness of all phenomena. Such a one has a perfect understanding of the natural and moral laws of cause and effect, and teaches others for the good of all. This is what is meant by a Buddha, or awakened one...[9]

So on a Buddhist understanding, the directions which the standards of morality provide are not commands given by a divine being, but are literally directions embedded in *Dharma* which tell us how to align ourselves correctly with the true structure of reality.

THE MORAL POINT OF VIEW AND THE RELIGIOUS POINT OF VIEW

Do the ethics of the World Religions have anything in common despite their differences? In the first place, the World Religions do have a largely shared morality: murder, lying, stealing, sexual impropriety, and so on are universally prohibited. Moreover, even more general principles are often shared among the World Religions. For instance, in the Chinese, Hindu, Buddhist, Zoroastrian, Christian, and Islamic traditions among others, we find a remarkably similar conception of how to treat others:

Do not impose on others what you yourself do not desire.[10]

> *The Analects*, XV:24, Confucius (551–479 BCE)

One should never do that to another which one regards as injurious to one's own self. This, in brief, is the rule of dharma. Yielding to desire and acting differently, one becomes guilty of adharma.[11]

> *Mahabharata* XIII:113,8

He who for the sake of happiness hurts others who also want happiness, shall not hereafter find happiness.

He who for the sake of happiness does not hurt others who also want happiness, shall hereafter find happiness.[12]

> *The Dhammapada* 131–2

That nature only is good when it shall not do unto another whatever is not good for its own self.[13]

> *Dadistan-i-dinik* 94:5

Love your neighbor as yourself.

> *Gospel of Mark* 13:33 (RSV)

No man is a true believer unless he desires for his brother that which he desires for himself.

> Muhammad, from the *Hadith*

While being moral is not sufficient for being religious, it is universally held that to be religious is in part to be moral. And though we noted some of the differences among the religious ethics of the World

Religions, difference implies commonality. To see what they have in common ethically, let us first consider what it means in general to take the moral point of view.

Drawing on some of our earlier observations, at least four characteristics of taking the moral point of view are these: (1) taking others into account in one's actions because one respects them as persons; (2) the willingness to take into account how one's actions affect others by taking into account the good of everyone equally; (3) abiding by the principle of universalizability – that is, the willingness to treat one's own actions as morally laudable or permissible only if similar acts of others in comparable circumstances would be equally laudable or permissible, and to treat the actions of others as morally impermissible only if similar acts of one's own would be equally morally culpable; and (4) the willingness to be committed to some set of normative moral principles.[14] Taking these in reverse order, of course different religious traditions, and different cultures, will specify the normative principles in (4) differently. But all traditions share universalizability (3), for as we saw when we discussed Kant's ethics, this is a logical feature of any morality. The willingness to take others into account (2) is a psychological feature of the moral life, and it, too, is shared by all the World Religions. This brings us to the key shared element of the religious ethics of all the World Religions (1): taking others into account in one's actions because one respects them as persons. This is the crux of taking the moral point of view and so the crux of the shared ethics of the World Religions.

Persons are social beings. Relationality, or relating to others as persons, is a salient and defining characteristic of moral agency. As a fundamental characteristic of taking the moral point of view, relationality supports Immanuel Kant's ethical dictum to "always treat others as ends in themselves and not merely as means to an end." Relationality is reflected in the Jewish thinker Martin Buber's justly famous notion of the "I–thou" perspective: "When I confront a human being as my You and speak the basic word I–You to him, then he is no thing among things nor does he consist of things."[15] Relating to persons *as persons* is radically different from treating people as mere objects, or in Buber's terms "its." As Buber puts the difference, whoever lives only by treating everything as an "it" "is not human".

The obligation to take the moral point of view is not a moral obligation, for that would be circular. However, relationality is a religious obligation, for on the view of the World Religions, one cannot relate to the Transcendent unless one relates to other persons. Hence taking the moral point of view is a religious obligation. Consequently, religion supervenes on morality. That is, religion encompasses but is more than morality. So just as there is a moral point of view, there is what I call a "religious point of view" which supervenes upon the moral point of view. Just as the moral point of view functions as the wellspring and the point of commonality and universality for moral value and truths, so too the religious point of view is the wellspring, the point of commonality, and the manifestation of universality in religion, even though the adherents of the World Religions have quite different specific religious worldviews.

In *Relationship Morality* James Kellenberger explains the moral point of view by arguing that "the ultimate grounding of obligation, and finally of all morality, is a single but universal relationship between each and all," suggesting that it is a realization of this "person/person relationship" to others which creates "a sense of duty grounded in a recognition of the intrinsic worth of persons."[16] Since religion supervenes on morality, to be genuinely religious is to realize the person/person relationship Kellenberger identifies, but with the added or supervening dimension of the realization of a single universal relationship both among all persons as spirits and with the Transcendent. I call this universal religious relationship a "spirit–spirit" relationship.

Clearly, this universal religious relationship is particularized in different ways for different people. For each person has a unique set of personal relations and, assuming that there is a Transcendent, each person has a unique relation to the Transcendent. But apart from these differences, to take the religious point of view is to direct one's life – through prayer and meditation, creed and text, ritual and social practice – toward a felt Transcendent – whether Allah, or Shiva, or YHWH, or God, or Ahura Mazda, or Akal Purakh, or the Tao, or the Dharmakaya – and by so doing, to treat other persons as spiritual beings. This means that one treats others as having the same spiritual value as oneself, as being on the same spiritual quest as oneself and with the same potential for salvation or liberation. As Buber says in monotheistic terms, "as soon as we touch a You we are touched by a breath of eternal life...the lines of relationships intersect in the Eternal You [God]."[17]

This analysis of the religious point of view in terms of interpersonal relationships obviously fits a personalistic conception of the Transcendent such as Buber's. But even those traditions with the least personal view of the Transcendent – such as Sri Lankan Theravada Buddhism and Japanese Rinzai Zen Buddhism – are religious precisely in that they do treat all persons as spirit, in the sense of potentially achieving liberation (even if this is as *anatman*), and hence they enjoin the spirit–spirit relationality of compassion for all living things. So while the moral point of view may not be logically connected to the religious point of view, the religious point of view is not only connected to but can serve as a fundamental ground for the moral life. For the religious person, the religious point of view motivates and enhances morality and brings an added (religious) significance to the moral life, the dimension of spirit–spirit relationality.

Further reading

INTRODUCTORY

Buber, Martin. *I and Thou*. Walter Kaufmann, trans. New York, Charles Scribner's Sons, 1970

Chapple, Christopher Key. *Nonviolence to Animals, Earth, and Self in Asian Traditions*. New York, State University Press of New York, 1993

Deutsch, Eliot. *The Bhagavad Gita: Translated, with Introduction and Critical Essays*. New York, University Press of America, 1968

Mascaro, Juan, trans. *The Dhammapada*. London, Penguin Books, 1973

Mill, John Stuart. *Utilitarianism*. George Sher, ed. Indianapolis, Hackett Publishing, 1979

Plato. *Euthyphro*. Benjamin Jowett, trans. New York, Bobbs-Merrill Company, 1956

Tzu, Lao. *Tao Te Ching*. John Oman, trans. London, Penguin, 1963

IN-DEPTH

Baier, Kurt. *The Moral Point of View*. New York, Cornell University, 1958

Byrne, Peter. *The Philosophical and Theological Foundations of Ethics*. London, Macmillan, 1999

Kant, Immanuel. *Kant's Theory of Ethics*, trans. T. K. Abbott. London, Longman, Green and Co., 1879

Kellenberger, James. *Relationship Morality*. Pennsylvania, Pennsylvania State University Press, 1995

MacIntyre, Alasdair. *After Virtue*. Notre Dame, University of Notre Dame Press, 1984

Porter, Jean. *Moral Action and Christian Ethics*. Cambridge, Cambridge University Press, 1995

Rawls, John. *A Theory of Justice*. Cambridge, Harvard University Press, 1971

Tierney, Nathan L. *Imagination and Ethical Ideals*. New York, State University of New York Press, 1994

12 PRUDENTIAL ARGUMENTS FOR RELIGIOUS BELIEF

If we are able to cultivate a mind benefiting other sentient beings, we will automatically accumulate great merit, the source of peace and happiness. Once we commit ourselves to fulfilling the purposes of other sentient beings, our own purposes will be fulfilled by the way. Therefore, I often tell people that if they want the best for themselves, they should work to benefit other people. Those people who ignore the welfare of other sentient beings and think only of themselves are trying to fulfill their wishes in a very foolish way.[1]

His Holiness Tenzin Gyatso, The Fourteenth Dalai Lama

We have assessed various metaphysical arguments for God's existence (chapters 4 and 5) as well as certain axiological arguments from morality to God's existence (chapter 11). In chapter 14 we will return to axiological arguments when we address love and devotion. Here we take up a very different sort of argument, namely prudential arguments. These are not arguments for the existence of God or of a Transcendent, for it is not a matter of prudence whether something is true or probable. Rather, these are arguments supporting the prudence of *belief* in God or a Transcendent; they are arguments suggesting that it is in the self-interest of humans to hold religious beliefs.

In *The Future of An Illusion*, Sigmund Freud argues (see chapter 10) that religious belief – at least belief in God – exacts an unacceptably high price in terms of restrictions on human freedom. Freud argues that religion is mere false hope, a "wish-fulfillment," which tells us nothing about the nature of reality. Since religion tells us nothing about reality, yet restricts human freedom, he concludes that it should be abandoned as too costly. We have seen that Freud's argument in support of this conclusion suffers from a number of logical fallacies. But another possible rejoinder to Freud is that religious belief is actually utilitarian, well serving human interest, and offering a considerable payoff which justifies its price.

PASCAL'S WAGER

One of the most famous arguments which attempts to support religious belief on the basis of self-interest is Pascal's Wager. Blaise Pascal (1623–1662) was a French mathematician, philosopher, and dedicated Roman Catholic. Like his older contemporary René Descartes, Pascal employed mathematical considerations to support religious belief, but where Descartes offered a deductive version of the ontological argument for God's existence, Pascal did not think that God's existence could be proven:

> If there is a God, he is infinitely beyond our comprehension, since, having neither parts nor limits, he bears no relation to ourselves. We are therefore incapable of knowing either what he is, or if he is...Who will then blame the Christians for being unable to provide a rational basis for their belief...It is by lack of proof that they do not lack sense.[2]

But much like Descartes, Pascal does have faith in the power of human reason and so in his *Pensées* goes on to suggest that religious belief can still be approached "according to natural lights." That is, even in the face of no proof of God's existence, rather than appealing to revelation or religious authority, he sets out to see what our natural human reasoning faculties can determine.

Assuming that arguments not only do not but could not prove God's existence, Pascal suggests that we should treat the situation as if what we are considering is a wager or a bet. We are trying to determine which side of the question of belief in God it is most rational to choose as the side, so to speak, to put our money on. Now you might suppose that you do not need to become engaged in this question. After all, there are many questions in life where, if we do not have sufficient evidence, what we normally do if we are rational is to suspend our judgment about the answers to those questions, perhaps waiting for future, clearer evidence. But Pascal suggests that the question of belief in God does not work that way. He says, "you have to wager. It is not up to you,

you are already committed. Which then will you choose?"[3] What Pascal means by "it is not up to you, you are already committed" is that if you do not choose – whether consciously or unconsciously – whether or not to believe in God, this has the same effect as choosing not to believe in God. There are those who believe in God, and there are those who do not believe – either because they consciously disbelieve or because they have not come to believe in God. This exhausts all the possibilities. So whether we like it or not, we in effect wager for one side or the other of belief in God.

Pascal then continues in the *Pensées* with the main argument for the wager:

> You have two things to lose: the truth and the good, and two things to stake: your reason and will, your knowledge and beatitude; and your nature has two things to avoid: error and wretchedness...But here there is an infinitely happy infinity of life to be won, one chance of winning against a finite number of chances of losing, and what you are staking is finite. That removes all choice: wherever there is infinity and where there is no infinity of chances of losing against one of winning, there is no scope of wavering, you have to chance everything.[4]

In effect what Pascal attempts to argue is this: we do not have any real proof that God exists or does not exist. Now, a probability is the likelihood that something may occur based on available knowledge. Hence regarding the question of God's existence, there is a fifty percent probability that God exists and a fifty percent probability that God does not exist. And the question of whether or not one should believe that God does exist will be much like any question of wagering, say at a racetrack. In a wager of this sort, we must consider two factors: (1) what is the chance that a particular horse will win; and (2) how much money can be made from betting on that particular horse. The difference is that in this case God is the only "horse" in the race. Or, to put the analogy in another way, suppose a one-horse race has been advertised and the only question facing you is whether to bet on the one horse which is supposed to be in the race. In effect the question is whether to bet that there is an actual horse and that the supposed race that has been advertised is not a fraud. With only one possible horse in the race, all one needs to consider in order to wager rationally is (1) the probability that the purported horse is an actual horse and (2) the size of the payoff if there is a horse versus what will be lost if there is no horse.

---◆---

SCHEMATIC OF PASCAL'S WAGER

1. We should (it is prudent to) act in our self-interest.
2. It is in our self-interest to know the truth and achieve the good.
3. If God exists, and
   a. One does believe that God exists, one has the opportunity for an infinite gain.
   b. One does not believe that God exists, one risks an infinite loss.
4. If God does not exist, and
   a. One believes that God exists, one will suffer a finite loss.
   b. One does not believe that God exists, one will achieve a finite gain.
5. It is equally probable (50%) that God exists as that God does not exist.
6. Therefore, one should (it is prudent) believe in God.

---◆---

One way to formalize Pascal's line of reasoning is given in the schematic above. Pascal's argument is clearly not going to be persuasive if we think that it is always wrong to act in our self-interest. Assuming then that premise 1 is acceptable, premises 3 and 4 are simply the four alternative combinations of the proposition that God exists and the proposition that God does not exist together with the proposition that one believes that God exists and the proposition that one does not believe, and the payoff to the believer or the disbeliever which is assigned to each alternative. Pascal's claim is that if we follow his argument, believing all of his premises, then there is only one rational conclusion, namely that we would not be prudent, and so we would not be rational, if we do not then believe in God.

How does Pascal assign the payoffs for the believer versus the disbeliever in premises 3 and 4? His reasoning follows that of the Augustinian theodicy (see page 104). If God exists and we do not believe in God, we risk an infinite loss: i.e. damnation (or lack of salvation), an eternally negative state. But if God exists and we do believe, then we have the opportunity for an infinite gain: i.e. salvation or beatitude. The other alternative is that God does not exist. In that case, if we believe that God does exist, then we are going to suffer a finite loss since we both hold a false belief and waste time in this life in religious ritual, etc. However, if God does not exist and we are atheists, then we will receive a finite gain: we will believe the truth in this life (and not waste our time and energy). In summary, if we consider just the payoffs, on the side of disbelief we have the possibility of an infinite loss counterbalanced by the possibility of only a finite gain, while on the side of belief we have the possibility of an infinite gain counterbalanced by the possibility of only a finite loss. Since the likelihood of our beliefs being true is equal all the way around (premise 5), anyone acting in his or her self-interest would be irrational if he or she did not believe in God.

On Pascal's wager, virtually all the weight of potential loss is on the side of disbelief, and virtually all the weight of potential gain is on the side of belief. If we are prudent and smart, we will choose to wager on the side with everything to gain and little to lose. In a certain respect, it is like standing on a set of railroad tracks and thinking we might hear the sounds of a train approaching from around the bend. We wonder if we should continue to stand on the tracks. We cannot see the train. If we are prudent, we will get off the tracks. It is possible, of course, that the apparent train noises are not noises from a real train; but then again, what if they are? The potential loss of staying on the tracks is rather large, and the potential gain (continuing one's life) if we exit the tracks is rather large. So if we are prudent, we will not stand on the tracks. If we are not so smart, we will continue to stand on the tracks, either wondering whether there is a train (agnosticism) or believing that there is no train (atheism).

Of course, this is not the end of the matter. Suppose Pascal convinces his readers that he is right. Even then, all he has presented thus far is an argument for the rationality of belief. The question still remains how the reader will then move beyond just believing that he or she *should* believe, and actually come to believe in God. Pascal addresses this issue:

> Realize that your inability to believe, since reason urges you to do so and yet you cannot, arises from your passions. So concentrate not on convincing yourself by increasing the number of proofs of God but on diminishing your passions. You want to find faith and you do not know the way? You want to cure yourself of unbelief and you ask for the remedies? Learn from those who have been bound like you, and who now wager all they have...Follow the way by which they began: by behaving just as if they believed, taking holy water, having masses said, etc. That will make you believe quite naturally, and according to your animal reactions.[5]

The way to come to believe in God, Pascal says, is to cultivate religious attitudes and habits of action: the way to come to believe is to become part of the community of believers.

RELIGION AS A LIVE OPTION

Unfortunately there are three salient problems with Pascal's argument: for those who are religious skeptics, it will not achieve its purpose; for those with a global outlook, it will not achieve its purpose, since it fails to account for similar arguments with similar purposes in other religions; and it has the wrong purpose. With regard to the first problem, here is the American philosopher William James's response to Pascal in James's essay "The Will to Believe":

> As well might the Mahdi write to us, saying, "I am the Expected One whom God has created in his effulgence. You shall be infinitely happy if you confess me; otherwise you shall be cut off from the light of the sun. Weigh, then, your infinite gain if I am genuine against your finite sacrifice if I am not!" His logic would be that of Pascal; but he would vainly use it on us, for the hypothesis he offers us is dead. No tendency to act on it exists in us to any degree.[6]

James uses this example of the lack of immediate appeal of Islamic messianic ideas for a Christian audience (the reverse would be true for committed Muslims regarding Christian messianic ideas) as a paradigmatic example of a "dead option." If we have a choice between options, those options which we take seriously as something we might actually act on are live options, those which we do not seriously consider as possible courses of action are dead. Pascal's wager offers a dead option – belief in God – for those indisposed to Christian belief; hence, it is unlikely to move those who do not already have faith in the Christian God, particularly as God is understood in the Augustinian theodicy. This restricts the potential value of Pascal's argument to its use as an apologetic device which might convince those who are disposed to believe in God but have some hesitation about the rationality of doing so. But can Pascal's argument even succeed as this sort of apologetic in our global world?

KARMA AND SAMSARA

This brings us to the second problem with Pascal's argument. Consider Pascal's statement in the *Pensées* that:

> Alone free from error and vice, the right to teach and correct men belongs only to the Christian religion...No other religion has held that we should hate ourselves. No other religion can therefore please those who hate

themselves and who are looking for a being who can be loved whole-heartedly. And they, if they had never heard of the religion of a humil-iated God, would embrace it at once.[7]

As his statement indicates, Pascal is an Exclusivist (see chapter 2). Unfortunately for his reasons supporting an exclusivist Christianity, other World Religions such as both Hinduism and Buddhism – two World Religions he was not aware of – also hold that we should "hate ourselves," in the sense of rejecting our illusory selves. Thus, founda-tional to the Hindu tradition are such texts as we find in the *Maitri Upanishad*:

> In thinking "This is I" and "That is mine," he binds himself with his self, as does a bird with a snare.[8]

Likewise, in the Mahayana Buddhist tradition we find among the best-known aphorisms, collected in the *Dhammapada*, this saying:

> If a man should conquer in battle a thousand and a thousand more, and another man should conquer himself, his would be the greater victory, because the greatest of victories is the victory over oneself.[9]

The Christian idea that humans are made in the image of God, which Pascal would endorse, parallels the Hindu idea of a pure inner atman, which either reflects or is Brahman, and for which we must forsake the false self of *maya*, while Buddhism enjoins its followers to recognize *anatman*, the no-self, as the reality underlying the illusory self, the self of *maya*, which must be conquered.

Bhakti forms of Hinduism in particular (see chapter 4) accord pre-cisely with the vision of true religion which Pascal thinks only applies to Christianity, when he says it is pleasing to "those who hate them-selves and who are looking for a being who can be loved wholeheart-edly." Of course, this same vision is also expressed in Judaism as well as Islam (which Pascal expressly opposes), particularly the self-abne-gating Sufi tradition of love of God. But even Buddhism, while not offer-ing a God to love, if anything offers an even stronger case than Christianity does for what Pascal unfortunately terms "self-hate." Quoting again from the *Dhammapada*:

> If a man watches not for Nirvana, his cravings grow like a creeper and he jumps from death to death like a monkey in the forest from one tree without fruit to another.

It is painful to leave the world; it is painful to be in the world; and it is painful to be alone amongst the many. The long road of transmigration is a road of pain for the traveler: let him rest by the road and be free.[10]

Indeed, along the lines of the Buddhist reasoning which we discussed in chapter 3 as the Argument from Impermanence, we can construct an argument which parallels Pascal's Wager but entails adherence to the Eightfold Path, not to the will of God. That reasoning is presented as a Prudential Argument for the Eightfold Path below. Of course this line of reasoning presents a dead option to Christians. What this shows is that Pascal's Wager – and parallel arguments in other traditions such as this hypothetical Prudential Argument for the Eightfold Path – are only convincing if the basic religious assumptions they appeal to are convincing to the hearer, and are only likely to appear strong if the hearer is not aware that other religious traditions can mount parallel exclusivist arguments for the prudential value of holding their views.

One has to accept the Augustinian sort of God Pascal assumes for premises 3 and 4 for the Wager to be accepted; one has to accept the assumption of karmic law in premises 3 and 4 of the Prudential

---

◆

A PRUDENTIAL ARGUMENT FOR THE EIGHTFOLD PATH

1. We should (it is prudent to) act so as to achieve release from *samsara*.
2. We can avoid the suffering of *samsara*, which is caused by *avidya* and the karmic law, if we achieve great merit and wisdom.
3. If the Eightfold Path is efficacious for release from *samsara*, and
   a. One follows the Eightfold Path, great merit and wisdom will be gained.
   b. One does not follow the Eightfold Path, an indefinitely large loss of merit and wisdom is risked.
4. If the Eightfold Path is not efficacious for release from *samsara*, and
   a. One follows the Eightfold Path, one will suffer a finite loss in this life.
   b. One does not follow the Eightfold Path, one will achieve a finite gain in this life.
5. Apart from one's own experience of the Eightfold Path, it is equally probable (50%) that the Eightfold Path is efficacious as that the Eightfold Path is not efficacious.
6. Therefore, it is prudent to follow the Eightfold Path.

◆

Argument for the Eightfold Path for that argument to be accepted. But further, any prudential argument for belief from the perspective of any religious tradition will not only reach an impasse with those for whom the religion in question is not a live option, it will have far less weight for those inclined to believe if they are sufficiently aware of the religious alternatives among the World Religions. For the real question faced by the prudent in our global world is not "either God or not God," but "either God or Brahman or Nirvana, etc. versus no Transcendent." To go back to our earlier analogy, one has to think that there are no trucks on the highway, despite the sounds of traffic, to think that stepping off the railroad tracks onto the highway to avoid the apparently oncoming train is the only option that has a huge potential payoff. One has to be unaware of alternatives among the World Religions to think that the choice for belief vis-à-vis the Transcendent could only be an either/or of belief in God.

IS RELIGION COST-EFFECTIVE?

However, most devastating for prudential arguments is a third problem that we can see with Pascal's Wager. This problem is exposed in William James's critique of Pascal's whole approach:

> You probably feel that when religious faith expresses itself thus, in the language of the gaming-table, it is put to its last trumps. Surely Pascal's own personal belief in masses and holy water had far other springs; and this celebrated page of his is but an argument for others, a last desperate snatch at a weapon against the hardness of the unbelieving heart. We feel that a faith in masses and holy water adopted willfully after such a mechanical calculation would lack the inner soul of faith's reality; and if we were ourselves in the place of the Deity, we should probably take particular pleasure in cutting off believers of this pattern from their infinite reward.[11]

Pascal's Wager is in a double-bind. It will not succeed as an argument for those outside the faith who do not share its basic assumptions, failing as "a last desperate snatch at a weapon against the unbelieving heart." And for the person who is already inclined to have faith in God, this desperate appeal to self-interest – the "last trumps" of the theological hand – is simply misplaced.

So why be religious? The reason cannot be for the payoff, if for no other reason than that concern for the payoff itself sullies one's ostensibly religious motives. This is reminiscent of the story of the ring of Gyges the Hydan which Plato uses in the *Republic* (II 359a–360b) to show that the reason to be moral cannot be concern for the payoff. Gyges finds a ring that, when the embossing is turned to the inside of the wearer's finger, turns the wearer invisible. In the ancient story, Gyges uses the ring to kill the king, sleep with the Queen, and inherit the kingdom. The question Plato poses is whether it is better to be like Gyges and act immorally, if one will not be caught and the payoffs are large, or better to be moral.

Plato concludes that "justice in itself is the best thing for the soul itself, and that the soul ought to do justice whether it possess the ring of Gyges or not."[12] However, the payoffs of the just life cannot simply be compared to the payoffs of the unjust life, as if the former would then win our allegiance. Rather, the just life (like the religious life) cannot even be understood from the point of view of a materialistic life. This is illustrated in Plato's dialogue *Apology* when Socrates faces death at the hands of the Athenians for disrupting the peace:

> If I say that this would be disobedience to God, and that is why I cannot "mind my own business," you will not believe that I am serious. If on the other hand I tell you that to let no day pass without discussing goodness and all the other subjects about which you hear me talking that a man can do, and that life without this sort of examination is not worth living, you will be even less inclined to believe me.[13]

The reason Plato gives in the *Republic* for how hard it is to see the value of the just life is this:

> To know its true nature we must view it not marred by communion with the body and other miseries as we now contemplate it, but consider adequately in the light of reason what it is when it is purified...it resembles that of the sea god Glaucus whose first nature can hardly be made out by those who catch glimpses of him, because the original members of his body are broken off and mutilated and crushed and in every way marred by the waves, and other parts have attached themselves to him, accretions of shells and seaweed and rocks, so that he is more like any wild creature than what he was by nature – even such, I say, is our vision of the soul marred by countless evils.[14]

Plato's metaphor of the obscuring accretions on the sea god Glaucus is not unlike the ancient Jain view of *karma*, where bad *karma* literally blocks clear moral and religious perceptions:

> The Jaina tradition presents a highly technical interpretation of *karma*, considering it to be a material, sticky, colorful substance, composed of atoms, that adheres to the life force and prevents ascent to the *siddha loka*, the world occupied by the liberated ones. This *karma* is attracted to the *jiva* by acts of violence, and persons who have committed repeated acts of violence are said to be shrouded in a cloud of blackish matter... "A hungry person with the most negative black-*lesya karma* uproots and kills an entire tree to obtain a few mangoes. The person of blue *karma* fells the tree by chopping the trunk, again merely to gain a handful of fruits. Fraught with grey *karma*, a third person spares the trunk but cuts off the major limbs of the tree. The one with orangish-red *karma* carelessly and needlessly lops off several branches to reach the mangoes. The fifth, exhibiting white *karma*, 'merely picks up the ripe fruit that has dropped to the foot of the tree.'"[15]

In sum, even if the religious and/or moral life is cost-effective and ultimately does have a substantial payoff, the nonreligious and the nonmoral could not see that this was so.

However, once clarity of thought is achieved – by means of the "examined life" for Socrates, the life of *ahimsa* in Jainism, the overcoming of *avidya* through wisdom in Buddhism, etc. – then not only is a different state of existence achieved, but the World Religions claim that the previous state of suffering on account of evil no longer applies. As the *Dhammapada* puts it:

> As a man who has no wound on his hand cannot be hurt by the poison he may carry in his hand, since poison hurts not where there is no wound, the man who has no evil cannot be hurt by evil.[16]

This Mahayana Buddhist perspective of the *Dhammapada* is almost precisely echoed by the Axial Age Greek philosopher Socrates:

> Nothing can harm a good man either in life or after death, and his fortunes are not a matter of indifference to the gods.[17]

If the religious life is not comparable to the materialistic life, then the proper motive for the religious life could not be that one wants to achieve a large payoff relative to what one would otherwise achieve materialistically. The proper motive for the religious life must be that one wants to be a certain sort of person, one who takes the religious point of view (see chapter 11). No argument can be given either for the universality of, or the obligation to take, the religious point of view.[18] Rather, the recognition of the religious point of view and of the significance of relationality would be a matter of intuition.[19] For as we shall see in the next two chapters, one either does or does not recognize the wisdom of the sort of perspective enunciated in the *Dhammapada*:

> Hold not a sin of little worth, thinking "this is little to me". The falling drops of water will in time fill a water-jar. Even so the foolish man becomes full of evil, although he gather it little by little.[20]

Further reading

Juan Mascaro, trans. *Dhammapada*. London, Penguin, 1973

Deutsch, Eliot, trans. *Bhagavad Gita: Translated, with Introduction and Critical Essays*. New York, University of America Press, 1968

H.H. Dalai Lama. *The Joy of Living and Dying in Peace*. London, Thorsons, 1997

James, William. "The Will to Believe" in *Essays on Faith and Morals*. Massachusetts, Meridian, 1911

Pascal, Blaise. *Pensées*. A.J. Krailsheimer, trans. London, Penguin Books, 1966

Plato. *Apology*. Edith Hamilton and Huntington Cairns, eds. Princeton, Princeton University Press, 1961

13 FAITH AND JUSTIFIED BELIEVERS

> Teach me to seek thee, and reveal thyself to me, when I seek thee, for
> I cannot seek thee except thou teach me, or find thee, except thou reveal
> thyself. Let me seek thee in longing, let me long for thee in seeking, and
> find thee in love and love thee in finding...for I do not seek to under-
> stand that I may believe, but I believe in order to understand.[1]
>
> St. Anselm (1033–1109)

We have repeatedly seen, whether in our discussion of attempted arguments for the existence of the Transcendent, or in the analysis of Kant's
defense of rational theology, or even in the failure of arguments mar-
shalled against religious belief on the basis of science, that reason is
insufficient in itself to support religious belief. On the other hand, religious faith is irrational if reason is rejected altogether. What, then, is
the relationship between religious faith and reason, and can the religious
person be justified in his or her faith?

One way to assess belief is on the basis of the likelihood that a belief
is itself true, given the means by which it was acquired. Sudden hunches
and desperate guesses are a weak basis for belief, while conclusions
drawn from carefully controlled experiments are epistemically strong.
This is because carefully controlled experiments are one form of belief-
forming procedure (or doxastic practice) which is generally favorable
for producing true beliefs. So the carefully controlled experiment justifies the beliefs acquired. Another way to assess belief is in terms of
whether the person who holds a belief is justified in holding that belief.
Someone who makes a wild guess at the answer to a problem in

chemistry is not justified (even if he is right), and the careful, painstaking chemist is justified (even if she is mistaken) in her conclusions.

Another example which applies to the same person might also help draw the contrast between these two senses of justification, the justification of the process by which beliefs are acquired versus the justification of the person acquiring the beliefs. If a young child is using a video game, the child's belief that there are real dragons in front of him is not epistemically justified since a fantasy setting is not an appropriate context for reliably acquiring true beliefs. But the *child* may be justified in believing that there are dragons, for the child has no reasons not to trust what otherwise are the reliable sources of knowledge he typically uses, such as his parents' encouragement, his perceptions, etc.

In earlier chapters we focused largely on attempts to justify religious beliefs. In this chapter we will primarily focus not on what would make the beliefs of the religious person justified, but what would make the religious *person* justified in his or her religious beliefs.

EVIDENTIALISM AND RELIGIOUS BELIEF

Skepticism about religious belief can lead to evidentialism. Evidentialism about religion usually amounts to a demand for evidence, holding that for religious people to be justified, they must acquire their beliefs in a rational manner, and to be rational, they must only acquire beliefs which are supported by evidence. Typically the evidentialist will attack the religious person as being insufficiently justified in his or her beliefs. In order to assess the evidentialist attack, we need to understand on what basis we are justified in holding our ordinary, non-religious beliefs, particularly the kind of belief which is a "basic belief."

A basic belief is a belief which is held immediately and is not based on other beliefs as reasons. A "properly basic belief" is a belief which one can hold as basic without violating any fundamental principles of knowledge. Typical properly basic beliefs are ordinary perceptual beliefs, memory beliefs, and beliefs ascribing mental states to other persons. So for instance, immediately coming to believe that the face in front of you is your wife's face, or immediately coming to believe that she dislikes the meal you just prepared as she wrinkles her nose, or immediately remembering that you forgot to add any salt, is to form properly basic beliefs. For being justified in believing that you see your wife's face, that she is displeased, or that you forgot to add salt does not depend on having *other* beliefs as reasons, such as believing that the nose you are looking at is your wife's, or that a wrinkled nose is more often than not a sign of displeasure, or that the absence of a salt cellar on the stove indicates your forgetfulness. Rather, these beliefs are justified because they are formed under the proper circumstances using reliable doxastic practices. The belief-forming practices in question, such as perception and memory, are "reliable" in the sense that they are innocent until proven guilty.

In the same manner, a religious person can properly believe, without inferring this from other beliefs as reasons, that "God should be thanked," or "Krishna loves me," or "all is Brahman." For a religious person often comes to hold these beliefs not on the basis of evidence or inference, but immediately. The religious person might be standing at the edge of the ocean, or hearing sacred music, or involved in quiet meditation. The experience of listening to the devotional songs of the Hindu woman saint Mirabai, or feeling the (putative) presence of Krishna in temple *darshan*, or feeling the (putative) presence of God during prayer or at the seashore, could serve as grounds for belief about the Transcendent and the Transcendent's relation to the world. And these doxastic practices are reliable (innocent) insofar as they have not been proven unreliable (guilty).

Thus, evidentialism does not show that the religious believer is unjustified. Moreover, remember Kant's defense of rational religion as alone sufficient to justify religious belief (chapter 9). For Kant the other side of this is that "it is impossible for revealed religion to provide sufficient epistemic justification for religious truth-claims" (premise 2 of the argument on page 154). But Kant's own observation that no empirical evidence could ever be sufficient to justify belief in God as the supremely perfect being turns out to be beside the point. Evidence, whether theoretical or empirical, is not needed to justify basic beliefs. If religious beliefs can be basic beliefs, then they can be properly basic beliefs appropriately grounded in the human experience of the revelation or manifestation of the Transcendent. Indeed if religious commitment is to be justified at all, it must be at least in part justified on the grounds of the self-revelation or manifestation of the Transcendent. For religious faith is the ultimate commitment that one has indeed confronted the Transcendent in the religious experience of the revelation or manifestation of the Transcendent. Consequently, contrary to Kant's view, scripture (which conveys fundamental religious experience) and revealed theology could, under the right circumstances, provide sufficient justification for the believer.

WHY RELIGIOUS BELIEFS ARE PROPERLY BASIC

Alvin Plantinga is a prominent proponent of the view that belief in God is basic for the believer:

> The mature believer, the mature theist, does not typically accept belief in God tentatively, or hypothetically, or until something better comes along. Nor, I think, does he accept it as a conclusion from other things he believes; he accepts it as basic, as a part of the foundations of his noetic structure. The mature theist *commits* himself to belief in God; this means that he accepts belief in God as basic.[2]

But as Plantinga himself acknowledges, different people will have quite different beliefs which they consider properly basic:

> there is no reason to assume in advance that everyone will agree on the examples. The Christian will of course suppose that belief in God is entirely proper and rational; if he doesn't accept this belief on the basis of other propositions, he will conclude that it is basic for him and quite properly so. Followers of Bertrand Russell and Madelyn Murray O'Hare may disagree, but...the Christian community is responsible to *its* set of examples, not to theirs.[3]

Thus, a belief is properly basic only for some individuals or community of individuals, which is to say that a belief is only properly basic relative to some particular worldview. To use William James's way of putting this point (see page 197), a belief must represent a live option before it can be acquired. A person cannot suddenly come to believe in God or suddenly become a Buddhist if she has no prior conception of God or of the Buddhist Middle Way, if belief in God or acceptance of the Four Noble Truths is not already a real option for her which could cohere with her current worldview. Consequently, atheistic beliefs, whether they are religious like Advaita Vedanta and Buddhism or secular, have the same *prima facie* claim to being properly basic *vis-à-vis* the relevant atheistic worldviews, as theistic beliefs have a *prima facie* claim to being properly basic relative to the worldview which the theist holds.

Religious beliefs could be properly basic, but what would actually make religious beliefs properly basic and the religious person justified in his or her beliefs? One approach to this question is to compare experiential religious beliefs to common perceptual beliefs since we have a better understanding of what can make the latter properly basic. A major proponent of this approach has been William Alston. Alston argues that we are *prima facie* justified in our perceptual beliefs insofar as we have no adequate reason for supposing that beliefs formed on the basis of our sense perception are unreliable. Alston then argues that religious beliefs about God, formed on the basis of religious experience, are similarly justified unless there is sufficient reason to believe otherwise.[4] An obvious objection to this suggested comparison is that religious experiences appear to vary far more than perceptual beliefs among similarly placed observers. Do we not regard our perceptual beliefs as reliable because – unlike religious experience – we all see, hear, and smell the same things?

But consider scientific beliefs, which might appear to be the most reliably invariant of our perceptual beliefs. In *The Structure of Scientific Revolutions* Thomas Kuhn builds a persuasive case that scientists with incompatible worldviews literally "live in different worlds."[5] On Kuhn's account, different scientific views do not just result in different interpretations of the same data available to all inquirers. Rather, differing theories actually result in different observational data. Galileans and Copernicans, Newtonians and quantum physicists, and pre- and post-Freudian psychologists do not see the same world differently; instead they see different worlds of phenomena. As the philosopher of science Norwood Hanson puts it, seeing is "theory laden" and the scientific observation of an entity X is "shaped by prior knowledge of X."[6]

The same effect of the worldview of the scientific perceiver on the data of experience can be seen in cases of common perception. One person hears a classic Scottish tune played on the bagpipe; another hears an obnoxious whining sound. One smells a fine Cuban Cohiba cigar; another smells a health hazard. One person savors Australian lamb and mint sauce; another pushes the dead, cooked animal away in vegan disgust. One person sees an admirably effective political leader; another sees the vile mustached face of Adolf Hitler. What we perceive is inextricably determined, in part, by the worldviews we bring to our experiences. And this is not different in kind from differences in religious perceptions. An uneducated Islamic or Christian fundamentalist who stepped off a plane in Kyoto, Japan, could not perceive the religious significance which the Zen priest would see there. And even among those from the same culture, four-year-olds native to Kyoto do not see the same world that native forty-year-olds see in Kyoto.

In general, to experience X is to experience X *as* something Y, where Y is a conceptualization determined by one's worldview. This applies whether what one is experiencing is a religious or a non-religious state of affairs.[7] This is why the theist but not the naturalist might well experience nature as the creation of God, an experience which could then ground the basic belief that "God created all this." And this is why the characteristics of particular religious experiences are not universal; for worldviews differ profoundly across traditions. But even people in the same religious tradition often have quite different religious experiences, for worldviews differ considerably even within the same religious tradition. This is why the monotheistic Ramanuja and not the monist Shankara might experience the world as God's body, an experience which could then properly ground Ramanuja's Vishishtadvaita basic beliefs (see chapter 4).

Now it might also be objected that while any observer can normally check the perceptual claims of another person, this is not generally true of the experiential claims of religion – and even when experiential religious claims can be checked, the World Religions assert that this is only possible if one understands those religious experiences from the perspective of the tradition in question. So to check, for example, a monotheist's experiential claims effectively, one would need at least to entertain theistic assumptions about how God might be manifesting Godself. And such a checking procedure, the objection goes, is circular. However, this circularity does not tell against the justification of the religious person.

The truth-claims of every doxastic practice can only be assessed by assuming the basic reliability of the practice. Thus you can only check the reliability of any of your particular perceptual beliefs by checking them against other perceptual beliefs, thereby assuming the general reliability of your perceptual doxastic practice. Even a doxastic practice like theoretical physics cannot be checked only on the basis of other doxastic practices such as sense perception. Phenomena postulated by theoretical physics – e.g. black holes, the weak and strong atomic forces, the Big Bang, or cosmic strings – can only be checked on the basis of the assumed reliability of both the more general theories of physics in which these specific theoretical entities are embedded, and the assumed reliability of the theorized relationship between perception and the theories in use. Since different theories result in different observational data, there is no neutral perceptual data against which to check the reliability of a scientific theory or to check the objectivity of the postulation of a scientific entity.

Even the idea that the reliability of our beliefs should be assessed in terms of what normal observers would perceive is a criterion for reliability which is internal to our worldviews. Individual beliefs derive their justification from the doxastic practice in which they are embedded. A person is justified in conforming to a doxastic practice, in turn, if he or she has no adequate reasons for thinking that this belief-forming practice is unreliable, which is in part to say if it conforms to what normal observers would experience. But normal observers are judged normal relative to the worldview in question, so it is those who hold the worldview who decide whether there are any reasons against supposing that the worldview itself incorporates normally acceptable doxastic practices.

Where does this leave us? One is justified in holding religious beliefs as basic beliefs if one has adequate grounds for one's beliefs. Religious experience could serve as grounds for religious beliefs as basic beliefs. But since the adequacy of religious experience as grounds for religious belief is relative to the individual's worldview, the acceptability of the religious worldview itself will determine whether the religious person is epistemically justified. This brings us to the nature of faith.

FAITH COMMITMENTS, WORLDVIEWS, AND CONVERSION

At the outset we must distinguish between *faith that*, where faith is basically equivalent to the cognitive state of belief, and *faith in*, which is roughly equivalent to commitment or trust. These are not two different types of faith, but rather two aspects of faith. The more fundamental notion of faith, *faith in*, denotes a dispositional state of a person. *Faith in* is inclusive of *faith that*. For instance, to have *faith in* God is to be in a certain dispositional state – *viz.* to be disposed, under the right conditions, to act in certain ways, such as worshipping or performing a superogatory moral act; to acquire and/or intensify certain attitudes, such as selflessly loving one's fellow creatures or being reverent toward God; and to acquire certain sorts of beliefs (*faith that*) about God. Collectively, these dispositions to act, to acquire attitudes, and to acquire beliefs spring from a fundamental disposition to experience the world in a certain way. The fundamental religious disposition of having *faith in* a Transcendent is the disposition to experience the world in terms of the Transcendent, to consistently and deeply experience the world as under the providence of or as a manifestation of, the Transcendent.

Paul Tillich famously captured the sense that *faith in* involves the whole person in a complex dispositional state of commitment which is manifested in various actions, attitudes, and beliefs, with the notion of "ultimate concern."[8] Faith understood as ultimate concern – the most fundamental way one experiences the world – applies to all the World Religions. Religious *faith in* can be personalistic – a faith in Allah or Ramanuja's Vishishtadvaita God – or it can be non-personal, such as Shankara's Advaitist faith in Brahman or Buddhist faith in the way of *Dharma*. *Faith in* essentially involves commitment to a worldview. Our faith commitment to our worldview determines how we will experience and understand the world, which in turn reinforces our worldview through the acquisition of new beliefs and concepts. And our commitment to our worldview is justified when our adherence is rewarded and we have no good reason to abandon our faith. Faith is innocent until proven guilty.

We first form our worldview on trust within the social context of our childhood. We may subsequently become attracted by a new worldview in the light of evidence which is awkward or cannot be easily accounted for on our present worldview. But if we shift our faith commitment to a new worldview, as happens when a person undergoes a conversion experience, it is only after that change of faith commitment that we seek conclusive evidence and argument to support our choice. For when confronted with a conversion issue of which worldview to choose, we face an external question about the acceptability of one worldview against alternative worldviews. These external questions about the acceptability of a new worldview cannot be settled on the basis of "neutral" evidence, for there is no evidence outside of *any* worldviews. Internal evidence is valuable for changing individual beliefs within a worldview, but it cannot provide sufficient grounds for the choice of a worldview. There is no evidence – whether it is Anselm's Ontological Argument for God's existence or the scriptural authority of the *Adi Granth* or of the *Pali Canon* – which is independent of faith commitment to some worldview. As Anselm says in the quote which opened this chapter, "I do not seek to understand that I may believe, but I believe in order to understand. For this also I believe – that unless I believed, I should not understand."

Worldviews themselves are neither true nor false. Questions of truth and falsity, and of what can serve as evidence in support of a belief, are matters internal to a presupposed worldview. It follows that the question of conversion is a matter of faith based on pragmatic considerations – for example, which worldview seems to be the view most helpful for our lives, which best accounts for our experiences, and which offers the most comprehensive resolution of the problems which are most significant to us. Different worldviews handle different problems with different gradations of importance. Buddhism preeminently offers a resolution of the problem of suffering, Christianity offers an explanation of cosmic origins, and Hinduism offers a resolution of the multiplicity of divine incarnation with the ultimate oneness of the Fullness of Being. Conversion to any one of these and other religious worldviews ultimately depends on what value you place on the questions addressed, and possibly answered, by the religious worldview in question.

RELIGION AS A GENUINE OPTION

What justifies the decision to make a faith commitment to a religious worldview? William James notes that "There are two ways of looking at our duty in the matter of opinion...We *must know the truth; and we must avoid error.*"[9] Evidentialism exclusively follows the second principle, insisting that if we are to be justified in our beliefs, we must always avoid error. A rather different attitude is expressed in the first principle, "seek the truth." It can be taken to mean that we are justified in our beliefs or doxastic practices unless we have adequate reasons to cease believing or cease conforming to those practices.

Extreme evidentialism was rejected above. But there are times when we should sometimes adhere to the more cautious evidentialist principle to "avoid error," and other times when it is best to follow the principle to "seek truth." In the sciences as well as in practical, everyday affairs, a wise course of action is to believe things only on sufficient evidence: for example, if the tires on your automobile are rated for 80 mph, it would be unwise to assume they could be driven at 140 mph; if a medical researcher thinks of a new way to remove tumors from the brain, he or she should acquire sufficient evidence about the feasibility of the procedure before recommending it to surgeons. However, there are circumstances when we should follow the invitation to seek truth and engage in a leap of faith without prior evidence of the probable outcome. In William James's terminology, this is the rational course of action when we are faced with a "genuine option."

A genuine option is a choice between alternative views which is (1) live; (2) forced on us; (3) momentous; (4) cannot be decided on the basis of evidence or argument; and (5) potentially self-verifying.[10] We have already noted that we can only make real choices between options which are live for us (1). And when possible, we should try to make choices among alternative views on the basis of evidence or argument (4). However, if we have insufficient evidence to decide a live choice, yet the choice is forced upon us (2), and if the choice has momentous consequences (3), then if we are inclined toward one side and our choosing of that side would potentially verify the correctness of the momentous choice, we will be rational to choose that side on faith. Regarding religion, this means that it is rational to engage in a leap of faith if one believes that there is some reasonable probability that this momentous choice will turn out to be correct.

The choice of a religious worldview will be a genuine option for those for whom it is a live option, for it is a momentous choice, and one either commits to a religious way of life, or one does not (so the choice is forced). Religious belief and the resultant religious life makes possible the verification of certain religious expectations which could not otherwise be verified. Accordingly, a leap of religious faith becomes a rational procedure if one expects that by so doing one is more likely to come to a satisfactory understanding of reality and the meaning of life, than if one does not act as if the religious worldview(s) in question were true. Or putting this in terms of basic beliefs, when we cannot decide a genuine option on intellectual grounds, the set of basic beliefs we acquire by virtue of coming to believe one side of the option can be a set of properly basic beliefs if they are potentially self-verifying. Since religious beliefs cannot be verified until one has already committed oneself to the appropriate religious faith stance, *faith in* is a pre-condition for substantiating our beliefs. It follows, then, that a person can be justified in his or her initial leap of faith commitment to a religious worldview.

This is not to endorse an unqualified fideism, which thinks of faith as needing no justification and even thinks of faith as acting as the judge of reason. The Danish philosopher Søren Kierkegaard develops just such a radical fideism when he argues that the most essential and valuable feature of religiousness is infinite passion, and that infinite passion requires that it is highly improbable that we know the object of our passion to be true. Kierkegaard concludes, therefore, that what is most essential and valuable in religion requires that the truth of religious belief be highly improbable. But surely the religious belief of a rational faith should seem most probably *true* to the believer. In our global world, a committed person in any of the World Religions needs to take into account World Religions other than his or her own, and it would be irrational not to think that one's own religion is most probably true, given the religious alternatives.

As children we were justified in simply holding the worldviews and doxastic practices inculcated in us by parents, friends, and social and religious authorities. As adults we have become all too well acquainted with the shortcomings of many of our previously held views. We are now in a position to consider alternative views, and in a global world we are in a position to be aware of the pluralism among the World Religions as well as the pluralism within each World Religion. Ultimately we settle on the worldview we do because our beliefs are confirmed by our own experience and the experience of those we trust, and because our worldview gives meaning to our lives and helps us fulfill our most fundamental goals. We retain our monotheistic or naturalistic, Buddhist or Advaita Vedantist worldviews because of internal considerations about what we value and why we value those things. When all is said and done, the only final justification for any faith commitment we may have is our deepest sense of what is valuable tempered by experience and a rational understanding of the real consequences of adhering to those values.

Further reading

INTRODUCTORY

Gilson, Etienne. *Reason and Revelation in the Middle Ages*. New York, Charles Scribner's Sons, 1966
James, William. *Essays on Faith and Morals*. New York, Meridian, 1974
Kierkegaard, Søren. *Fear and Trembling and the Sickness Unto Death*. Walter Lowrie, trans. Princeton, Princeton University Press, 1954

St. Bonaventure. *The Mind's Road to God*. George Boas, trans. Indianapolis, Bobbs-Merrill Company, 1953

Tillich, Paul. *Dynamics of Faith*. New York, Harper Torchbooks, 1957

IN-DEPTH

Alston, William P. *Perceiving God: The Epistemology of Religious Experience*. London, Cornell University Press, 1991

James, William. *Pragmatism and the Meaning of Truth*. Cambridge, Harvard University Press, 1978

Kellenberger, James. *Kierkegaard and Nietzsche: Faith and Eternal Acceptance*. London, Macmillan, 1997

Kierkegaard, Søren. *Concluding Unscientific Postscript*. David F. Swenson and Walter Lowrie, trans. Princeton, Princeton University Press, 1954

Kuhn, Thomas. *The Structure of Scientific Revolutions*. Second edition. Chicago: The University of Chicago Press, 1962, 1970

Plantinga, Alvin. *Warrant: The Current Debate*. Oxford, Oxford University Press, 1993

Plantinga, Alvin. *Warrant and Proper Function*. Oxford, Oxford University Press, 1993

Swinburne, Richard. *Faith and Reason*. Oxford, Clarendon Press, 1981

14 LOVE AND THE MEANING OF LIFE

What is the meaning of human life, or of organic life altogether? To answer this question at all implies a religion. Is there any sense then, you ask, in putting it? I answer, the man who regards his own life and that of his fellow-creatures as meaningless is not merely unfortunate but almost disqualified for life.[1]

Albert Einstein (1879–1955)

The World Religions not only hold that life has a meaning; they see that meaning as ultimately grounded in relationships, relationship to the Transcendent and relationship to others. Over against this religious sense of ultimate meaning, many people are resigned to the vision of life which Macbeth presents in Shakespeare's play:

> Out, out, brief candle!
> Life's but a walking shadow, a poor player,
> That struts and frets his hour upon the stage,
> And then is heard no more. It is a tale
> Told by an idiot, full of sound and fury,
> Signifying nothing.[2]

If a person thinks that as humans we have only our short lifespan and only our own resources, if a person thinks there is "no appeal" from life, then as Albert Camus suggests, Sisyphus becomes the quintessential heroic figure. Sisyphus, you will recall, was the greedy king of Corinth whom the gods condemned to roll a rock ceaselessly up a hill only to have it roll down again as soon as he reached the top, necessitating another round of futile struggle with the rock. In Camus's words:

> Sisyphus...contemplates that series of unrelated actions which becomes his fate, created by him, combined under his mind's eye and soon sealed by his death. Thus, convinced of the wholly human origin of all that is human, a blind man eager to see who knows that the night has no end, he is still on the go. The rock is still rolling...The struggle itself toward the heights is enough to fill a man's heart. One must imagine Sisyphus happy.[3]

On this view, the view of Religious Antipathy (see chapter 2), our only hope is to struggle within this world for human happiness, and the only source of the good is our own humanity.

VALUES AND THE RELIGIOUS DIMENSION OF MEANING

The World Religions, on the other hand, consider this single focus on human happiness self-centered, self-defeating, and ultimately meaningless. The World Religions enjoin their followers to give up a self-centered craving for life, for possessing things of this world, and for power over others. But why? Why does religion offer this wholly different picture of the universe and our place in it? For the humanist like Camus *we* create the only value, and things have value only in so far as they have value from our point of view. The scientific humanist even more specifically holds that science now creates some of the highest of human values. What alternatives do the World Religions portray as the source of value and meaning?

We saw in chapter 10 that if we ask not only "*what* am I?" but "what does it *mean* that I am?," scientific humanism does not have the resources to answer our question. To limit oneself to scientific explanation is to limit one's explanations. Scientific explanation cannot fully account for *values*, for it cannot account for those values outside the values implied by a commitment to the scientific method itself. However good our biological or sociological or psychological or physical theories and descriptions, they do not and cannot explain either *what* we ought to do or *why* we ought to do the things we ought to do. Importantly, scientific explanations cannot explain either that we ought to love or why we ought to love. While ought implies can, the reverse is not true: what *is* the case does not tell us what ought to be the case.

To see this better, we must first determine what is meant by a "value." There are two ways to think about values. There might be a plurality of values, or there might be only one value, where all other things derive any value they might have from the one and only value. For example, some people have supposed that pleasure is the only value, or that only things that give pleasure have value. This is metaphysical hedonism. A metaphysical hedonist is not necessarily someone who thinks "wine, women, and song" are the only things of value, for a sophisticated hedonist will hold that art and friendship and so on are also valuable – but only valuable because they provide pleasure. Here is how John Stuart Mill explicates this view in his book *Utilitarianism*:

> Some kinds of pleasure are more desirable and more valuable than others ... Few human creatures would consent to be changed into any of the lower animals for a promise of the fullest allowance of a beast's pleasures; no intelligent human being would consent to be a fool, no instructed person would be an ignoramus, no person of feeling and conscience would be selfish and base, even though they should be persuaded that the fool, the dunce, or the rascal is better satisfied with his lot than they are with theirs.
>
> It is better to be a human being dissatisfied than a pig satisfied; better to be Socrates dissatisfied than a fool satisfied. And if the fool, or the pig, are of a different opinion, it is only because they only know their own side of the question.[4]

An alternative way to argue that while there is only one value, there are degrees of that one value, is to argue that the one value is happiness, but that happiness comes in degrees. However, against such monistic views of value, you might hold that there is a plurality of values and that the many values cannot be reduced to just one value. In that case, either you might think that all values are roughly equivalent or, more likely, you might think that there is a hierarchy of values. If you think there is a hierarchy of values, then you probably think there are ultimate values.

Another important distinction when assessing values is between intrinsic and extrinsic values. Many of us would say that certain works of art are intrinsically valuable. However, if your approach to art is to collect it, put it away in a vault, wait twenty years, let it go up in monetary value, and, when the price is right, sell it, then for you the art has only (or primarily) extrinsic value. In contrast, the intrinsic value of a thing does not depend on any external circumstances, such as how much others will pay for it.

Another way to put this is that if something has intrinsic value, that value comes from the nature of the thing itself. Of course, the same thing can have both intrinsic and extrinsic value(s): the Rembrandt etching treasured by the family because of its profound psychological impact (intrinsic value) might be sold in a time of financial need.

Now, keeping these distinctions in mind, to understand the religious dimension of value, we need to consider the connection between intrinsic value and meaning. Regarding the former, in *The Examined Life* Robert Nozick suggests that something has intrinsic value to the degree it is "organically unified".[5] The degree to which something is organically unified is determined by how much diversity is being unified as well as the degree of unity that is achieved within that diversity.[6] In short, the greatest intrinsic value results from the greatest integration of the greatest diversity. This is why human life has greater value than works of art or than plant life. (Even Jains, who attribute *jiva* to plants, would agree, for the *jiva* of plants are far less complex *jiva* than the *jiva* of humans.) In humans, not only a great complexity of physical aspects, but also mental and spiritual aspects, become integrated.

Moreover, the value of a thing is enhanced by meaning. Meaning comes from a thing's connectedness to other things. Of course, any distinct thing is related to other distinct things. (Buddhists particularly emphasize this in the doctrine of dependent origination [*pratitya-samutpada*], though on a Buddhist view "things" turn out to be illusory – in a certain sense, on a Buddhist view a "thing" just is a set of relations.) Some relations with other things are not meaningful, such as being heavier than something else. But some relations with other things are meaningful, such as being the father or lover of someone. When relations are meaningful, they add to a thing's organic unity and thereby increase that thing's intrinsic value. Importantly, our human lives have the special meaning they do through our connectedness to other persons. Our relationships with others add more than just extrinsic value, for the meaning which comes from our connection to others is both integrative and adds to the richness and diversity of our own lives.

Finally, we can only attain *ultimate* meaning if we are connected to and integrated with something outside us which is ultimate or unlimited in value. Just as the meaning of our lives as an integrative connectedness with things of value outside ourselves enhances the value of our lives, the degree of value derived from our connection, if any, to unlimited value will be proportionate to the degree of integration which results from our connection to unlimited value. With respect to the World Religions, this would mean that to the extent that there is a lived connection or reciprocity with the Transcendent, the religious life has ultimate meaning because it brings one into contact with ultimate value: the religious life, it is held, serves as a connective bridge to ultimate value.

SCIENCE AND RELIGION REVISITED

As we saw in chapter 10, scientific humanism opposes this religious search for meaning. The British biologist Richard Dawkins opens his book *The Selfish Gene* by citing with approbation the zoologist G. G. Simson's assessment of historical attempts to give an answer to the meaning of life:

> All such attempts to answer that question before 1859 [the date of publication of Darwin's *Origin of Species*] are worthless and...we will be better off if we ignore them completely.[7]

But it is implausible if not unscientific to dismiss so quickly the insights of other minds throughout most of human history.

History displays a remarkable panoply of lived faith within diverse religious traditions with highly developed philosophical views. The philosophy of religion has been a global phenomenon for more than two millennia. With the recent rise of science, Western philosophical religion has more often come into conflict with science than have the Asian philosophical religious traditions. This is both because science is the step-child of Western philosophy and because Western monotheism is concerned with orthodoxy, or right belief, and science can seem to contravene religious orthodoxy. Asian traditions like Buddhism might initially find an easier accord with science because they are more oriented toward orthopraxy, or right practice. However, all the World Religions ultimately run aground on the idea of science as a total explanation of the universe. For it is not just that God's existence might be called into question, as when the well-known scientific humanist Julian Huxley says that values are not "absolute or transcendental in the sense of being vouchsafed by some external power or divinity: they are [merely] the product of human nature interacting with the outer world."[8] Even more fundamentally, what is called into question is the very idea of a

Transcendent – whether personalistic like Allah or Ahura Mazda or Akal Purakh, or nonpersonal like the Tao or Nirguna Brahman or Nirvana or the Jain *siddha loka*.

The World Religions are all in the same epistemic boat *vis-à-vis* science. Where good science is judged by repeatability and predictability, good religion is judged by the "fruits of the spirit." Where science prizes probabilities, the World Religions prize wisdom. Further, when compared to science, the World Religions are all in the same axiologic boat. While science values the temporal and the physical, religion values the eternal, or timeless, and is directed toward the Transcendent, even if that Transcendent is immanent in the world. For the naturalist, all value must be found in the natural order, and religion must be explained in a reductionist fashion: "The actual gods of historical religions," Julian Huxley says, "are only personifications of *impersonal* facts of nature and of facts of our *inner* mental life."[9] Against this, adherents of the World Religions believe there is a Transcendent which is the ground of all value.

In effect, humanism holds that an understanding of humanistic values is itself sufficiently comprehensive so that parsimony then argues against the postulation of an extraneous entity such as God or Brahman to explain values. As Huxley says, "it is among human *personalities* that there exist the *highest* and most valuable achievements of the universe."[10] True, if we initially exclude all but the natural order, the human mind (say, by employing mathematical laws) can offer an elegant explanation of what is left. But this sense of "parsimony" begs the question. Hindus, Jews, Christians, Muslims, Buddhists, and so on would want to argue that the Transcendent contains all explanation and all value. And this is another sort of parsimony of explanation, an elegant answering of the evaluative "why" question of the universe, thereby providing the simplest comprehensive explanation. So on this religious view, the *prima facie* extraneous Transcendent, once postulated, actually offers the simplest (comprehensive) explanation. Hence, the issue between scientific humanism and the World Religions comes down to this: what counts as the most parsimonious explanation is determined by the more fundamental question of what count as the most important questions to answer. The issue, then, comes down to a question of values.

SERAPHIC LOVE

Science values the intellect, and to restrict ourselves to scientific explanation is to limit ourselves to the way of the intellect. As we saw in the
Introduction, some philosophical religion also characterizes the way of
the intellect as the preeminent religious path. But as we also saw in the
Introduction, there is another way, the way of love, which emphasizes
relationality. The World Religions value relationality in some form or
other as a high value, for it is not merely the existence of the
Transcendent that matters but our relationship to it and thereby to other
beings. A fundamental characteristic of relationality is encapsulated in
the Golden Rule, the moral imperative to do unto others as you would
have them do unto you, found in some form in all the world's great
religious traditions (see page 187). One way to express the Golden Rule
is in terms of love: "You shall love your neighbor as yourself" (Matt.
22:37–39). And within the World Religions, the only appropriate object
of this sort of unconditional love is the Transcendent, and anything
made, or manifest, in the image of the Transcendent.

What kind of love is this unconditional love of which all the World
Religions in some manner speak? We can find the beginnings of an
answer in Paul Tillich's suggestion that "faith as the state of being ultimately concerned implies love, namely, the *desire and urge* toward the
reunion of the separated."[11] This kind of love of the Transcendent
involves the passionate devotion characteristic of *eros*. In eros is the desire
to be with the beloved. Indeed, there is an important sense in which eros
contains the passionate desire even to *be* the beloved. For example, we
see this in the Hindu poet-saint Nammalvar's portrayal of the devotee's
relation to Krishna in terms of this passionate desire for union:

> While I was waiting eagerly for him
> saying to myself,
> "If I see you anywhere
> I'll gather you
> and eat you up,"
> He beat me to it
> and devoured me entire.[12]

In religious devotional poetry, such as Nammalvar's, or Rumi's
Sufi poetry, or the poetry of St. John of the Cross, Divine Love is
characterized as interested, not *dis*interested. I shall refer to the ultimate

love of the Divine, as well as that human love which is modeled in the World Religions on Divine Love, as "seraphic love." "Seraphim" comes originally from a Hebrew root for "burning." The greatest ardor for the Divine, a burning, intense, egoless love of God, is what I am calling seraphic love.

Now Christianity has often traditionally spoken of *agape* or altruistic love as the highest love. And usually agape is distinguished from eros. Instead, we might think of agape and eros (or passionate love) not as two distinct kinds of love but as the two poles of seraphic love. For we can ask what motivates agape. And the motive for agape is the passionate, devoted love which is eros. So agape and eros form a dynamic pair. We can see how eros provides the motive for agape in this dynamic pair if we consider Eliot Deutsch's analysis of *karma-yoga* in the *Bhagavad Gita* in which he finds a pairing of duty toward others with passionate devotion (*bhakti*):

> For Arjuna, *karma-yoga* is expressed in its *bhakti* mode as a loving sacrifice...
>
> In order to act without attachment to the fruits of action (otherwise, action means a loss of freedom), it is necessary that one perform one's action in the spirit of sacrifice, *yajna*. This means to perform action with loving attention to the Divine; it means to redirect the empirical self away from its ego-involvement with needs, desires, passions.
>
> And from this unity of man with the Divine, a man is able to fulfill his *dharma*. He acts in the knowledge that all action is essentially the Divine's action. He becomes an instrument of the Divine. He imitates the Divine by acting in the spirit of non-attachment and in so acting his freedom is realized.[13]

Eros (or *bhakti*) is that dynamic pole of seraphic love which brings humans also to have agape (or egoless love). Put in Hindu terms, seraphic love combines *bhakti-yoga* and *karma-yoga*, passionate devotion and selfless duty.

SIX CHARACTERISTICS OF EROS[14]

Another way to see the role of eros as a dynamic pole of divine or seraphic love is to consider the appropriateness of the traditional Western bridegroom metaphor for God. As the Christian bride mystic St. Bernard of Clairvaux says, in the "loving descent of God into the soul," the soul:

Will be far from content that the Bridegroom should manifest Himself to her in the manner which is common to *all*...She desires that He whom she loves...should be, as it were, impoured into her; that He should not merely appear to her, but should enter into and *possess* her.[15]

The metaphor of God as a husband or a bridegroom brings out the relational dimension of the love of God, in response to which the devout are to love God with their whole "mind, soul and strength." Similarly, Krishna is lover/bridegroom of all devotees in *bhakti* Hinduism.[16] As the *Bhagavad Gita* says:

> But those who dwell in godlike nature
> and know Me, those of Mighty Soul,
> love Me with undivided mind
> as Source of Beings, Unchangeable.
>
> They glorify Me constantly
> with zeal and steadfast vow,
> and integrated giving worship
> in love to Me they bow.[17]

Now, there are six salient elements of eros which make this metaphorical or analogical way of referring to the love joining the human and the Transcendent appropriate. These six elements are: relationality, surrender, vulnerability, integration, union and equality. First, as we have already noted, eros fundamentally involves the reciprocity of relationship. In Hinduism this is made explicit through the iconography of the model for love, the divine couple – Shiva and Parvati, Krishna and Radha, and so on – and within Buddhism, the fundamental doctrine of dependent origination (*pratitya-samutpada*) is clearly relational. Second, because eros is relational, eros involves vulnerability. To allow ourselves to be truly loved by someone is to allow them to know our weakness and faults. Otherwise it is not we ourselves who are lovable. Mahadeviyakka, the twelfth-century Indian saint, says this to Shiva:

> Finger may squeeze the fig
> to feel it yet not choose
> to eat it.
> Take me, flaws and all.
> O Lord[18]

Third, because eros is relational, eros requires surrender. The development of *bhakti* out of the rule-bound background of Vedic Hinduism and the initial development of Christianity out of Judaism both exemplify movements away from the obedience of ritual and sacrifice to the vulnerability of love and surrender (though Judaism also contains these latter elements). Eros both reflects and is reflected by this spiritual surrender to the Other.

Fourth, eros is not only relational; eros is fundamentally integrative. Thus the passionate directedness of the devotee toward the Transcendent becomes one's ultimate concern, and as Tillich says:

> Ultimate concern is the integrating center of the personal life...the center unites all elements of man's personal life, the bodily, the unconscious, the spiritual ones. Faith...is the centered movement of the *whole* personality toward something of ultimate meaning and significance.[19]

Fifth, because eros is integrative, eros brings union. St. Bernard argues that "Man and God...are with strict truth called 'one spirit' if they adhere to one another with the *glue of love*. But this unity is effected not by coherence of essence but by concurrence of wills."[20] Making one's will congruent with the will of the Divine is part of a divine command theory of ethics. The *bhakti* Hindu saint Devara Dasimayya expresses this union when he says to Shiva:

> God of my clan,
> I'll not place my feet
> but where your feet
> have stood before:
> I've no feet
> of my own.
>
> How can the immoralists
> of this world know
> the miracle, the oneness
> of your feet
> and mine,
>
> Ramanatha?[21]

In a non-theistic metaphysics like that of Advaita Vedanta or Buddhism this state of union or understanding of inseparability from interrelation is designated "bliss."

Sixth, since eros is unitive, eros entails the equality of acceptance. As St. John of the Cross says regarding mystical union with God, "the property of love is to make the lover equal to the object loved. Wherefore, since its love is now perfect, the soul is called Bride of the Son of God, which signifies equality with Him."[22] And Rumi analogically compares human–human love with human–divine love:

> Just before dawn, lover and beloved awake...
> She asks, "Do you love me or yourself more?
> Really, tell the absolute truth."
> He says, "There's nothing left of me.
> I'm like a ruby held up to the sunrise.
> Is it still a stone, or a world
> made of redness? It has no resistance
> to sunlight."
> This is how Hallaj said, I am God,
> and told the truth![23]

As we noted in chapter 11, to take the religious point of view is to treat others as spirit, entering fully into spirit–spirit relationship. We can now say that to take the religious point of view is to be genuinely open to seraphic love with its dynamic poles of agape and eros – both an egoless love and the passionate love for concurrence of wills, or unitative bliss, with others and with the Transcendence.

THE ARGUMENT FROM LOVE

With this extended analysis of eros and of seraphic love, it is now clear why love cannot be accounted for by science alone. Consider the Darwinian world the biologist Richard Dawkins describes: "all we have a right to expect from our theory," he says, "is a battleground of replicators, jostling, jockeying, fighting for a future in the genetic hereafter."[24] As an empirical theory, presumably predictive of how things should have turned out, Dawkins, radical sociobiological worldview is seriously deficient in a world of seraphic love. Moreover, as a value theory, this Darwinian sociobiology would make a proclamation like Jesus' that "the meek shall inherit the earth," or Gandhi's commitment to satyagraha and ahimsa, or Shakyamuni Buddha's claim that humans have an inappropriate attachment to self, the quaint delusions of three genetic dead ends.

The problem for Darwinian sociobiology is far greater than the difficulty of explaining the altruism of agape. For it could be argued that agape is just self-deceptive selfishness, that our apparent altruism is just a ruse for getting other people to like us, help us, admire us, etc. As we saw in chapter 12, even Buddhism can regard *metta* (benevolence) or *karuna* (compassion) as *upaya* – a skillful means to the end of release from *samsara* – fitting Dawkins' theory as a type of self-interested view. The deeper problem for Darwinian sociobiology is how to explain eros, and so seraphic love. On the surface, eros certainly appears selfish, and indeed lust is the vice of adolescent eros. But mature eros, or genuine eros, is not self-centered. In genuine eros, the value of vulnerability, the need for surrender, the drive for integration and union and the hope for equality make no sense if life is really just a battleground of replicators. It is obvious that genuine eros is contrary to the "selfish gene." Indeed, an argument for God is even implied by the presence of eros as a component of seraphic love, a line of reasoning which is not susceptible to some of the objections which confront other arguments from the evidence of the world to God.

For instance, contemporary theists often attempt to support religious belief in God in our scientific world by asserting that consciousness cannot be explained by science alone. It is argued that the question of why and not just how the universe has evolved conscious beings can only be answered by positing a transcendent being that is the exemplar and source of our consciousness. Darwinians might try to respond that once consciousness emerged through genetic mutation, the development of the conscious ability to calculate has obvious survival value and so would be replicated over time. Perhaps this Darwinian counter-argument does not work. But even if it did, it would not serve as an objection to a parallel argument, namely the notion that the presence of love in the universe and the obligation to love implies a transcendent love. Love and any obligation to love imply a higher form of consciousness than the mere facility to calculate, and they imply a higher form of consciousness than even self-reflective calculation. Consequently, if there is an obligation to love, an argument for the existence of God might be formulated along the lines of the argument on the next page.

An argument like the Argument from Love is almost diametrically opposed to Pascal's Wager (see page 195). The religious philosopher Blaise Pascal assumes that we should act in our self-interest, arguing that it is only prudent to believe in God since positive belief has a 50/50 chance of an infinite positive payoff, and disbelief a 50/50 chance of an

---

◆

ARGUMENT FROM LOVE TO GOD'S EXISTENCE

1. We ought to love fully – that is, we ought to have seraphic love towards all persons.
2. The obligation to love implies the ability to love.
3. Therefore, we have the ability to love seraphically.
4. To have seraphic love is not purely in one's self-interest since it involves vulnerability, surrender, and equality.
5. Therefore, the physical-biological-social laws of the universe which provide supporting conditions for selfish behaviour do not explain our *ability* to love seraphically.
6. Therefore, the physical-biological-social laws of the universe do not explain our *obligation* to love seraphically.
7. Therefore there must be an extra-natural source of this obligation to love seraphically.
8. Seraphic love is a perfection.
9. The cause of a perfection must itself possess that perfection.
10. Therefore, there is something extra-natural – which we call God – possessing the perfection of love – which we call Divine Love.

◆

---

infinite negative payoff. In contrast, the Argument from Love is not prudential; indeed, the reasoning goes against pure self-interest, taking the Other into account in spirit–spirit relations. Thus, the Argument from Love is opposed to the sort of utilitarian arguments for universal love which, for example, the Confucian philosopher Mo Tzu apparently gave. Of Mo Tzu's thought Burton Watson writes:

> I have said previously that it is the business of the benevolent man to try to promote what is beneficial to the world and to eliminate what is harmful. Now I have demonstrated that universality is the source of all the great benefits in the world and partiality is the source of all the great harm. It is for this reason that Mo Tzu has said that partiality is wrong and universality is right.
> ...One who loves will be loved by others, and one who hates will be hated by others. So I cannot understand how the men of the world hear about this doctrine of universality and still criticize it![25]

To some extent the Argument from Love is a transcendental argument, that is, an argument based on the necessary conditions for experience.

In that respect it shares some affinities with Kantian moral arguments for God's existence which we discussed in chapter 11.

The most obvious objection to the line of reasoning encapsulated in the Argument from Love is to deny premise 1, to deny the obligation to love seraphically. Now of course scientific humanists may do just that, but just because some people get off the bus at earlier stops does not mean that the final destination of the bus is not worth arriving at. More pointedly, early departures by some passengers do not mean that the bus does not eventually arrive at the final destination. Another objection would be that non-theistic religious traditions like Theravada Buddhism or Advaita Vedanta Hinduism or Taoism would not see this argument as supporting the existence of God, but rather as supporting the Way of Truth. The Truth or *Dharma*, as broadly conceived in Hinduism and Buddhism and Taoism, implies the obligation to love, or in Buddhist terms "to cultivate the Buddha mind of compassion," if one wants to align oneself with the *Dharma*. We might say that, using Kant's terms, if the obligation to love seraphically is a categorical imperative, the particular obligation to love God versus the obligation to conform to *Dharma* as part of one's seraphic love is a hypothetical imperative. That is to say, if one believes that God exists, then one ought to enter into seraphic relation with other persons and with God. And if one believes in Dharma, then one ought to cultivate compassion. But does this Argument from Love succeed?

FAITH, LOVE, AND RELIGION

No argument can of itself convince us to have the willingness and the courage to act seraphically. In the words of the Sufi poet Rumi,

> The way of love is not
> a subtle argument.
>
> The door there
> is devastation.[26]

The Argument from Love will be no more rationally convincing to the religiously apathetic than other arguments for belief in a Transcendent which we have considered. Perhaps the Argument from Love could be used as part of a cumulative case made with multiple types of arguments for the existence of a Transcendent, or more specifically, of God.

For instance, Keith Ward suggests the outlines of a teleological argument in *God, Chance, and Necessity* when he says:

> One may think of God as having a universe-long intention to bring conscious beings into a community of freely chosen loving relationships. This intention will shape the initial laws of the universe and the emergence of more complex possibilities within it. In general, God will exert the maximum influence for good, compatible with the preservation of the relative autonomy of nature and its probabilistic laws, and with the freedom of finite agents.[27]

And it is an old cosmological argument that the Transcendent attracts by eros. But a cumulative case would still only provide a more rationally convincing case for those inclined to religious belief, and it will not provide an incontrovertible proof for the a-religious of the existence of God or the Transcendent.

In the end one must repeatedly make the hard choices to be a certain kind of person, to have a certain *karma* (character) involved in the risk of making transforming choices against self-centeredness. One must repeatedly risk to cultivate attitudes and habits which will eventually enable one to better act relationally. It is this life commitment – this directedness toward relationality – that makes premise 1 attractive, and the Argument from Love convincing. But this requires a faith commitment. Perhaps humans have an innate disposition, like our disposition to be moral, to recognize spirit–spirit relations and the religious point of view. However, one cannot recognize anything without the relevant conceptual resources, and one cannot choose freely – or take an informed leap of faith – unless one knows what choices there are to make. Therefore, in order to acquire the conceptual resources for the religious point of view, one would need to develop a commitment to at least some rudimentary religious worldview.[28] One would need to cultivate in oneself religious habits of action and learning if one hoped to achieve a religious outlook.

This is why wisdom is meant to be coupled with virtuous action and meditation in the Buddhist way; why in the Fourth Gospel Jesus says "If you continue in my word, you are truly my disciples, and you will know *the truth* and *the truth* will make you free," adding "I am the way, *the truth*, and the life" (John 8:31–32 and 14:6); why the Islamic *shahada* "there is but one God, and Muhammad is his messenger" is an indication of a path followed, not an end of understanding. One cannot follow the religious way which purports to bring freedom from false self unless one is willing to commit to take the religious point of view – to have ultimate concern not for the transitory, but for spirit–spirit relations and for the Transcendent.

Genuine religion is a search for meaning wherein the search itself is thought to give meaning to human lives through spirit–spirit relations, and conjunctively through relation with the Transcendent, the source of the Good. In this, genuine religion proposes a meaning to life very different from humanism. Reason alone will never convince the humanist of the validity of religious faith, whether Hindu or Buddhist, Christian or Muslim, Sikh or Baha'i, Jewish or Jain. But to paraphrase J. S. Mill, from the perspective of the World Religions, it is better to be Mahatma Gandhi dissatisfied than a materialist satisfied; better to be St. Anselm dissatisfied than a religiously apathetic person satisfied. And if the materialistic and religiously apathetic disagree, the religious person can only say that materialism and religious antipathy prevent one from having convincing religious experiences.

Further reading

Barks, Coleman, trans. *The Essential Rumi*. San Francisco, HarperSanFrancisco, 1995

Dostoevsky, Fyodor. *Crime and Punishment*. Constance Garnett, trans. Toronto, Bantam, 1958

Hanh, Thich Nhat. *Cultivating the Mind of Love*. Berkeley, Parallax Press, 1996

H.H. Dalai Lama. *Ethics for the New Millennium*. New York, Penguin Putnam, 1999

Hick, John. *The Fifth Dimension: An Exploration of the Spiritual Realm*. Oxford, Oneworld, 1999

Rossi, Philip J., S.J. *Together Toward Hope: A Journey to Moral Theology*. Notre Dame, University of Notre Dame Press, 1983

Runzo, Joseph and Nancy M. Martin, eds. *The Meaning of Life in the World Religions*. Oxford, Oneworld Publications, 1999

Tolstoy, Leo. *Great Short Works of Leo Tolstoy*. Louise and Aylmer Maude, trans. New York, Harper and Row, 1967

Tutu, Desmond. *No Future Without Forgiveness*. New York, Doubleday, 1997

GLOSSARY OF RELIGIOUS AND PHILOSOPHICAL TERMS

abhidharma	canonical teachings presenting the truth of Buddhist teachings in a systematic and analytical way.
Adi Granth	the *Guru Granth Sahib*, the principle Sikh scripture.
Advaita Vedanta	the school of Vedanta in Hinduism that emphasizes the nonduality of reality.
agnosticism	uncertainty about whether it can be known whether to believe that there is a God or a future life.
ahimsa	"non-violence;" in Jainism, a reverence for all living things.
Ahura Mazda	the Zoroastrian god of light; the Wise Lord who is the highest deity.
Akal Purakh	"Timeless Being;" God (Sikhism).
Allah	"God" in Arabic (Islam).
Amesha Spentas	the higher spirits directly under Ahura Mazda; they are modes of divine being that bear names of ethical virtues, such as "Good Thought" (Zoroastrianism).
Amitabha	"the Buddha of Endless Light and Infinite Life;" who presides over the Pure Land or Western Paradise, which may be reached by faith in this Buddha's vow that all who call upon his name will be reborn there.
Analects (Lun-yu)	the collected sayings of Confucius.
anatman	"no-self," no unchanging soul or self-nature; one of the three characteristics of existence in Buddhism along with impermanence and suffering.
anekantavada	the view that knowledge is always from a particular perspective and that no one perspective encompasses the whole truth (Jainism).
Angra Mainyu	the evil spirit who opposes Ahura Mazda (Zoroastrianism).
annica	impermanence; the Buddhist doctrine that there are no permanent entities.

apocalypse	a revelation and/or a prophetic vision of the destruction of evil and the salvation of righteous people.
arhat	"noble one," one who has conquered all lust, hatred, and delusion and is assured of Enlightenment (Buddhism).
Aryans	Indo-Europeans who entered the Indus Valley prior to 1000 BCE.
atheism	lack of belief in God either (1) because of conscious disbelief or (2) because of the lack of the concept of God.
Atman	the true soul or self, which is held to be identical with Brahman – the ultimate reality (Hinduism).
atman	the individual self.
Avalokiteshvara	"the Lord Who (Kindly) Looks Down," the *bodhisattva* of endless compassion who protects those who call on him; originally male, this celestial being is female in Chinese and Japanese Buddhism (see Kuan Yin and Kannon).
avatar	a descent or incarnation of God (Hinduism).
Avesta	the scriptures of Zoroastrianism believed to have been revealed to Zoroaster.
avidya	delusion, ignorance (Hinduism, Buddhism).
Baha'i	a faith arising out of the Islamic Babi movement in Persia; a universalist religion stressing the unity of all faiths, education, sexual equality, monogamy, and the attainment of world peace.
bardo	the intermediate state that intervenes between one life and another (Tibetan Buddhism).
basic belief	a belief not based on other beliefs.
Bhagavad-Gita	"Song of the Lord," a long devotional poem in which Krishna teaches the secret of non-attached action.
bhakti	devotion to a personal god; one of the paths to liberation from the ignorance that mistakes the ego-self for the true Self (Atman) according to Krishna in the *Bhagavad-Gita* (Hinduism).
bhikkhu	a Buddhist monk.
Bible	scriptures of the Christian Church composed of the Old Testament (Hebrew Scriptures) and the New Testament.
bodhichitta	enlightened mind (Buddhism).
Bodhidharma	the monk who brought meditative Buddhism to China. His example inspired Ch'an (in Japan, Zen) Buddhism.
bodhisattva	a being destined for buddhahood; an enlightened being who, out of compassion for others, vows not to enter *nirvana* until all beings have attained liberation (Mahayana Buddhism).
Brahma	the creator god; along with Vishnu and Shiva comprises a "trinity" (Hinduism).
Brahman	"that which makes great," ultimate reality; the eternal, unchanging Absolute that underlies all things (Hinduism).
Brahmin	highest, priestly caste (Hinduism).

Brihadaranyaka Upanishad	the oldest Upanishad, *c.* eighth century BCE, famous for teaching the supremacy of the Self (Atman).
Buddha	"the awakened," an enlightened being, one who has achieved the state of knowledge of the true nature of things.
Buddhism	a way of thought and practice that emphasizes moral practice, meditation, and wisdom, leading to enlightenment, founded by Siddhartha Gautama, the Buddha.
Ch'an	Chinese form of Mahayana Buddhism emphasizing meditative insight, known in Japan and the West as Zen.
Chandogya Upanishad	an early Upanishad, noted for teaching the identity of Atman and Brahman in the phrase, "You are That."
ch'i	energy, especially the psychophysical energies through which full humanness (*jen*) can be achieved (Confucianism).
Chinvat Bridge	the bridge of judgment that a soul must walk over after death (Zoroastrianism).
Christ	Greek word meaning "the anointed one." The Hebrew word for this conception was "messiah." The first Christians were those who believed that Jesus was the long-awaited Messiah.
Christianity	a Western religion begun after the death of Jesus in 30 CE; Christianity is a trinitarian monotheism, God is the creator and saves humankind through the divine son, Jesus the Christ.
conceptualism	the epistemological view that the possession of relevant conceptual resources is a necessary condition for experience.
conceptualization	the mind's ordering of experience.
Confucius (Kung Fu Tzu)	the Chinese founder of Confucianism. Primarily a teacher, he sought to develop good government through a responsible ruler and ethical people.
Confucianism	Chinese tradition based on the teachings of Confucius and his followers, particularly Mencius and Hsun-tzu.
Dalai Lama	Tibetan Buddhism's spiritual and political ruler, understood as an incarnation of Avalokiteshvara.
darshan	vision, being in the presence of divinity (Hinduism).
deism	(1) the belief that a Supreme Being created the law-abiding universe and does not interfere with its operation to answer prayers and perform miracles or (2) a view rejecting revelation and appealing to reason alone (seventeenth-century usage).
deontological	based on a sense of one's duty.
dependent origination	the causal connection among moments, arising and decaying in the endless process of life; explains the cause and effect pattern characterizing ego-ridden existence (Buddhism).
Devi	the Great Goddess (Hinduism).
Dhammapada	"Path of Truth," Buddhist collection of wisdom sayings.
dharma	"that which maintains everything else," the Law in the sense of (1) the path of liberation, the truth, the way, the norm,

righteousness; (2) teachings of the Buddha; (3) one's own proper social behavior; virtuous behavior; social duty; acting in prescribed ways (Hinduism).

dharmas	the true ultimate constituents of existence (Buddhism).
Diamond Sutra	brief Mahayana scripture outlining the bodhisattva way.
Dogen	thirteenth-century founder of Soto Zen in Japan. His *Shobogenzo* is universally regarded as a masterpiece of Zen Buddhism.
doxastic practice	a systematic method employed consciously or unconsciously for acquiring beliefs of some type.
dualism	a metaphysical view that categorizes all existence into two fundamentally different kinds.
duhkha	the suffering of all humans and sentient beings (Buddhism).
Dvaita Vedanta	the dualistic school of Vedanta championed by Madhva (Hinduism).
Eightfold Path	the Fourth Noble Truth of Buddhism, the middle path between worldliness and asceticism taught by the Buddha; the path of deliverance, namely, right knowledge, intention, speech, action, livelihood, effort, mindfulness, and concentration.
empiricism	the broad epistemological view that (1) sense experience is the test of truth and (2) knowledge can only be derived from sense experience.
emptiness	the teaching that separate and permanent existence is devoid of reality (Mahayana Buddhism).
epistemology	a theory or philosophical study of the nature of knowledge
evidentialism	the epistemological view that one should not believe anything without sufficient evidence.
external question	a question about the acceptability of one worldview against alternative worldviews.
fideism	the view that the truth of religious beliefs cannot be established by unbiased arguments and so must be held on the basis of faith.
five precepts	the basic Buddhist moral precepts, namely to refrain from hurtful activity, from taking what is not given, from improper sexual activity, from wrong speech, and from alcohol and other drugs.
foundationalism	the epistemological view that while some beliefs are held on the basis of other beliefs, some beliefs must be held immediately and not based on other beliefs.
Genku (Honen Shonin)	founder of the Jodo Buddhist sect in Japan which focuses on faith in Amitabha Buddha's liberating vow.
gnosticism	the doctrine that knowledge (*gnosis*) is the way to salvation for humans as spirits who are trapped in the prison of the flesh.

gospel	"good tidings," the positive proclamation about Jesus Christ in the Christian tradition.
Great Ultimate	the fundamental source and principle of existence that operates through the polarities of yin and yang (Neo-Confucianism).
guru	a teacher, particularly of religious duties. For a student, the guru represents the divine in human form (Hinduism); title given to the ten early spiritual leaders in Sikhism.
hadith	"report" or "account;" a tradition about Muhammad – what he said or did on a particular occasion; the hadiths were collected as a record of the Prophet's Sunna or tradition, which is second only to the *Qur'an* in authority for Muslims.
halakhah	Jewish law that was developed in rabbinic writings.
Hasidism	a mystical Jewish religious movement which emerged in eighteenth-century Eastern Europe.
Heart Sutra	the encapsulation of Mahayana Buddhist teaching, emphasizing the emptiness of separate and permanent self-existence.
hell	(1) in Hinduism and Buddhism, one of the six levels of existence, some of which are hot, some cold, but not eternal destinies – they are more like the Catholic purgatory; (2) in Christianity and Islam, a place where the unrighteous are eternally punished by God.
henotheism	a belief that affirms one deity among many, without denying the existence of the others, and often without holding that one deity is supreme over the others; ascribing all the attributes of God to one deity among many.
Hillel	a prominent Jewish teacher and founder of the Hillel school of rabbis in the first century. He was considered more liberal in his views than the conservative Shammai.
Hinayana	"the lesser vehicle, the narrow path," the term used by Mahayana (Great Vehicle) Buddhists to designate traditions of Buddhism such as Theravada, which teach monasticism as the way to *nirvana.*
Hinduism	European term for the religious practices of India. Hinduism is tied together by a commonality of belief in Brahman, a plurality of manifested deities, *samsara*, *karma*, and *moksha.*
Hindus	eighth-century Muslim term for the inhabitants of "the land beyond the Indus River."
holy	set apart for a sacred purpose or possessing a special quality derived from God; God.
Holy Spirit	in the Hebrew Scriptures God exercises creative power by his spirit ("breath"); in the Christian New Testament the Holy Spirit functions as Jesus' alter ego after his death; the third person of the Trinity.

Hsun-tzu	Confucian thinker who claimed innate human intelligence rather than inherent goodness to be the basis of virtue.
humanist	a person who believes that human values are the highest in the universe, or that all values come from the human.
idolatry	worship of human-made gods.
imam	"exemplar," (1) the leader of the Muslim worship; (2) the charismatic leaders of the Shi'a descended from 'Ali.
iman	"faith," in Islam; it has three elements – conviction, profession, and works.
incarnation	to invest God in human flesh. Christians consider the Christ as God in human form.
internal question	a question which must be decided from within some particular world-view.
ishtadevata	"the god of one's choosing;" one's chosen god within henotheism (Hinduism).
Ishvara	"the one who is able;" Brahman seen as God in the general sense, the supreme Lord of the universe.
Islam	"submission;" an Abrahamic religion, emphasizing worship of one God. Adherents believe that Muhammad is the last and most important of the prophets of God.
Jahiliya	the pre-Islamic Arabian age of "ignorance," marked by barbarism and unbelief; Islam came to end this evil age, according to Muslim belief.
Jainism	an indigenous Indian system of thought and practice founded before the sixth century BCE by Mahavira, that stresses liberation from (physical) karmic bondage. Strong emphasis on knowledge, morality, and asceticism to overcome suffering and death.
jen	the source and principle of humanity; what makes a person human, fellow-feeling (Confucianism).
Jina	"Spiritual conqueror," a person who has conquered rebirth – origin of term "Jainism".
jinn	spirit beings created from fire who are intermediate between humans and angels, which can be believers or unbelievers; if they are unbelievers, they are demons (Islam).
jiva	the soul, the life-principle of a person and other beings (Jainism).
jnana-yoga	path of release based on intellectual knowledge and meditative realization (Hinduism).
Jodo	The Japanese sect of Pure Land. It was founded in the twelfth century CE by the monk Genku. Salvation comes by grace, through faith in Amitabha's vow that those who call on his name will be reborn in the Western Paradise.
Judaism	the oldest of the Western monotheisms; includes belief in a creator God, *Torah*, and a messiah.

junzi (chun-tzu)	the gentleman or superior man; a role model for the conduct (Confucianism).
Kabbalah	Jewish mysticism first developed in the Middle Ages.
kalam	"disputation;" medieval Islamic term for scholastic and apologetic theology.
Kali	"the black one;" great Hindu goddess, consort of Shiva, destroyer of evil, but also addressed as mother.
kalpa	a long period of the created world. One world ends and new period begins with another creation (Indic).
Kannon	Japanese form of Avalokiteshvara or Kuan Yin, the Bodhisattva of Compassion.
karma	(1) action; (2) character – that is, the effects of action that inevitably accrue to the agent, producing bondage. In Hinduism *karma* is an explanation of caste and other aspects of life defined by birth. In Buddhism *karma* is primarily psychological. In Jainism it is understood in primarily physical terms.
karma-yoga	disciplined action whereby one acts without attachment to the fruits of one's actions (Hinduism).
karuna	compassion (Buddhism).
kerygma	the core message or proclamation of the early Christians.
koan	"public case;" a paradox or puzzle which cannot be solved by conventional, rational means used in Zen Buddhism to break up dualistic thinking.
Krishna	an incarnation of Vishnu; the chariot driver for the warrior Arjuna in the *Bhagavad Gita* and the Divine Beloved of Hindu devotion.
Kuan Yin	Chinese term for Avalokiteshvara, the Bodhisattva of Compassion, represented as male in India, but as female in China.
Kukai (Kobo Daishi)	founder of the Japanese Buddhist Shingon sect.
lama	"supreme being;" an enlightened teacher (Tibetan Buddhism).
Lao-tzu	purported sixth-century BCE Taoist sage, regarded as the founder of Taoism and traditionally believed to be the author of the *Tao-Te-Ching*.
Law of Karma	the principle that a person's thoughts and deeds are followed eventually by deserved pleasure or pain (Hinduism).
li	(1) in Confucianism, the norm of propriety, it can refer to ritual and correct conduct in society; (2) in Neo-Confucianism, the principle which gives things their nature and connects them to each other.
lila	joyful play, especially divine play; in Hinduism the universe is spontaneously brought about as a manifestation of *lila*.
Lin-chi	school of Ch'an that emphasized sudden enlightenment and

	koan practice (Chinese Buddhism). In Japan called *Rinzai Zen*.
linga	iconic or aniconic phallic representation of Shiva.
Logical Positivism	a philosophical view of the first half of the twentieth century holding that only tautologies and verifiable empirical statements are genuine. Metaphysical and religious assertions are unverifiable and hence meaningless.
Lotus Sutra	Mahayana Buddhist scripture explaining the superiority of the Mahayana path. A primary vehicle for the spread of Buddhism throughout East Asia.
Madhva	thirteenth-century Dualistic Vedantist who emphasized the differences between God and self; God and matter; individual selves; self and matter; and between individual things.
Madhyamika	the Buddhist philosophy that the phenomenal objects that one experiences are not ultimately real. Nagarjuna was the founder of the Madhymika school.
Mahavira	most recent of the twenty-four Jinas (sixth century BCE), according to Jaina tradition.
Mahayana	"the great vehicle, the wide path;" form of Buddhism prevalent in Tibet and East Asia. Emphasizes the Buddha's example of compassion and effort to bring all beings to enlightenment by means of Buddhas and Bodhisattvas as well as monastic discipline.
Mahdi	the expected one, a messianic figure (Islam).
Maitreya	"the friendly one, the benevolent one;" the celestial *bodhisattva* who now resides in heaven and will come to earth as the Buddha of the next age.
Makiguchi	founder of Soko Gakkai (Value Creation Society) of Japan in 1937.
mandala	a geometric pattern used in worship.
Mani	a Zoroastrian gnostic who taught the fulfillment of Zoroastrian, Christian and Buddhist beliefs, teaching that matter is evil.
maya	illusion, the appearances of things which prevents one from seeing things truly, thus concealing that deeper reality (Hinduism).
Mencius	the second great Confucian teacher after Confucius. His work was a key factor in the successful propagation of Confucianism throughout East Asia.
Messiah	God's long-awaited anointed king who will restore the world to rights; the one whom the Jews expected to come and deliver Israel from oppression and establish a kingdom of righteousness. It can refer to a historical person or to a supernatural being (Judaism, then Christianity).
metaphysics	a theory or philosophical study of the structure of reality. Metaphysics has two branches: ontology (a theory of the

	kinds of being) and cosmology (a theory of the origin of the universe).
metta	loving kindness, benevolence to all without discrimination; one of the four Buddhist virtues.
Middle Way	characterization of the Buddhist path to liberation because it is "midway" between indulgence and asceticism, between being and nonbeing, and between determinism and indeterminism.
midrash	rabbinic exposition explaining the meaning of the scriptures (Judaism).
miracle	an event that is judged to be brought about by divine intervention in the ordinary events of history.
Mishnah	"Oral Law;" the collection of oral law compiled in the second century CE (Judaism).
moksha	release, liberation from all constraints, including the cycle of birth-and-death (*samsara*): the goal of the spiritual quest in much of Hinduism.
monism	a belief that reality is of one kind; monism rejects any dualism of body versus mind, flesh versus spirit, or natural versus supernatural.
monotheism	belief that there is one, but only one, divine being; often used more specifically for belief in the supreme personal creator-God of Judaism, Christianity, and Islam.
Mo Tzu	an anti-Confucian pragmatic philosopher who founded Mohist philosophy, advocating universal love, which included sharing equally the essentials of food, clothing, and shelter. Confucians objected to Mohist universal love because it did not allow for special feelings for kin and because they believed more than the affirmation to love was required to shape a virtuous and harmonious society.
Muhammad	the prophet of Islam to whom God revealed his full message to humankind in the *Qur'an*.
Muslim	follower of Islam, one who has submitted to God.
mystical experience	an inordinate experience in this life of a (felt) profound, direct encounter or union or identification, with a supernatural, or transcendent, or possibly divine reality.
Nagarjuna	the Buddhist philosopher who established the Madhyamika school of philosophy.
Nataraj	"lord of the dance;" symbolic representations of Shiva as creator, preserver, and destroyer, dancing and so producing the cycles of the eons (Hinduism).
Neo-Orthodoxy	the most influential school of Christian orthodoxy in the twentieth century, begun by the work of Karl Barth.
New Testament	the canon of Christian scriptures codified in 382 CE which, together with the Hebrew scriptures, constitutes the Christian Bible.

Nichiren	a monk in Japan who established a school based on faith in the *Lotus Sutra*.
nirguna	having no qualities, a term sometimes used to characterize Brahman or God in devotional Hinduism.
nirvana	"extinction;" the goal of Buddhist practice, the liberation from *samsara* and the extinction of greed, hatred and delusion; deliverance from rebirth and all suffering; (1) earthly nirvana (2) final nirvana. In Pali, nibbana.
nonattachment	nonattachment to the fruits of action is the key to fulfilling one's duties without accumulating karmic bondage according to the *Bhagavad-Gita*; fundamental also to Buddhism.
noumena	"things-in-themselves;" in Kant's theory of knowledge, this includes God and the non-empirical self.
nyaya	argumentation, Hindu system that focuses on logic and epistemology.
pan-en-theism	the belief that "God" permeates everything, but is not identical to it.
pantheism	the belief that the whole cosmos is divine, usually equating "God" and nature.
paramitas	the surpassing virtues of generosity, enthusiasm, patience, morality, meditation, and wisdom that characterize the life of a *bodhisattva*.
parinirvana	"beyond nirvana;" the final state that one who has reached earthly nirvana passes into after death.
Parvati	a Great Goddess and consort of Shiva, whose alter ego is Kali.
Pentateuch	the first five books of the Hebrew scriptures.
phenomena	"things-as-they-are-experienced;" in Kant's theory of knowledge, a subject's experience of an object that is different from the object itself.
Pillars of Islam	the basic institutions of Islamic law for every responsible male believer; five for the Sunnis: the profession of faith, worship, almsgiving, pilgrimage, and fasting; Shi'ites add recognition of the imam.
polytheism	a belief in many gods among whom are divided the powers of nature.
pratitya-samutpada	see dependent origination.
properly basic belief	a belief which is held as basic without violating any fundamental epistemic principles.
Pure Land (Ching-tu)	the paradise established by Amitabha Buddha by reason of his great merit and out of his compassion for suffering beings, who, by faith, may enter his paradise at death where rapid completion of the Buddhist path is facilitated.
purgatory	a Roman Catholic conception of a state between this life

and heaven, where the sins of this life are expiated in preparation for heaven itself (see hell, Buddhist).

Qur'an the sacred scripture of Islam, regarded as the word of God dictated to Muhammad through the archangel Gabriel; the *Pentateuch* and Psalms from the Hebrew Scriptures, Christian Gospels and *Qur'an* comprise the complete Islamic scriptures.

rabbi a learned man who has received ordination to preach and teach (Judaism).

Ramanuja eleventh-century Hindu Vedantist philosopher whose qualified nondualism allowed him to regard Brahman as the soul and the world as the body of reality; author of *Vedartha Samgraha*.

rationalism the broad epistemological position that (1) reason is the test of truth and (2) knowledge can only be acquired through reason.

reductionism with respect to religion, rejecting metaphysical claims and retaining only ethical content.

reincarnation the view that the spirit or soul of a person repeatedly assumes a new bodily form after death.

resurrection the belief that a person who has died will be restored as a whole, living person.

Rig Veda oldest and philosophically most important of the Vedas, the sacred texts that form the foundation of Hinduism; compiled between twelfth and tenth centuries BCE.

rita cosmic order (Vedic Hinduism).

roshi "venerable teacher;" a Zen master.

sacred set apart to worship as a deity or as worthy of worship.

saddha the faith or trust which is acknowledged in Buddhism as necessary until wisdom is achieved.

saguna with qualities; in Hinduism, saguna Brahman is a manifest form of the divine as opposed to nirguna Brahman, or unqualified divinity.

salvation a divine favor freely given by God through grace.

samsara "continuous wandering;" the ceaseless process of birth, aging, suffering, death, and rebirth; (sansar in Sikhism).

sannyasin renouncer; the last stage in the order of life in Hinduism.

sasatavada eternalism, the belief that the soul continues eternally.

sati mindfulness, a factor of enlightenment.

satori Japanese term for the Zen experience of enlightenment.

satyagraha "seizing the truth;" the term used by Gandhi to describe his method of nonviolent opposition to social and political injustice.

scriptures sacred writings.

shahada witnessing; the Islamic profession of faith "there is but one God, and Muhammad is his messenger (rasul)."

shakti	the feminine divine power (Hinduism).
Shakyamuni	the historical Buddha, sage (muni) of the Shakya clan.
Shankara	most famous Advaita Vedanta philosopher, eighth century CE.
Shari'a	the "way" of Islam, including law and governance, according to the *Qur'an* and Sunna.
Shekhinah	"the divine presence;" the most general term for the immanence of God in the world (Judaism).
sheol	shadowy realm of the dead (Judaism).
Shi'a	"party" of 'Ali; the Shi'ites believe that Muhammad designated his son-in-law, 'Ali, to succeed him as leader of the *Umma* of Islam; the Shi'ite community constitutes about twenty percent of the total Muslim community.
Shingon	Japanese term for the Chinese Ch'en Yen school of Buddhism; a form of esoteric, tantric Buddhism.
Shiva	supreme deity for many Hindus; god of yoga, known as the god of creation and destruction and Nataraj.
Shivite	a worshipper or devotee of Shiva.
shruti	"that which is heard;" revealed knowledge in Hinduism.
shu	reciprocity; treating others as they would like to be treated (Confucianism).
shunyata	emptiness of separateness and permanence; devoid of own-nature; voidness; fundamental Buddhist teaching.
Siddartha Gautama	the historical Buddha, founder of Buddhism, born in northeast India in the sixth century BCE.
Sikh	"learner;" follower of Nanak and his successors.
Sikhism	an offshoot of Hinduism with certain Islamic elements which began in the fifteenth century with Guru Nanak.
sin	disobedience of the will of God (Christianity).
skepticism	a religious skeptic denies that there are any reasonable grounds for religious belief.
Soto Zen	school of Zen established in Japan by Dogen which emphasizes *zazen*, sitting meditation.
spirit	the form of a being apart from any material properties.
Sufism	Islamic mysticism emphasizing personal devotion and sincerity as key to realizing God's presence.
Sunnis	the majority of Muslims, who believe that any good Muslim can be a leader; they prefer to reach agreements by means of consensus and do not recognize special sacred wisdom in their leaders as Shi'ites do.
Talmud	collection of oral law and commentary compiled in the fifth century CE in Palestine and the sixth century CE in Babylonia (Judaism).
tanha	craving; identified in the second Noble Truth as the cause of suffering.
Tao	"the way;" (1) in Taoism, referring to the path, course, or

	way of the universe (2) in Confucianism, referring to the way of both the cosmic and social order.
Taoism	Chinese tradition based on following the natural way (*tao*).
Tao-Te-Ching	"Book of the Way and its Power," foundational Taoist text.
tariqa	"way" of Sufism as a whole as the mystical path of Islam in contrast to the Shari'a, the religious law; tariqa also refers to a specific Sufi organization or method of meditation.
tawhid	the divine unity, Islam's central doctrine.
Ten Command-ments	ten laws given by God to Moses as recorded in Exodus chapter 20.
theism	belief in a personal creator God.
theodicy	an attempted justification for the presence of evil in a universe created by a powerful, wise, and loving God.
theology	the discipline that describes and explains God and God's relation to the world.
Theravada	"The way of the elders;" the tradition of Buddhism prevalent in South and Southeast Asia whose followers believe they are following the original Buddhism, the way taught by the Buddha in early discourses, and in which senior monks hold primary authority in matters pertaining to the Buddha's way.
Tirthankara	"ford-maker;" another name for Jina, emphasizing the conqueror's ability to find a way across the ocean of suffering (Jainism).
Torah	teaching of God to the Jews. The *Torah* includes (1) the written *Torah* of the Hebrew Bible and (2) the oral *Torah* later recorded in the *Talmud*, both said to have been revealed on Mount Sinai.
transcendental idealism	the Kantian view that the *a priori* conditions of experience can be deduced (transcendentally).
trikaya	three bodies of the Buddha: dharmakaya, celestial buddhas, and Shakyamuni, the earthly Buddha (Mahayana).
Trinity	the Christian doctrine that God is three persons in one: Father, Son, and Holy Spirit.
ucchedavada	annihilationism, the denial of any continuity or future after death (Hinduism).
Upanishads	"sitting closely to a teacher;" concluding portion of the Vedic literature containing sacred knowledge of reality, Brahman and Atman.
upaya	skillful means for arriving at the direct perception of truth (Mahayana Buddhism).
utilitarianism	a secular ethic in which good and bad, right and wrong, are determined by the sum of human happiness produced.
Vaibhashika	Buddhist philosophical school of the Theravada tradition that regards the dharmas – ultimate units of existence – as both real and many.

Vaishnava	a worshipper or devotee of Vishnu or his avatars, particularly Krishna.
Vedanta	"End of the Vedas;" Hindu philosophical tradition rooted in the Upanishads; concerned to understand the relation between Brahman and the world.
Vedartha Samgraha	Ramanuja's summary and interpretation of Vedic teachings.
Vedas	four foundational Indian religious texts – *Rig, Sama, Yajur,* and *Atharva* – composed prior to 1000 BCE.
vipaka	"ripen;" the consequence of an action, according to the law of karma.
viraga	"without lust or greed;" non-attachment.
Vishishtadvaita Vedanta	the qualified non-dualistic school of Vedic philosophy represented by Ramanuja (Hinduism).
Vishnu	supreme deity for many Hindus; associated with 10 incarnations, including Krishna and Buddha, known as "the preserver."
voidness	an alternate translation of *shunyata* or emptiness (Buddhism).
worldview	all the cognitive elements which the mind brings to experience – i.e. concepts, their interrelationships, laws of logic, persistent beliefs.
wu-wei	no-action, accomplishing tasks without assertion by following the way of the Tao; individuals in harmony with the Tao can accomplish more than those not in harmony.
yang	one of a pair of complementary principles in Chinese thought (the other principle is yin) characterized as sunny, warm, hard, dry, and active.
YHWH	the sacred name of God which is never pronounced in Judaism.
yin	one of a pair of complementary principles in Chinese thought (the other principle is yang) characterized as feminine, dark, soft, moist, cold, and yielding.
yoga	a path of discipline (Hinduism).
Yogacara School	a Mahayana Buddhist school which focuses on calm meditiation and denies the independent existence of matter while affirming consciousness; said to be founded by Asanga and Maitreyi (the latter a reference either to Asanga's teacher or to the future Buddha who may have inspired him) and Asanga's brother, with important foundational literature also written by Vasubhandhu.
Zen	a form of Mahayana Buddhism that flourished in Japan; emphasizes direct meditative insight.
zhongyong	Doctrine of the Mean; path between the extremes (Confucianism).

Zoroaster   Greek for the Persian name Zarathushtra, founder of Zoroastrianism.

Zoroastrianism   founded in sixth century BCE in Persia by Zarathushtra, the first tradition to teach heaven and hell and resurrection of the body. In Zoroastrianism a good "God" is opposed by an evil spirit; see Ahura Mazda and Angra Mainyu.

NOTES

ACKNOWLEDGMENTS

1. Shusaku Endo, *Deep River*, trans. Van C. Gessel (New York: New Directions Books, 1994), pp.117–118.

INTRODUCTION

1. Bertrand Russell, *The Problem of Philosophy* (New York: Oxford University Press, 1959), pp. 155–157.
2. Fyodor Dostoevsky, *Crime and Punishment*, trans. Constance Garnett (New York: Bantam Books, 1958), p. 279.
3. Peter Berger, *The Heretical Imperative* (Garden City, N.Y.: Doubleday, 1979).
4. Paul Tillich, *Dynamics of Faith* (New York: Harper & Row, Harper Torchbooks, 1957), p. 18, 16.
5. Ibid., p. 17.
6. Robert Funk, *Honest to Jesus: Jesus for a New Millennium* (San Francisco: HarperSanFrancisco, 1996) p. 11.
7. Ibid., p. 11, 306.
8. Ibid., p. 300.
9. Ibid., p. 298.
10. Moses Maimonides, *The Guide for the Perplexed* (New York: Dover Publications, 1956), pp. 384–386.
11. Ch.12 v.1. Parrinder, Geoffrey, trans. *The Bhagavad Gita: A Verse Translation* (Oxford: Oneworld, 1996) p.81.
12. Ch.12 v.5. Ibid., p. 81.
13. Ch.11 v.54. Ibid., p. 80.
14. St. Anselm, *Proselogium* in *St. Anselm: Basic Writings*, trans. S.M. Deane (Lasalle: Opencourt, 1966), pp. 6–7.
15. St. Bonaventure, *The Mind's Road to God*, trans. George Boaz (New York, Bobbs-Merrill, 1953), p. 3.
16. Ibid., pp. 44–45.

CHAPTER 1: RELIGION AND PHILOSOPHY

1. Of these nearly two billion Christians, over half are Roman Catholic, a quarter are in various Protestant denominations and half of the remainder are in the traditions of Eastern Orthodoxy.
2. Socrates, *Apology* 36b-c and 38a in *Plato: The Collected Dialogues*, ed. Edith Hamilton and Huntington Cairns (Princeton: Princeton University Press, 1941), p. 21.
3. William James, *Some Problems of Philosophy* (New York: Greenwood Press, 1968), p. 15.
4. Bertrand Russell, *The Problem of Philosophy* (New York: Oxford University Press, 1959), pp. 155–157.
5. Clarence Irving Lewis, *Mind and the World Order* (New York: Dover Publications, 1929), pp. 18–19.
6. See, respectively, Bertrand Russell, *Why I am not a Christian*, ed. Paul Edwards (New York: Simon and Schuster, 1957); A. J. Ayer, *Language, Truth and Logic* (New York: Dover, 1952); Jean-Paul Sartre, *The Devil and the Good Lord* (New York: Random House, 1960), p. 141.
7. Etienne Gilson, *Reason and Revelation in the Middle Ages* (New York: Charles Scribner's Sons, 1938), p. 18.
8. Richard Rorty, *Philosophy and the Mirror of Nature* (Princeton: Princeton University Press, 1979), p. 367.
9. Ibid., p. 360.
10. Paul Tillich, *Systematic Theology* (Chicago: University of Chicago Press, 1951), Vol. 1, p. 3.

CHAPTER 2: WORLDVIEWS AND RELIGION

1. William James, *The Varieties of Religious Experience* (New York: Random House, The Modern Library, 1902), p. 120.
2. On this point see R. C. Zaehner, "Religious Truth," in *Truth and Dialogue in World Religions: Conflicting Truth-Claims*, ed. John Hick (Philadelphia: Westminster Press, 1974), p. 3.
3. His Holiness the Dalai Lama, *The Joy of Living and Dying in Peace* (London: HarperCollins, 1997), p. xxi.
4. See His Holiness the Dalai Lama, *Ethics for the New Millennium* (New York: Riverhead Books, 1999).
5. His Holiness the Dalai Lama, *The Joy of Living and Dying in Peace*, p. 19.
6. Ludwig Wittgenstein, *Philosophical Investigations*, 3rd edition, trans. G. E. M. Anscombe (New York: Macmillan Co., 1953), I. 268 b.
7. John Hick, *Problems of Religious Pluralism* (New York: St. Martin's Press, 1985), p. 34.
8. John Hick, *God Has Many Names* (Philadelphia: Westminster Press, 1982), p. 96.
9. John Hick, *Problems of Religious Pluralism*, p. 29.
10. Ibid., p. 41.
11. Ibid., pp. 42–43. See also *God Has Many Names*, p. 59.
12. *Nostra Aetate* ("Declaration on the Relationship of the Church to Non-Christian

Religions"), in *The Documents of Vatican II* (America Press, 1966), pp. 660–662 and 667.

13. Karl Rahner, *Theological Investigations* (London: Darton, Longman & Todd; New York: Seabury Press, 1961–1984), vol. 6, p. 391.
14. Zaehner, "Religious Truth," pp. 18 and 17.
15. Inclusivism is typically based on the notion that one's own religion most fully possesses a particular element which is most essential to religion. Zaehner looks to the integration of the personal and collective; Kant holds that true religiosity is identical to the moral life; Schleiermacher proposes that underlying genuine religion is "the feeling of absolute dependence;" Rudolph Otto emphasizes a numinous sense of the holy, a sense of the *mysterium tremendum*; *Nostra Aetate* declares that "from ancient times down to the present, there has existed among diverse peoples a certain perception of that hidden power which hovers over the course of things and over the events of human life;" and John Baillie suggests that all humans have a knowledge of God through a felt presence of the divine such that all people "already believe in Him." (John Baillie, *Our Knowledge of God* (New York: Charles Scribner's Sons, 1959), p. 255.)
16. Frank Whaling, *Christian Theology and World Religions: A Global Approach* (Basingstoke: Marshall Pickering, 1986), p. 87. "Other religions can have their own fulfillment theology. Sri Aurobindo sees the world religious process converging on Mother India rather than the Cosmic Christ, and Sir Muhammad Iqbal sees it converging upon a kind of ideal Islam."
17. Rahner, *Theological Investigations*, vol. 5, p. 132.
18. Parrinder, Geoffrey, trans., *The Bhagavad Gita: A Verse Translation* (Oxford: Oneworld, 1996), pp. 52, 62–63.

CHAPTER 3: RELIGIOUS METAPHYSICS WITHOUT GOD

1. Eliot Deutsch and J. A. B. van Buitenen, eds., *A Source Book of Advaita Vedanta* (Honolulu: The University Press of Hawaii, 1971), p. 130.
2. G. M. A. Grube, trans., *Plato's Republic* (Indianapolis: Hackett Publishing Company, 1974) pp. 170–171.
3. *Majjhima Nikaya*, sutta 63, in John M. and Patricia Koller, eds., *A Source Book in Asian Philosophy* (New Jersey: Prentice Hall, 1991), pp. 244–246.
4. Deutsch and van Buitenen, eds., *A Source Book of Advaita Vedanta*, p. 180.
5. Leo Tolstoy. "The Death of Ivan Ilyich," in *Great Short Works of Leo Tolstoy*, Louise and Aylmer Maude, trans. (New York: Harper and Row Publishers, 1967), pp. 247–302.
6. His Holiness the Dalai Lama, *The Joy of Living and Dying in Peace*, p. 53.
7. Ibid., p. 134.
8. Damien Keown, *Buddhism: A Very Short Introduction* (Oxford: Oxford University Press, 1996), p. 40.
9. His Holiness the Dalai Lama, *The Joy of Living and Dying in Peace*.
10. Don Cupitt, *The New Christian Ethics* (London: SCM Press Ltd., 1988), p. 36.
11. Don Cupitt, *Crisis of Moral Authority* (London: SCM Press Ltd., 1972), pp. 27–28, and Cupitt, *The New Christian Ethics*, p. 15.
12. First, Cupitt thinks that "modern people demand autonomy," and, second, he thinks that autonomy is a necessary condition of moral action (and also of the

religious requirement to "fulfill our highest possible destiny as spiritual, self-conscious beings"). Don Cupitt, *Taking Leave of God* (New York: Crossroad, 1981), pp. ix and 94. Cf. p. 85.

13. Cupitt, *The New Christian Ethics*, p. 1.

14. Ibid., pp. 4, 6, 52 and 115 (italics mine).

15. In our religiously pluralistic world it is important to keep in mind that the considerations here about the relation between theism and ethics go far beyond Christianity. Cupitt explicitly endorses, and so I address, *Christian* humanism, but many of the considerations below more broadly apply to "religious humanism."

16. Cupitt, *The New Christian Ethics*, pp. 18–19.

17. Julian Huxley, "The Creed of a Scientific Humanist," in *The Meaning of Life*, ed. E. D. Klemke (New York: Oxford University Press, 1981), pp. 68 and 65.

18. Kaufman is also aware of this problem (*Theology for a Nuclear Age* [Manchester: Manchester University Press, 1985], p. 37).

19. Cupitt, *The New Christian Ethics*, p. 155.

20. Bhikkhu Chao Chu, "Buddhism and Dialogue Among the World Religions: Meeting the Challenge of Materialistic Skepticism," in Joseph Runzo, ed., *Ethics, Religion, and the Good Society: New Directions in a Pluralistic World* (Louisville: Westminster/John Knox, 1992), p. 168.

CHAPTER 4: RELIGIOUS METAPHYSICS WITH GOD

1. Sarvepalli Radhakrishnan and Charles A. Moore, eds., *A Sourcebook in Indian Philosophy* (Princeton: Princeton University Press, 1957), p. 552.

2. Alfred North Whitehead, *Religion in the Making* (New York: New American Library, 1960), p. 50.

3. A God distinct from the world can also be immanent in the world.

4. Deutsch and van Buitenen, eds., *A Source Book of Advaita Vedanta*, p. 162.

5. Radhakrishnan and Moore, eds., *A Sourcebook in Indian Philosophy*, p. 551.

6. The ideas of premises 9 and 11 come from Surendranath Dasgupta, *A History of Indian Philosophy*, Vol. IV (Cambridge: Cambridge University Press, 1955), pp. 77, 80, 178.

7. Radhakrishnan and Moore, eds. *A Sourcebook in Indian Philosophy*, p. 543.

8. Ibid., p. 544.

9. Ibid., p. 562.

10. Ibid., p. 567.

11. See, e.g., Sallie McFague, "The World as God's Body" in *The Meaning of Life in the World Religions*, Joseph Runzo and Nancy M. Martin, eds. (Oxford: Oneworld Publications, 1999) and McFague, *Models of God: Theology for an Ecological, Nuclear Age* (Philadelphia: Fortress Press, 1987).

12. Radhakrishnan and Moore, eds., *A Sourcebook in Indian Philosophy*, p. 552.

13. Ibid., p. 552.

14. Though it is slightly ambiguous, for ease of discussion, I will here understand "greatest conceivable being" as equivalent to "the being than which no greater can be conceived."

15. St. Anselm, *Anselm's Basic Writings* 2nd ed., trans., S. W. Deane (La Salle, Illinois: Open Court Publishing Company, 1962).

16. Since God is perfectly good, on Leibniz's view the world God chose to create is, in the now famous phrase, "the best of all possible worlds."

17. Plantinga's version of the argument begins with the assumption that God should be thought of as "maximally great." Being maximally great entails being "maximally excellent." That is, if God exists, God necessarily possesses the most perfect set of properties which would make a being great. (Alvin Plantinga, *The Nature of Necessity* [Oxford, Clarendon Press, 1974] p. 213 f.) Thus, a maximally excellent being would be omnipotent, omniscient, and perfectly good. But further, a being could not be maximally excellent unless it existed in every possible world. Now, Plantinga argues that the property of maximal greatness *could* be possessed by a being. So there is some "possible world" – some way in which the world could have turned out – in which the maximally great being, God, exists. But any being which is maximally great in some possible world would exist in *all* possible worlds, for that being would have the property of being maximally excellent. Therefore, God exists necessarily, for there is no possibility (no possible world such that) that God does not exist.

18. Alvin Plantinga, *God, Freedom and Evil* (New York: Harper & Row, 1974), p. 112.

19. Stephen H. Phillips, *Classical Indian Metaphysics* (Chicago: Open Court, 1995), p. 83.

CHAPTER 5: A POSTERIORI ARGUMENTS FOR GOD'S EXISTENCE

1. Jean-Paul Sartre, *The Devil and the Good Lord*, trans. Kitty Black (New York: Vintage Books, 1960), Act III, scene x.

2. Bertrand Russell and F. C. Copleston, "A Debate on the Existence of God," repr. in *The Existence of God*, ed. John Hick (New York: Macmillan, 1964), pp. 173–175.

3. See Thomas Aquinas, *Summa Theologiae* (Manchester: Blackfriars, 1970).

4. For a comprehensive analysis of the principle of sufficient reason, see William Rowe, *The Cosmological Argument* (Princeton, N.J.: Princeton University Press, 1975), ch. 2.

5. Samuel Clarke gave an earlier, modern version of this argument in the eighteenth century.

6. Russell and Copleston, "A Debate on the Existence of God," pp. 173–175.

7. Some philosophers, like Samuel Clarke and Leibniz, have held the even stronger view that the principle of sufficient reason is a necessary truth, but it is doubtful that such a strong view could be made convincing to those already skeptical of God's existence.

8. See David Hume, *Dialogues Concerning Natural Religion*, ed., Nelson Pike (Indianapolis: Bobbs-Merrill, 1970).

9. Ibid., pp. 55, 57.

10. This parallels an argument Alvin Plantinga presents in *God and Other Minds* (Ithaca: Cornell University Press, 1967) to make a similar point.

11. Hume, *Dialogues Concerning Natural Religion*, p. 32.

12. Regarding (a), in addition to the foregoing sorts of considerations against specific arguments for God's existence, Immanuel Kant provides a fundamental reason

why all such arguments will ultimately fail. Note that Kant's moral argument is not intended as a proof of God's existence but as support for the conviction that God exists: "I must not even say, '*It is* morally certain that there is a God, etc.', but ' *I am* morally certain, etc.'" (Kant, *Critique of Pure Reason*, trans., Norman Kemp Smith [London: Macmillan, 1973], B 857.) By distinguishing between phenomena and noumena, Kant is able to draw the epistemological conclusion that we could never *know* the existence or nature of God *qua noumenal*: "Through concepts alone, it is quite impossible to advance to the discovery of new objects and supernatural beings; and it is useless to appeal to experience, which in all cases yields only appearances." (Kant, *Critique of Pure Reason*, p. 530.)

CHAPTER 6: EVIL: AN ARGUMENT AGAINST MONOTHEISM

1. Fyodor Dostoyevsky, *The Brothers Karamazov*, trans., Andrew McAndrew (Toronto, Bantam, 1987).

CHAPTER 7: EMBODIMENT, GENDER AND GOD

1. Part of this chapter comes from my "The Symbolism of Sex and the Reality of God" in *Love, Sex, and Gender in the World Religions*, Joseph Runzo and Nancy M. Martin, eds. (Oxford: Oneworld Publications, 2000) where a more detailed analysis can be found.
2. Shusaku Endo, *Deep River* (New York: A New Directions Book, 1994), pp. 140–141.
3. Parrinder, trans., *The Bhagavad-Gita*, p. 30.
4. And looking to the other end of time, this is why the Christian Scriptures speak of a "new heaven and a new earth." See Isaiah 65:17 and Revelation 21:01.
5. See Lee Seigel, *Fires of Love, Waters of Peace* (Honolulu: University of Hawaii Press, 1983), p. 95.
6. Sallie McFague, *Models of God: Theology for an Ecological, Nuclear Age* (Philadelphia: Fortress Press, 1987), p. 106.
7. Ibid., p. 111.
8. Ibid., p. 112.
9. Ibid., p. 73 and 138.
10. Ibid., p. x.
11. See Thomas Aquinas, *Summa Theologiae* Pt. I, Q 13, Art. 5.
12. St. Teresa of Avila, *Autobiography* (New York: Columbia Press, 1911), Ch. 29, p. 215. This experience occurred in 1559.
13. *Song of Songs* (RSV) 1:13 and 1:16.
14. Gershom G. Sholem, *Major Trends in Jewish Mysticism* (New York: Schocken, 1954), p. 227.
15. Jalalu'l-Din Rumi in Reynold A. Nickolson, trans., *Rumi: Poet and Mystic* (Oxford: Oneworld, 1995), p. 45 (*Math* V, 372).
16. *Zohar: The Book of Splendor*, ed., Gershom G. Sholem (New York: Shocken, 1949), p. 89. See also Charlotte Fonrobert, "To Increase Torah is to Increase Life," in Runzo and Martin, eds., *The Meaning of Life in the World Religions*, p. 81.

17. Gershom Scholem, *Major Trends in Jewish Mysticism*, p. 235.
18. Carl G. Jung, *Man and His Symbols* (London: Penguin, 1990) p. 75. On p. 78, he says "the unconscious seems to be guided...chiefly by instinctive trends, represented by corresponding thought forms – that is, by the archetypes." Unlike Freud, Jung thinks religion is valuable for modern persons, but he is, even so, a non-realist about the Transcendent.
19. It can be argued that this epistemic distance between humans and God actually preserves human free will from what would otherwise be the constant overwhelming presence of God.
20. Jung, *Man and His Symbols*, p. 67.
21. Robert Nozick, *The Examined Life* (New York: Simon and Schuster, 1989), p. 67.
22. Paul Tillich, *The Dynamics of Faith*, pp. 41–43.
23. Faith is our ultimate directedness toward that which transcends finite reality. This is why as Tillich says, "the language of faith is the language of symbols." Tillich, *The Dynamics of Faith*, p. 45.
24. A. K. Ramanujan, trans. *Speaking of Siva* (New York: Penguin, 1973), p. 125.
25. McFague, *Models of God*, pp. 33–34. This critique follows my review of *Models of God* in *Faith and Philosophy*, 7, 3, pp. 360–364.
26. McFague, *Models of God*, p. 39.
27. Ibid., p. 35.
28. Basavanna, in *Speaking of Siva*, p. 89.

CHAPTER 8: LIFE AFTER DEATH

1. William Shakespeare. *Hamlet* III.I.59–67, 77–81 in *The Riverside Shakespeare* (Boston: Houghton Mifflin Company, 1974), pp. 1135–1197.
2. Juan Mascaro, trans., *The Dhammapada* (London, Penguin Books, 1973), p. 40.
3. Parrinder, trans., *The Bhagavad-Gita*, p. 14.
4. John Searle, *Minds, Brains and Science* (London: British Broadcasting Corporation, 1984), p. 32.
5. Ibid., p. 37.
6. His Holiness The Dalai Lama, *The Joy of Living and Dying*, pp. 152–153.
7. From *Milindapanha*, trans., V. Trenckner (London: Royal Asiatic Society, 1928), pp. 25f. quoted in Wm. Theodore de Bary, ed., *Sources of Indian Tradition*, Vol. 1 (New York: Columbia University Press, 1958), pp. 104–105.
8. From *Milindapanha* (Trenckner, p. 40).
9. From *Milindapanha* (Trenckner, p. 70).
10. Keith Ward, *In Defence of the Soul* (Oxford: Oneworld, 1998), p. 142.

CHAPTER 9: RELIGIOUS EXPERIENCE

1. Immanuel Kant, *Lectures on Philosophical Theology*, p. 161.
2. The *Talmud* is the total codified Jewish civil and religious law, comprised of the Mishnah (*c.* 200 CE) and the Gemara, a commentary on the Mishnah.
3. John 8:31 (RSV).
4. I Corinthians 1:18 and 21 (RSV).

5. Rudolf Otto, *The Idea of the Holy* (London: Oxford University Press, 1923), p. 7.
6. Walter Stace, *Time and Eternity* (Princeton: Princeton University Press, 1952), pp. 33 and 39. Italics mine.
7. Meister Eckhart, "Sermon on Lk. 10:38", in *Meister Eckhart*, ed., trans., Raymond B. Blakney (New York: Harper & Row, Harper Torchbooks, 1941), p. 211. (See also Eckhart's sermon on Lk. 2:42, in *Meister Eckhart*, pp. 118–119.)
8. Anton Poulain, *The Graces of Interior Prayer*, 6th ed. (London: Kegan Paul, Trench, Trubner & Co., 1912), p. 3.
9. David Hume, *Dialogues Concerning Natural Religion*, ed., Nelson Pike (Indianapolis: The Bobbs-Merrill Co., 1970), Part IV, p. 40.
10. Otto, *The Idea of the Holy*, p. 22.
11. The ideas in this section are drawn from my article "Kant on Reason and Justified Belief in God," in Philip J. Rossi and Michael Wreen, eds., *Kant's Philosophy of Religion Reconsidered* (Bloomington: Indiana University Press, 1991) pp. 22–39.
12. Kant, *Lectures on Philosophical Theology*, trans. Allen W. Wood and Gertrude M. Clark (Ithaca and London: Cornell University Press, 1978), pp. 52–54.
13. Ibid., p. 54.
14. See Kant's essay, "What is Enlightenment?," in *Kant on History*, ed., Lewis White Beck (Indianapolis: Bobbs-Merrill, 1963).
15. Immanuel Kant, "What is Orientation in Thinking?" in *The Critique of Practical Reason and Other Writings in Moral Philosophy*, trans., Lewis White Beck (New York: Garland, 1976), p. 305n.
16. Immanuel Kant, *Religion Within the Limits of Reason Alone*, trans., Theodore M. Greene and Hoyt H. Hudson (New York: Harper & Row, Harper Torchbooks, 1960), pp. 142–143.
17. Allan Wood identifies this reasoning as central in "Kant's Deism." In *Kant's Philosophy of Religion Reconsidered*, ed. Philip J. Rossi and Michael Wreen (Bloomington: Indiana University Press, 1991).
18. Kant, *Lectures on Philosophical Theology*, p. 160.
19. Moses Maimonides, *The Guide for the Perplexed*, trans., M. Friedlander (New York: Dover Publications, repr. 1956), p. 395.
20. Kant, *Religion Within the Limits of Reason Alone*, pp. 152–153.
21. Ibid., p. 142n.
22. Immanuel Kant, *Prolegomena* (Indianapolis: Bobbs-Merrill Company, 1950), p. 106.
23. Karl Barth, *The Epistle to the Romans* (London: Oxford University Press, 1972), p. 230.
24. Ibid., p. 242. Italics mine.
25. Tillich, *Dynamics of Faith*, p. 78. Italics mine.

CHAPTER 10: USING SCIENCE TO ARGUE AGAINST RELIGION

1. Richard Dawkins, *The Selfish Gene* (Oxford: Oxford University Press, 1989), pp. 192–193.

2. Carl Sagan, introduction to Stephen Hawking, *A Brief History of Time: From the Big Bang to Black Holes* (New York: Bantam, 1988), p. x.
3. Albert Einstein, *The World as I See It*, trans., Alan Harris (New York: Carol Publishing group, 1998), p. 5.
4. Ibid., p. 1.
5. Hawking, *A Brief History of Time*, p. 136.
6. Dawkins, *The Selfish Gene*, p. 2.
7. Ibid., p. 256.
8. Ibid., p. 266.
9. Ibid., p. 265.
10. Ibid., p. 265.
11. Ibid., p. 2.
12. Charles Darwin, *The Origin of the Species by Means of Natural Selection* (first published 1859; Harmondsworth: Penguin, 1985), p. 263, quoted by Keith Ward, *God, Chance, and Necessity* (Oxford: Oneworld Publications, 1996), p. 62.
13. Dawkins, *The Selfish Gene*, pp. 245, 263, 265. Italics mine.
14. Ibid., p. 192–193.
15. Paul Davies, *The Mind of God: The Scientific Basis for a Rational World* (New York: Simon & Schuster, 1992), p. 152.
16. Marvin Harris, *Our Kind: Who We Are, Where We Came From, Where We Are Going* (New York: Harper & Row, 1989), p. 127.
17. Ibid., p. 399.
18. Ibid., p. 414.
19. Ibid., p. 446.
20. Sigmund Freud, *The Future of an Illusion*, trans., W. D. Robson-Scott, (Garden City, N.Y.: Doubleday & Co., 1964), p. 92.
21. Ibid., p. 49.
22. Ibid., p. 48.
23. Ibid., p. 90.
24. Ibid., p. 92.
25. Einstein, *The World As I See It*, p. 26.
26. Ibid., pp. 7–8.
27. Luke 17:33.

CHAPTER 11: MORALITY, ETHICS AND RELIGION

1. Within Utilitarianism, an "act" utilitarian says that for any alternative set of actions (within the range of choices) one should perform the action which will produce the greatest possible balance of good over evil in the nonmoral sense. A "rule" utilitarian asks the question: Which action fits the rule which produces the greatest possible balance of good over evil? A "rule" utilitarian argues that if we do not have general rules in the system, when we get to the situation requiring a moral decision, we will end up choosing a lot of actions which have disutility because we are trying to decide actions one by one.
2. Dorothy Sayers, "Dilemma," in *In the Teeth of the Evidence* (New York: Harper & Row, 1987).
3. Dostoevsky, *Crime and Punishment*, p. 58.

4. Likewise this is a problem with the "veil of ignorance" which John Rawls proposes should be employed when deciding what is just.
5. Eliot Deutsch, *The Bhagavad Gita: Translated, with Introduction and Critical Essays* (London: University Press of America, 1968), p. 161.
6. Ibid., p. 162.
7. Ibid., pp. 162–164.
8. William K. Frankena, "Is Morality Logically Dependent on Religion?" in Gene Outka and John P. Reeder, eds., *Religion and Morality* (Garden City, NY: Anchor Press/Doubleday, 1973), pp. 303–304.
9. Bhikku Chao Chu, "Buddhism and Dialogue Among the World Religions: Meeting the Challenge of Materialistic Skepticism," in *Ethics Religion and the Good Society: New Directions in a Pluralistic World*, ed., Joseph Runzo (Louisville, Kentucky: Westminster, 1992), pp. 168–170.
10. Confucius, *The Analects* (London: Penguin, 1979), p. 135.
11. In Christopher Key Chapple, *Nonviolence to Animals, Earth, and Self in Asian Traditions* (New York: State University of New York Press, 1993), p. 16.
12. Juan Mascaro, trans., *The Dhammapada*, p. 54.
13. E. W. West, *Pahlevi Texts* (Oxford: Clarendon Press, 1882), p. 271.
14. Cf. Runzo, "Ethics and the Challenge of Theological Non-Realism," in *Ethics, Religion, and the Good Society*, ed., Runzo, p. 90, n.45.
15. Martin Buber, *I and Thou*, trans. Walter Kaufmann (New York: Scribner's, 1970), p. 59.
16. James Kellenberger, *Relationship Morality* (University Park, Penn.: Pennsylvania State University Press, 1995), pp. 42 and 53.
17. Buber, *I and Thou*, pp. 113, 123.

CHAPTER 12: PRUDENTIAL ARGUMENTS FOR RELIGIOUS BELIEF

1. His Holiness the Dalai Lama, *The Joy of Living and Dying in Peace*, p. 25.
2. Blaise Pascal, *Pensées and Other Writings* (Oxford: Oxford University Press, 1995), p. 153.
3. Ibid., p. 154.
4. Ibid., p. 154.
5. Ibid., pp. 155–156.
6. William James, "The Will to Believe" in William James, *Essays on Faith and Morals* (Massachusetts: Meridian, 1911), p. 37.
7. Pascal, *Pensées and Other Writings*, pp. 75, 77.
8. *Maitri Upanishad* in Radhakrishnan and Moore, eds., *A Source Book on Indian Philosophy*, p. 94.
9. Mascaro, trans., *The Dhammapada*, p. 50.
10. Ibid., pp. 78, 83.
11. James, "The Will to Believe", p. 37.
12. Plato, *Republic* 612b in *Plato: Collected Dialogues*, Edith Hamilton and Huntington Cairns, eds. (Princeton: Princeton University Press, 1941), p. 837.
13. Plato, *Apology* 37e–38a in *Plato: Collected Dialogues*, Hamilton and Cairns, eds., p. 23.

14. Plato, *Republic* 611c–d in *Plato: Collected Dialogues*, Hamilton and Cairns, eds., p. 836.
15. Christopher Key Chapple, *Nonviolence to Animals, Earth and Self in Asian Traditions*, p. 13.
16. Mascaro, trans., *The Dhammapada*, p. 53.
17. Plato, *Apology* 40d in *Plato: Collected Dialogues*, Hamilton and Cairns, eds., p. 25.
18. The conviction that one should act so as to respect others as spirit in relation to the Transcendent, while it might be *supported* by reasons as I have tried to do, it seems to me is itself a basic belief, and in the right epistemic circumstances, a properly basic belief. That is, while a justified belief, it is not *based on* other beliefs as reasons.
19. By "intuition" I mean what G. E. Moore intended in *Principia Ethica*: "When I call...propositions 'Intuitions,' I mean *merely* to assert that they are incapable of proof; I imply nothing whatever as to the manner or origin of our cognition of them." G. E. Moore, *Principia Ethica* (Cambridge: Cambridge University Press, 1965), p. x.
20. Mascaro, trans., *The Dhammapada*, p. 52.

CHAPTER 13: FAITH AND JUSTIFIED BELIEF

1. St. Anselm, *Proselogium*, in *St. Anselm: Basic Writings*, pp. 6–7.
2. Plantinga, "Is Belief in God Rational?", p. 27.
3. Ibid., p. 46.
4. See, e.g., Alston, "Christian Experience and Christian Belief," in Plantinga and Wolterstorff, eds., *Faith and Rationality*, pp. 112–113.
5. Thomas S. Kuhn, *The Structure of Scientific Revolutions* (Chicago: University of Chicago Press, 1962), pp. 109, 115–116.
6. Norwood Hanson, *Patterns of Discovery: An Inquiry into the Conceptual Foundations of Science* (Cambridge: Cambridge University Press, 1958), p. 19.
7. I give an extended argument for this analysis of perception in *World Views and Perceiving God* (New York: St. Martin's Press, 1993).
8. Paul Tillich, *The Dynamics of Faith*, p. 1. Cf. Tillich, *Systematic Theology* (Chicago: Univ. of Chicago Press, 1951), Vol. 1, pp. 11–12.
9. James, "The Will to Believe," p. 48.
10. Ibid., p. 42.

CHAPTER 14: LOVE AND THE MEANING OF LIFE

1. Albert Einstein, *The World As I See It* (New Jersey: Carol Publishing, 1984), p. 1.
2. William Shakespeare, *Macbeth* V.V.19–28.
3. Albert Camus, "The Absurdity of Human Existence," in *The Meaning of Life*, ed., E. D. Klemke.
4. J. S. Mill, *Utilitarianism* (Cambridge: Hackett Publishing Company, 1979), pp. 8–10.
5. Nozick, *The Examined Life*, p. 164.

6. As Leibniz put it, not just the quantity but the variety of goodness makes for the "best of all possible worlds."
7. Richard Dawkins, *The Selfish Gene*, p. 1.
8. Julian Huxley, "The Creed of a Scientific Atheist" in *The Meaning of Life*, ed., E. D. Klemke, p. 63.
9. Ibid., p. 65.
10. Ibid., pp. 67–69.
11. Tillich, *Dynamics of Faith*, pp. 113–114. Italics mine.
12. A. K. Ramanujan, trans., *Hymns for the Drowning* (New Delhi: Penguin Books, 1993), p. 69.
13. Eliot Deutsch, *The Bhagavad Gita: Translated, with Introduction and Critical Essays*, pp. 161–169.
14. I discuss these in "Eros and Meaning in Life and Religion" in Runzo and Martin, eds., *The Meaning of Life in the World Religions*, pp. 187–201.
15. St. Bernard of Clairvaux, *Sermon on the Canticles*, xxxi, 5–6, quoted in Nelson Pike, *Mystic Union* (Ithaca: Cornell University Press, 1992), p. 81.
16. Krishna as the lover is the common metaphor; Krishna as bridegroom is less common.
17. Parrinder, trans., *The Bhagavad Gita*, p. 61.
18. A. K. Ramanujan, trans., *Speaking of Siva*, p. 133.
19. Tillich, *Dynamics of Faith*, p. 106.
20. St. Bernard of Clairvaux, *Sermons on the Canticles* #71, quoted in Pike, *Mystic Union*, p. 36.
21. Devara Dasimayya in *Speaking of Siva*, A. K. Ramanuja, trans., p. 106.
22. St. John of the Cross, *Spiritual Canticles* #2, quoted in Pike, *Mystic Union*, p. 81.
23. Rumi, *The Essential Rumi*, trans., Coleman Barks (San Francisco: HarperSanFrancisco, 1995), pp. 100–101.
24. Dawkins, *The Selfish Gene*, p. 256.
25. From Burton Watson, *Basic Writings of Mo-Tzu, Hsun Tzu and Han Fei Tzu* (New York: Columbia University Press, 1967), reprinted in Koller and Koller, *A Sourcebook in Asian Philosophy*, pp. 463, 467.
26. Rumi, *The Essential Rumi*, trans. Coleman Barks, p. 243.
27. Keith Ward, *God, Chance and Necessity*, p. 80.
28. This would constitute a fourth element of the religious point of view.

INDEX

jiva 46, 48, 63, 114, 175
jnana-yoga 11–12
Judaism 6, 9, 37, 54, 60,
68–69, 76, 144, 172, 198, 221,
225, 231
Jung, Carl 118, 120, 253 (ch.7 n.18)

Kabbalism 116–117
Kali 65–68
Kant, Immanuel 7, 20, 25–26, 73,
82, 143, 152–157, 161, 165,
178–181, 184, 188, 204, 206,
229, 249 (ch.2 n.15), 251 (ch.5
n.12)
karma 31, 51–52, 64, 105–106,
124–125, 173, 182, 203, 230
karma-yoga 11, 182, 184, 223
karuna 152, 227
Kellenberger, James 189
Kierkegaard, Soren 20, 25 26, 92,
98, 213
Kitaro, Nishida 20
Krishna 11, 24, 43, 66–68, 111,
114, 120, 144, 151, 206, 222,
224, 258 (ch.14 n.16)
Kuhn, Thomas 209
K'ung Fu Tzu 19

Lao Tzu 165
Leibniz, Gottfried 75, 107, 128, 251
(ch.5 n.7), 258 (ch.14 n.6)
Lewis, C.I. 22, 248 (ch.1 n.5)
Lewis, C.S. 184–186
liberation 19, 35, 37, 40, 53, 57,
106, 124
lila 69
Locke, John 138
love 10, 77, 111, 118, 120, 122,
162–163, 166, 198, 216–231
Luther, Martin 20

Madhva 20, 24, 37, 46–47, 61–64,
77, 125
Mahadeviyakka 119, 224
Mahavira 19, 165
Maimonides, Moses 10, 20, 24, 37,
54, 111, 154–155
Malebranche, Nicolas 128
Manicheanism 25, 106

materialism 22, 126, 129, 137, 231
maya 7, 55, 141, 170, 198
McFague, Sallie 65, 77, 112–114,
117, 120
meaning 131–132, 171, 216–231,
219 (def.)
Mencius 19, 24
metaethics 173–174, 183
metaphors 113–115, 120–121, 224
metaphysics 10, 25–26, 44, 46–48,
50, 60–61, 69, 111, 152, 154,
183
realist 44–45
Mill, J.S. 82, 177, 180–181, 218,
231
Mirabai 206
Mishnah 31
moksha 46, 124, 127, 141
monotheism 37, 39, 44, 53, 55, 58,
60–61, 64, 68, 82, 95–97, 99,
124–125, 139, 156,
165–166–167, 184–186, 209,
214, 220
Moore, G.E. 257 (ch.12 n.19)
moral argument 93, 184, 229, 252
(ch.5 n.12)
morality 172–173
moral point of view 187–190
Mo Tzu 228
Mozart, Wolfgang 165
Muhammad 13, 20, 25, 69, 165,
187, 230
mystical 9, 148
mystics 32, 149, 151

Nagarjuna 20
Nammalvar 222
Nanak 37
Native American traditions 5
naturalism 185, 214
Newton 165, 208
Nirvana 19, 31, 44–45, 47, 52–53,
68, 125, 136, 141, 156, 198,
200, 221
nishkama karma 183
non-attachment 51, 182
non-realism 57
religious 56
theological 55
normative ethics 173–174, 179–181

God, Chance and Necessity

KEITH WARD

The 'new materialism' argues that science and religious belief are incompatible. This book considers such arguments from cosmology (Stephen Hawking, Peter Atkins), from biology (Charles Darwin, Richard Dawkins) and from sociobiology (Michael Ruse), and exposes a number of crucial fallacies and weaknesses.

With a carefully argued, point by point refutation of scientific atheism, *God, Chance and Necessity* shows that modern scientific knowledge does not undermine belief in God, but actually points to the existence of God as the best explanation of how things are the way they are. Thus its sets out to demolish the claims of books like *The Selfish Gene*, and to show that the overwhelming appearance of design in nature is not deceptive.

'At last, God is beginning to argue back'
Clive Cookson in the *Financial Times*

'A witty, clear and probing critique'
John Polkinghorne in the *Times Higher Educational Supplement*

'Beautifully and clearly written'
Peter Atkins in *The Observer*

'A profound and richly satisfying book'
James le Fanu in the *Catholic Herald*

ISBN 1–85168–116–7
Price: UK £10.99, US $14.95, Can $19.99

Keith Ward is Regius Professor of Divinity at Oxford University and a Canon of Christ Church.

God, Faith and the New Millennium

Christian Belief in an Age of Science

KEITH WARD

Does being a Christian in the modern scientific age require intellectual suicide?
What future for Christianity in the Third Millennium?

In *God, Faith and the New Millennium* Keith Ward has produced a powerful and upbeat study of Christian belief that tackles questions such as these head on. In what he describes as a summary of his life's work on Christianity, religion and science, Ward's new and positive interpretation presents a Christian faith in harmony with the scientific worldview while remaining true to its traditions.

This is a cutting-edge study that will provoke and inspire anyone interested in the debate on the role of faith in the modern world. Through his examination of key issues such as creation, evolution and the divine purpose, Ward demonstrates that there is a 'natural fit' between the scientific worldview and mainstream Christian beliefs – Christian faith gives insight into the meaning and purpose of the universe, the physical structure of which modern science has marvellously discovered.

ISBN 1–85168–155–8
Price: UK £9.99, US $14.95, Can $19.99

In Defence of the Soul

KEITH WARD

Is there such a thing as the human soul?
Are we tiny cogs in a vast cosmos, or do we have special value?

In the modern scientific age, questions such as these become more and more difficult to answer. In this book, however, Keith Ward presents a balanced, strongly argued and convincing case for the existence of the human soul in the context of scientific discovery.

Drawing on a range of disciplines and writers, from Nietzsche, through Darwin, Freud and Marx, to contemporary philosophers and scientists, Ward's study of the key protagonists in the debate on the souls is authoritative and comprehensive. Covering such thorny issues as individual freedom, morality, the role of religion and the limits of scientific investigation, *In Defence of the Soul* builds rational bridges between apparent contradictions to shed light on an area we would all like to understand more fully.

ISBN 1–85168–040–3
Price: UK £8.99, US $13.95, Can $18.99

Concepts of God

Images of the Divine in Five Religious Traditions

KEITH WARD

Is there a universal concept of God?
Do all the great faiths of the world share a vision of the same supreme reality?

In an attempt to answer these questions, Keith Ward considers the doctrine of an ultimate reality within five world religions – Hinduism, Buddhism, Islam, Judaism and Christianity. He studies closely the works of definitive, orthodox writers from each tradition – Sankara, Ramanuja, Asvaghosa, Maimonides, Al-Ghazzali and Aquinas – to build up a series of 'images' of God, a common core of belief.

Ward discovers that while the great religious traditions of the world retain their differences, there are convergences of thought at the deepest level, with a broad similarity of structure in concepts of God. He concludes that a recognition of these beliefs, as well as encouraging a clearer acceptance of the mystery of the divine, might also lead to an increase in understanding and tolerance of other faiths, to the enrichment of one's own.

ISBN 1–85168–064–0
Price: UK £9.99, US $14.95, Can $19.99

The Fifth Dimension

An Exploration of the Spiritual Realm

JOHN HICK

Many of us today, living in our highly technological western culture, are all too willing to accept a humanist and scientific account of the universe which considers human existence as a fleeting accident.

The triumph of John Hick's gripping work is his exposure of the radical insufficiency of this view. Drawing on mystical and religious traditions ancient and modern, and spiritual thinkers as diverse as Julian of Norwich and Mahatma Gandhi, he has produced a tightly argued and thoroughly readable case for a bigger, more complete, picture of reality, in which a fifth, spiritual, dimension, plays a central role.

Hick's elegant study tackles such fundamental issues as the meaning of life, the nature and validity of religious experience and the science versus religion debate. Few readers will fail to re-examine their vision of the spiritual landscape in response to this stimulating investigation.

John Hick, a world-renowned theologian and philosopher of religion, is the author of numerous books, many of which have become classics in their field. He received the Grawemeyer Award for significant new thinking in religion in 1991.

'This book illustrates the meaning of life from various angles. It is simply expressed, but rich.'
Professor Ninian Smart, University of California, Santa Barbara

'. . . essential reading for anyone concerned with spirituality in the modern world.'
Professor Keith Ward, University of Oxford

'John Hick opens new possibilities for an interreligious, multicultural search on the meaning of human life.'
Professor Mahmoud Arkoun, the Sorbonne, Paris

ISBN 1–85168–191–4
Price: UK £10.99, US $17.95, Can $25.99

The Psychology of Religion

A Short Introduction

KATE M. LOEWENTHAL

Designed for students and general readers alike, this new introduction to the Psychology of Religion offers a thorough coverage of the subject, from its troubled history to the latest theories.

Drawing from a wide variety of cultures and faiths, the book considers the key themes of the psychology of religion. A jargon-free approach, accompanied by helpful diagrams and case studies, ensures that readers of all levels will gain an understanding of such complex topics as the relationship between religion and moral belief and the development of faith. Other areas covered include:

- prayer, prophecy and conversion: the nature of religious behaviour
- religious beliefs, and their influence on emotional well-being
- disorders of the mind: the relationship between religion and psychopathology
- the controversial question of religion and prejudice

A concise and intelligent study, this book will be valued equally by scholars, students and all those interested in the subject.

Kate M. Loewenthal is a Reader in Psychology at Royal Holloway, University of London, where she runs a highly popular course on the psychology of religion. As a respected expert in this field, her work has been widely published in both book and journal form.

'The book contains a wealth of current material, presented with a critical eye. I would like to take this opportunity to congratulate the author.'
Christopher Lewis, University of Ulster

ISBN 1–85168–212–0
Price: UK £9.99, US $15.95, Can $22.99

Pluralism in the World Religions

A Short Introduction

HAROLD COWARD

From the challenges facing Christianity to the future of Islam in a multi-cultural world, this is a coherent introduction to the teachings and debates within the various traditions on the subject of religious pluralism.

Drawing on a combination of scripture, scholarship and the words of great thinkers past and present, Harold Coward evaluates six major world faiths and their attitudes towards pluralism and religious tolerance. Balancing the historical context of each religion with its responses to the modern pressures of globalization and multi-cultural living, he tackles complex and problematic areas in an accessible manner, to produce a succinct survey of the issues and arguments surrounding inter-religious relationships. Among the key topics covered are:

- Muslim relations with the West and with Christianity
- the Jewish diaspora within the multi-cultural world
- assimilation and mutual criticism within Hinduism, Buddhism and Taoism
- the future of religion: how to reach new levels of tolerance and understanding

Harold Coward is the Director of the Centre for Studies in Religion and Society at the University of Victoria. Author and editor of nearly forty books, he is a well-known expert in the fields of Hinduism, philosophy and comparative religion and a Fellow of the Royal Society of Canada.

'Clear, lapidary, sympathetic, insightful in its perceptions and suggestions.'
Journal of Ecumenical Studies

'A useful and concise survey.'
Religious Studies Review

ISBN 1–85168–243–0
Price: UK £9.99, US $15.95, Can $22.99

The Library of Global Ethics and Religion

EDITED BY JOSEPH RUNZO AND NANCY M. MARTIN

Joseph Runzo is Professor of Philosophy and Religious Studies at Chapman University and Life Fellow of Clare Hall, Cambridge University. The recipient of five Fellowships and Awards from the National Endowment for the Humanities, he has published widely in philosophy and theology on issues of religious pluralism and religious ethics.

Nancy M. Martin is Assistant Professor of Religious Studies at Chapman University. The recipient of a Graves Award for the Humanities, her research has involved extensive fieldwork in Rajasthan, and she is an acknowledged expert on devotional Hinduism and the religious lives of women.

The Meaning of Life in the World Religions

Bringing together in one volume the work of some of the world's most prominent religious scholars, this is a clear and concise exploration of the religious perspective on the meaning of life.

Written in non-technical language, this collection of essays by such distinguished thinkers as John Hick, Huston Smith, Ninian Smart, Sallie McFague and Keith Ward not only addresses the distinct views of the major religious traditions, but also offers comparative analysis and original insight. The result is a detailed but accessible study that underlines the power of cumulative wisdom to educate and enlighten, and allows the reader to arrive at an informed personal understanding of the meaning of life.

The first volume in Oneworld's *Library of Global Ethics and Religion*, this authoritative book will stimulate and absorb students, scholars and the interested general reader alike.

ISBN 1–85168–200–7
Price: UK £14.99, US $23.95, Can $33.99

Love, Sex and Gender in the World Religions

This new volume offers wide-ranging and enlightening new perspectives on the role of love, sex and gender in a variety of different faiths. Among the issues covered are gender politics, sexual symbolism and religious ecstasy and their role in religions as diverse as Christianity and Tibetan Buddhism. This exciting new collection combines classic sources of text and tradition with innovative ideas and modes of thought, to create a detailed but accessible study.

Ideal for students, scholars and the interested general reader alike, this clear and concise book will challenge the reader to think creatively about both past and present concepts of sexuality, relationships and the role of women in the world faiths.

ISBN 1–85168–223–6
Price: UK £14.99, US $23.95, Can $33.99

Ethics in the World Religions

This thought-provoking book considers the way in which the world faiths offer resources for resolving modern ethical issues and conflicts.

Featuring work from such well-known authorities as Keith Ward, Vasudha Narayanan, Elliot Dorff, and William LaFleur, this volume examines the role of ethics in all the major religious traditions, from Confucianism to Christianity. Topics covered include the Buddhist approach to organ transplants and the Islamic perspective on gender issues, in an exciting collection that combines textual and traditional sources with current debate on the challenging issues of today, to create a detailed but accessible study.

Ethics in the World Religions is not only a definitive guide to religion and ethical issues, but also offers the key to a more harmonious future, showing how mutual religious understanding can help to resolve the most difficult of conflicts.

ISBN 1–85168–247–3
Price: UK £14.99, US $23.95, Can $33.99